TRADITION IN A ROOTLESS WORLD

TRADITION IN A ROOTLESS WORLD

WOMEN TURN TO ORTHODOX JUDAISM

LYNN DAVIDMAN

University of California Press
Berkeley • *Los Angeles* • *Oxford*

University of California Press
Berkeley and Los Angeles, California

University of California Press, Ltd.
Oxford, England

© 1991 by
The Regents of the University of California

Library of Congress Cataloging-in-Publication Data
Davidman, Lynn, 1955–
    Tradition in a rootless world : women turn to
Orthodox Judaism / Lynn Davidman.
        p.   cm.
    Includes bibliographical references and index.
    ISBN 0-520-07282-0 (alk. paper).
    1. Women, Jewish—United States—Religious life—
Case studies.   2. Jews—United States—Return to
Orthodox Judaism—Case studies.   3. Orthodox
Judaism—United States—Case studies.   I. Title.
BM726.D38   1991
296.8'32'082—dc20   90-25881
                                                     CIP

Printed in the United States of America

1 2 3 4 5 6 7 8 9

This book is dedicated to the loving memory of
two generations of people
whose love has nurtured and sustained me:
my grandparents,
Edith Rochwarger Zuckerman and Udah Jacob Zuckerman,
and my mother,
Shirley Zuckerman Davidman.

And the end of all our exploring
Will be to arrive where we started
And know the place for the first time.

T.S. Eliot, *Four Quartets*

Contents

Acknowledgments

Many times while writing this book I fantasized about writing my acknowledgments. It is a joy and honor to thank the many people and institutions whose help was invaluable in my work.

I owe a particularly large debt to the people in the two communities I studied who so willingly shared their lives with me. At both Lincoln Square Synagogue and Bais Chana I was welcomed as a friend and potential member. The openness of the people I met and their thoughtfulness in recounting their experiences are the foundation on which this study rests. Rabbi Ephraim Buchwald, then of Lincoln Square Synagogue and now of the National Jewish Outreach Center, played an instrumental role in facilitating my entrée into Lincoln Square Synagogue. His interest in the project and faith in me made him a vital source of information and support. He read and extensively commented on the manuscript, offered his own thoughts and reactions, and thanked me for what he learned. Thank *you*, Effie.

The first stages in the development of this book occurred while I was a graduate student at Brandeis University. I was fortunate to have a dissertation committee composed of people—Peter Conrad, Karen Fields, Shulamit Reinharz, and Irving Kenneth Zola—who taught me by their example and by direct feedback on my work. Shulamit Reinharz, my major adviser, encouraged and directed me while having the wisdom to teach me to develop my own insights and interpretations. Over the years we have become colleagues, collaborators, and friends who share work as well as the stories of our daily lives. Karen Fields taught me to be a sociologist of religion. Her comments often pushed me beyond what I thought were my intellectual limits. She forced me to confront my own assumptions about religion and women and thus enabled me to hear more fully the experiences of the people I was meeting. I was honored when Judith Plaskow agreed to be my "outside reader." Her work has always inspired me and influenced my thinking. Her insightful comments on the original dissertation helped shape its further evolution into this book.

It is truly a pleasure for me to thank the several institutions whose faith in my work was reflected in their grants. The Barnard College Alumnae Fellowships, the Woodrow Wilson Foundation, the Memorial Foundation for Jewish Culture, and the Center for Modern Jewish Studies at Brandeis, under the directorship of Marshall Sklare, all provided assistance that was essential to the completion of this project. Larry Sternberg, assistant director of the Center for Modern Jewish Studies, played a crucial role in acting as intermediary on my behalf. These grants made it possible for me to have my interview tapes transcribed and to take time off from teaching to write. More recently, a faculty development grant from the University of Pittsburgh provided the support for me to return to New York and further pursue some of my developing ideas.

I am also pleased and honored to thank the many friends and colleagues whose comments, encouragement, and assistance spurred me along. Shelly Tenenbaum was a partner in every stage of this process. When we started graduate school together, we immediately began to do collaborative work. Together we shared the struggles and joys of giving birth to our dissertations and then working on our books. Over the years our friendship has grown along with our ability to help each other develop our ideas and writing. I look forward to our future projects. My uncle, Alan Zuckerman, who for years has been my academic role model and mentor, read the entire manuscript and offered critical and loving feedback. He, too, appreciates and greatly misses the people to whom I have dedicated this book.

I am grateful to everyone who read all or portions of the manuscript: David Bromley, Robert Buchsbaum, Aidel and Ephraim Buchwald, Jean Carr, Denise Connors, Phyllis Coontz, Blu Greenberg, Rosanna Hertz, Barbara Hargrove, Samuel Heilman, Susannah Heschel, Bernie Levinson, Ida Mann, Esther Sales, Lynn Schlesinger, Larry Sternberg, Ella Taylor, Becky Thompson, Wesley Ward, and R. Stephen Warner. Jeffrey Hadden had the vision to see a good book in a just-completed dissertation. His suggestions and enormous enthusiasm gave me the confidence to do the necessary work. In the last few years, the work of, and my conversations with, Mary Jo Neitz and Steve Warner have pushed me to rethink some of my basic assumptions about religion in the modern world. Their ideas have greatly shaped the direction of this book; I appreciate our developing collegiality and friendships. I owe an especially enthusiastic thanks to Larry Greil, who patiently went through the entire manuscript several times and worked closely with me on each successive draft. During his sabbatical in Pittsburgh, we helped each other to complete our books. Our close contact turned writing from a solitary activity into a shared one; I hope we will have the opportunity to do that again in the future.

Bonnie Goltz Reiser transcribed most of my tapes and shared with me her insights about the women whose words she typed out. My colleagues at the University of Pittsburgh have made me feel welcome and supported in my work. The members of the staff, particularly Rochelle Cook and Peggy Sestak, cheerfully spent hours helping me to get the manuscript in shape. Deborah Gould, a student of mine from the University of Pittsburgh, provided skillful and enthusiastic research assistance. Many of the students in my courses at Wellesley College, Brandeis University, Brown University, and the University of Pittsburgh, and the members of the audiences at my public talks, often managed to ask those pesky questions that prodded me to further refine my analysis.

Naomi Schneider, my sponsoring editor at the University of California Press, provided a well-balanced combination of suggestions and support, often at just the right moment. Jan Kristiansson, my copy editor, and Amy Klatzkin, my production editor, approached this book with interest and enthusiasm; their careful attention is reflected on every page.

Steven Freedman cheered me on in the last few years of my work on this book. He read and commented on portions of the manuscript and helped me to come up with its title. His caring and support were shown in ways large and small and helped to create an environment that fostered my intellectual development.

1

A Day in the Life of
Two Jewish Women

It is Saturday morning, about 9:30. The streets of the Upper West Side of Manhattan are empty, except for a few hardy joggers puffing along with their Walkmen. As Stephanie,[1] a thirty-two-year-old advertising executive, approaches her destination, the large, modern, white-stone synagogue at the corner of West 69th Street, she begins to notice the dressed-up people converging on the streets, all seemingly heading to Shabbat[2] (Sabbath) services. She draws her breath and follows them into the synagogue.

Inside the building, in the red and black carpeted lobby, people are milling about. The women are fashionably dressed and bejeweled, and several are wearing stylish hats. Little children run around, comfortable in the shul (synagogue). Some of the men wear long white shawls, with black stripes and fringes at the ends, over their suits.

Stephanie hesitates. The people in the lobby appear so at ease, whereas she feels awkward and conscious of not having been in a synagogue for years. Recently, Stephanie and her boyfriend of three years had split up, and she had been going through a rough time at work. She had mentioned to a friend, an Orthodox woman, that she was looking to do something new and exciting, something that would be intellectually as well as socially stimulating. As the two of them had recently been talking about Judaism, her friend suggested that she go to the Beginners' Service at Lincoln Square— a lively, fascinating service led by a dynamic rabbi and attended by many young, attractive people. Stephanie decided to give it a try, and today is the day.

She glances around, trying to get a feel for the place. On her left, through a pair of glass-paned doors, she sees an unusual sanctuary. It is built in the round, with women and men seated on wooden benches in separate semicircular sections leading upward toward stained glass windows. The men also occupy the floor space in the center of the circle, and the men's and women's sections are divided by six-foot-high plexiglass. Stephanie decides that this room looks too formal to fit her friend's description of the Beginners' Service. A man in a white shawl notices her bewildered look and asks if she's new here. She nods. He says, "Don't worry; we all began sometime" and directs her upstairs to "Effie's minyan (prayer service)." First hurdle overcome, Stephanie heads up the concrete flight of stairs.

At the top of the stairs she steps into a long corridor where she is confronted with a confusing array of sounds, people, and doors. Through a doorway across the hall and slightly off to the left of the stairs, she hears singing. She glances through that open door and sees the women's section. The people in the room all seem perfectly able to follow the Hebrew service, so she heads down the corridor to a small classroom with a waist-high wooden divider down the middle. Men are seated on the left, women are on the right, and a rabbi is standing up front in the middle explaining the service. Stephanie realizes this must be the Beginners' Service, but she hesitates to enter because getting to the women's section requires walking around the rabbi as he leads the prayers. She asks a woman standing next to her in the hall if there's another entrance to the room. The woman replies, "Oh, that's okay. You can just go right in." She shows Stephanie how to fold her coat on top of an already jam-packed coatrack and says with a smile, "This is the hardest part; after this it's simple." Once Stephanie has placed her coat on the rack, she draws a breath and walks in.

As she enters, she passes a poster on the door that says:

> Welcome to this service for people with little or no background. Take a Bible (blue book) and a siddur (black book) [prayer book] and find a seat and prayer shawl (men). Remember, other people in here didn't know what they were doing when they first came but they learned quickly, and you can learn too. . . . Please follow along.

When she walks past the rabbi, he nods quickly at her and points with his chin to the women's section. She doesn't immediately see the books she's supposed to pick up, so rather than standing in the front looking, she takes a seat. While he continues to lead the prayers, the rabbi walks over to her and hands her the two thick books as well as a handout welcoming newcomers to the service and explaining a little about it.

She relaxes a bit and looks around the room. The service is already in progress, and the room, which holds about seventy people, is half full. The somewhat larger women's section has about forty seats. All the people in the service look professional: they are well groomed, nicely clothed, and fashionably coiffed. Most are young, in their mid-twenties to late thirties, although there are also some middle-aged and elderly people in the room. She notes that although most of the participants "look Jewish," a Chinese woman and a black man are seated in the room and are easily following the service.

In the front of the room hang several handwritten cardboard posters explaining the service. In the center is a large poster announcing:

> If you do not *yet* read Hebrew, you may sign up for the free crash course in Hebrew reading; you only need to call the synagogue office to make arrangements. Meanwhile, just try to follow along and get into the rhythm of the prayers and chanting.

Reading this sign, Stephanie thinks, "Crash course in Hebrew? It's nice that they offer it, but who's got the time?"

The other posters—in transliterated Hebrew and in English—describe aspects of the service. One displays the order of the prayer service:

Berchot Hashachar (morning blessings)

Pesukei Dezimrah (Psalms of Praise)

Shema (Hear, O Israel) and its blessings

Amidah (silent devotion)

Torah (Pentateuch) reading

Return of the Torah

Mussaf (additional *Amidah*)

Aleinu (It is our duty)

Adon Olam (Lord of the Universe)

As Stephanie struggles to pronounce these words, she suddenly realizes that "Torah" is the only one she recognizes. She wonders how it is that she went to Reform Sunday School for eight years, and even was confirmed, and yet never heard of most of these words.

Another poster, this one extending over two sheets of oak tag, lists the three *brachot* (blessings) that precede the *Shema* and the three blessings within it. A small sign nearby says, "Have you greeted the person next to you? Shabbat shalom." "Well," she thinks, "at least I understand that one."

Glancing around the room, Stephanie notices additional signs on the left wall, mostly about Hebrew. A large printed poster demonstrates the vowels of the Hebrew language and the pronunciation of the sounds. Numerous sheets of paper contain each of the letters of the Hebrew alphabet and their English equivalents. Stephanie begins to realize how central Hebrew is here; she wonders if she can catch up and whether it is even worth trying.

Stephanie also looks at the handout, which explains that the service is for those with little or no background and is intended to teach newcomers the structure of the Sabbath prayer services and provide a forum for learning about traditional Jewish life. The handout instructs newcomers to follow, sing along, and relax: "If the service gets too heavy, take a break and go out into the hall. Don't worry, we won't be hurt."

Having taken in her physical surroundings, Stephanie turns her attention to the service. Nearly all of the prayers are read aloud—either by the rabbi alone or by the rabbi and the congregation—in English or in Hebrew, with a few read in both languages. All present follow along in English, and a few of the participants also chant with the rabbi in Hebrew. The rabbi frequently announces the page and the part of the service now being performed. When a prayer is sung in Hebrew, many of the people in the room join in, humming the tune if not singing the words. Stephanie feels awkward about joining in, but nevertheless the sound of the chanting feels good and reminds her of visits to the synagogue with her grandparents when she was a girl. Some of the prayers are particularly lively, and the rabbi pounds on the pulpit and shouts, "Sing!"

As the service progresses, the rabbi occasionally pauses to explain the structure and meaning of a prayer. When they get to the

Amidah, the rabbi explains that it is a silent meditation that is the core of the service. He tells them that the entire lengthy prayer is to be read silently, standing up, and he shows them how to take three steps forward to open the prayer and three steps backward at its end. He explains that even though they're always in God's presence, in this central prayer they reaffirm that by taking three steps forward. This enables them to become especially conscious of standing before God, like bowing before an earthly king. The three steps backward after the prayer signify the ending of this intimate moment of communion with God.

During a prayer proclaiming that God has chosen "us" from among the nations, the rabbi pauses and asks what it means that the Jews are a chosen people. When no one responds, he recounts a fable, which Stephanie actually remembers from Sunday school, about how God went to all the other nations and asked them if they wanted the Torah. They all asked what this would entail, and for each group accepting the Torah meant keeping a particular commandment the group was in the habit of breaking. So they all declined God's offer. But when he got to the Jews they joyously said, "We will act and we will listen." Thus, to be chosen means that the Jews have a special relationship with God and that to fulfill that relationship they have to meet certain obligations. Stephanie smiles at the fable. She also begins to get a more vivid sense of the power of belonging to a people with such a long tradition and strong sense of group identity.

Participants frequently stop the rabbi to ask questions about the prayers, their tunes, or some other matter in Jewish life. This morning one of the questions is about evolution and whether Judaism is compatible with evolutionary theory. The rabbi explains that Judaism has no problem with evolutionary theory because the order of creation presented in the Bible does follow an evolutionary pattern. He says, "We know that time in the Bible was expressed in different terms from our contemporary understanding. Since in those days people lived nine hundred years and we don't know what that means, so similarly, the six days of creation could easily refer to a much longer time span by contemporary standards."

Stephanie's attention is captured by this exchange. To the extent that she had thought about Judaism and modern science, they had appeared to her to be fundamentally incompatible. "This man doesn't fit the stereotype of an Orthodox rabbi who is out of touch with the modern world," she thinks. "He knows all the traditional texts, but he's also well read and informed about contemporary issues."

When the first part of the service is completed, the rabbi explains the reading of the Torah. One chapter is read aloud each week in services, and the entire Torah takes a year to read in this way. He says that although in regular services Torah scrolls are taken out from the ark (*aron hakodesh*) and a trained person, a *ba'al koreh*, chants the weekly portion in a distinct tune, beginners in their service read it aloud together from their Hebrew-English Bibles. Prior to the reading, however, the *dvar torah*, a brief talk related to the weekly portion, is given by a member of the service.

The rabbi calls up the speaker for the week, Michelle, and introduces her. She begins by describing the *parsha* (Torah portion) for that week. It is the story of Moses ascending Mount Sinai to receive the Ten Commandments. He was on the mount for forty days and nights, and the people of Israel got impatient and distrustful. They collected all of their gold jewelry and made a golden calf, which they then worshipped. The golden calf was a symbol that was odious to Moses and God because it was used by the Hebrews' Goddess-worshipping neighbors, the Canaanites. Their polytheistic religion was anathema to the leaders of the emerging monotheism. Moses' wrath, reflecting God's, erupted on viewing the pagan rituals, and he smashed the tablets containing the Ten Commandments God had given him for the people. From this story Michelle had gotten the image of a wrathful God who was to be feared. Michelle tells the group that she is a "yeshiva [institution of Jewish education] girl" who had strayed and that she has always been troubled by God's wrathfulness and judgment. She wants to figure out why God is so unforgiving.

She then describes three incidents she observed at a rock concert at Watkins Glen in the early 1970s. All of these, she explains, shook her. First, in a traffic jam on the way to the concert, when a man started honking his horn, the driver from the car in front got out and started beating the horn honker up. Second, at the concert she saw a couple giving their five-year-old daughter sips of wine from their wineskin and tokes of their joint. Third, she witnessed a teenager performing a sexual act.

Now she understands that the phrase "the people . . . have corrupted themselves" (Exodus 32:7) in this week's Bible portion is also a reference to present-day immoral acts. She can begin to comprehend why God is so angry. And even though she still doesn't have all the answers to life's fundamental questions, at least she realizes that she needs to be asking them and that Orthodox Judaism is the framework within which to do so. Stephanie is touched by what Michelle is saying. She, too, had begun to feel uncomfortable with some of the contradictions in the hippie culture in which she had come of age, and she found Michelle's words an apt expression of her own thoughts and feelings. Michelle finishes talking; people in the service call out, *"Yasher coach"* (You did well); and she returns to her seat.

The rabbi then goes through the *parsha* in English, elaborating on numerous points within the reading. When he comes to the enumeration of the thirteen attributes of God, he emphasizes the attribute of mercy, saying that God is truly a loving, forgiving God who remembers good deeds for thousands of generations but sins for only four. If four generations of Jews don't observe the Sabbath or the commandments, then they really don't know what it is to be Jewish anymore. Stephanie thinks about her grandparents, and her own assimilated life, recognizing that she is the second generation of unobservant Jews in her family. For some time now she has been wondering whether she will want to pass on to her children, when she has them, any sense of the tradition and just what she will be able to convey. Participants ask the rabbi questions about the reading. When this section is completed, the service resumes.

By noon, Stephanie is getting tired and hears her stomach grumbling: she hadn't eaten breakfast because she had no idea that services would last for three hours. The Reform services she had occasionally attended with her parents as a child and as an adult had lasted only one hour. She's feeling tired; it's been a very full morning. "It will take a while to sort this out," she thinks.

At this point the rabbi pauses for announcements, which include the times of the Saturday afternoon services, the meal in between them, and other events in the synagogue that week, such as the visit of a rabbi who will be available to check the condition and kashrut (in this case, ritual propriety) of the congregants' mezuzot (plural of mezuzah, the sacred scroll hung on doorposts of Jewish homes and rooms) and the men's tefillin (phylacteries that Orthodox Jewish men wear when praying). While Stephanie wonders what these words refer to, the rabbi announces the important life events that had occurred to synagogue members that week: births, deaths, weddings, engagements, and bar mitzvahs, as well as the list of people who'd left to study in Israel. The rabbi invites all present to participate in the kiddush (benediction over wine) following the services, saying that there will be wine and grape juice. He explains that this week's kiddush is special because it is in honor of a participant's recent engagement and is sponsored by her mother. He asks people to fold their chairs, make sure to put their Bibles and prayer books back in place, and then come to the back of the room.

He then says that they've reached a special part of the service where newcomers are asked to be extrafriendly and introduce themselves. A few people present, including Stephanie, say their names, and some add where they are from (particularly if from out of state or out of the country) or introduce a fiancé or spouse who has come along. After each person's introduction, the rabbi greets her or him warmly, saying, "Welcome," or "We're glad to have you." Following these introductions, the group sings the *Adon Olam.*

Much to Stephanie's relief everyone now stands up, and she joins the others who are hurriedly folding the chairs and placing them against a side wall. She follows the group (which is now coed) to the back of the room, where people cluster around a table bearing tiny plastic cups of wine and grape juice and paper plates offering bite-size pieces of chocolate and carrot cakes. The rabbi makes his way to the back of the room, stopping to wish a "good Shabbos [Sabbath]"[3] and exchange a few hurried words with several people. He invites participants to follow along with the blessings for the wine and cake, and the group recites them together. Stephanie notices that other people are reading these blessings from an English transliteration on a poster on the back wall. At the last few words she softly chimes in. While those assembled recite the blessings, a few women pass around the plates with the beverages and cakes. Stephanie helps herself to some wine and chocolate cake and takes a sip from her plastic cup. "Sweet wine," she grimaces. "I'd forgotten about this." The cake is good, however, and she helps herself to some more.

A few people smile at her, and she smiles back. One woman introduces herself as Judy. While they're talking, the rabbi comes over and says, "Stephanie, do you have a place for Shabbos lunch?" "Excuse me?" she asks, while marveling that he remembers her name. "Shabbos lunch," he repeats. "That's the meal following services. I'll send you to a family." "Uh . . . no thank you," she says dubiously. He insists, "Really, we do this all the time; there are families who especially ask for newcomers for their table." She hesitates. "Okay," he says. "I'll let the Cohens know you're coming."

Not having any idea what she has got herself into, Stephanie resumes her conservation with Judy, who remarks that she, too, occasionally goes to families' homes for Shabbat meals and that Stephanie will enjoy herself. As they're talking, the rabbi shouts to the group, "Hey! Let's celebrate this engagement!" He begins to sing a lively tune, and within a minute several people have joined in. Stephanie notices that many people who hadn't been at the service have now entered the room. As the singing gets livelier, the rabbi grabs a young man and begins to dance energetically with him, the two of them running around in a circle. Judy explains to Stephanie that the man dancing with the rabbi is the fiancé of the woman whose mother sponsored this kiddush. Other men join the circle, and within a few minutes a group of women have formed a circle of their own. The lively dancing continues for a while to the accompaniment of a variety of joyous Hebrew songs.

While she watches, a medium-build, bespectacled man approaches her and introduces himself as Philip Cohen. Stephanie tells him her name, and he invites her to come along. Once outside, he introduces her to a small group of men and women, ranging in age from their late twenties to late fifties, who are waiting to join them. "This is the crew," he smiles, and they all head west to his home.

As they walk, a young man named Michael falls in step with Stephanie and asks her about herself. This is her first time here, she explains, laughing self-consciously. He grins. "I know what that's like; I myself began a couple of years ago. The first time is the hardest; after that it really does get easier. And you'll see, Effie's great: you can ask any question at all, and you really can go at your own pace. And you'll be surprised at how quickly you pick things up. Within a year and a half most people graduate to the main service."

"Did you feel dumb when you first walked in?" she asked. "It felt so weird to walk into a Jewish service, as a Jew, and have no idea what's going on! I'm not used to feeling so incompetent!"

He laughs. "Yeah, we all go through that. The Hebrew killed me at first; I felt so inept. But that crash course is great; I really learned to read."

She frowns a little about the crash course but is relieved to hear he had the same feelings. She's about to ask him more, but they've reached the Cohen's apartment building. The group enters the lobby and walks past the bank of elevators to a door leading to a concrete staircase. Stephanie looks at Michael dubiously; he laughs and says, "Their house isn't so bad; it's only on the eleventh floor. I've been to apartments on the twenty-fourth!" She remains skeptical. "I thought this was supposed to be a day of rest," she thinks.

Huffing and puffing (some more than others) the group finally reaches the Cohen's apartment. They are met at the door by a pretty seven-year-old girl, whom Philip introduces as his daughter, Sarah. Philip's wife, Sharon, comes out of the kitchen in an apron to greet her guests. She already knows several, but she warmly welcomes the new people and wishes everyone a good Shabbos. She ducks back into the kitchen while Philip assembles the guests and his three children around the lavishly set dining room table.

As Sharon enters and takes her place, Stephanie looks around the table at the ten assembled people. She wonders if the Cohen's Saturday lunches are always so large. Philip fills his own and everyone else's wine glasses, offering a choice of red or white wine. He recites a longer version of the blessing over the wine than she had heard that morning. Everyone sips wine, and then all ten people leave the table and head toward the kitchen. "We're washing for *hamotzieh*, the blessing over the *challah* [special braided bread for the Sabbath]," Michael whispers to Stephanie.

In the kitchen everyone assembles around the sink, and one at a time each person pours water over her or his hands from a large mug with handles. Sharon waits for Stephanie to reach the sink and then shows her how to perform the ritual: the mug is held in the right hand and water is poured over the left and vice versa; the entire activity is then repeated. Stephanie feels awkward but copies Sharon's actions. Sharon then hands Stephanie a towel and recites with her, word for word, the Hebrew blessing.

When they all are seated around the table again, Philip uncovers two large loaves of *challah*, slices one of them, and takes a piece. He puts salt on his plate, dips his piece of *challah* into the salt, says a blessing out loud, and eats the bread. Meanwhile, he has passed around the table a plate with the rest of the bread slices. Stephanie imitates the other guests and dunks her *challah* into salt before taking a bite.

Now the meal begins in earnest. For the first course Sharon hands out small plates, each with an oval-shaped piece of gefilte fish on it. Stephanie smiles; she remembers her grandmother's gefilte fish. She hopes this is homemade; any of the bottled versions she'd bought as an adult were never as good. She spoons the red horseradish on her fish, takes a bite, and smiles with pleasure.

While they eat, Sharon, who is seated next to Stephanie, asks her about herself: where she grew up, what kind of Jewish background she had, where she lives, and what kind of work she does. Philip overhears them talking and tells Stephanie that he and Sharon also did not grow up Orthodox but instead came to it as adults. He explains that when his mother died, he was looking for a place to recite the kaddish, the prayer for the dead said for a year following the death of a parent. He went shul "shopping" in the neighborhood, and when he entered Lincoln Square he was so taken with the warmth of the community, and particularly with the rabbi of the main congregation, that he kept coming back. A man at the table chimed in, "Yeah, there's no way you can come there for a year and not get hooked!"

Sharon said that at first she didn't want any part of it, but after Philip had been going for six months and talking so enthusiastically about it, she began to be curious and to feel more open. One day during that time the two of them ran into the rabbi on the street. She was taken by his warmth and impressed that he knew her name. She, too, went to shul the following Saturday. Philip has gone weekly ever since; Sharon frequently joins him. "That was five years ago," she smiles.

The first course finished, Sharon goes into the kitchen and comes out with the next course. There is a salad, a platter of chicken, and a bowl holding some brown food that Stephanie doesn't recognize. As the platters are passed around Stephanie helps herself to chicken and salad and is about to skip the bowl that she now sees contains a curious combination of meat, beans, and potatoes. Philip grins at her, "Try it. My wife makes the best *chulent* on the Upper West Side." Stephanie dubiously puts a little on her plate. Philip explains that *chulent* is a traditional Shabbat lunch dish because it can continue cooking in the warm oven since before the beginning of the Sabbath on Friday evening, and thus they can have hot food for lunch without having to turn on the stove on the Sabbath. Stephanie takes a small mouthful, gulps, and swallows. This dish is a little strange to her, but the rest of the food is delicious, and she eats happily.

During the meal several conversations go on at once. Some of the guests talk with Stephanie about the synagogue and offer suggestions about how to get involved slowly and which adult education classes they'd found helpful. Philip is engaged in a heated discussion with one of the men about the shul's search for a new rabbi now that the founding rabbi has moved to Israel. The children keep chiming in, too, making an altogether lively scene. Several guests enthusiastically discuss various rabbinic commentaries on the Torah portion read that morning.

When the main course is cleared away, the group sings several Hebrew songs. Stephanie has never heard any of them, but she enjoys the sound and feel of their rhythms. The two oldest children sing along. The singing is followed by dessert—fruit and homemade cake—and tea (made from an urn of hot water that is plugged in for the entire Sabbath), and Philip then leads the group in the *bentching*, which, he explains to Stephanie, is the grace after meals. This, too, is sung aloud.

Finally, two hours after they arrived, the guests get up from the table and slowly leave. Stephanie warmly thanks her hosts. They tell her it was a pleasure to have her and that she is welcome back any time. They wish her good luck, and she leaves, this time taking the elevator down. Exhausted, she hops on a bus uptown to her studio apartment, which in contrast feels quiet and empty.

•   •   •

Beth pulls the covers over her head, trying to block out the sound of the loudspeaker. "*Modeh ani l'fanecha* [I give my thanks to you]," a female voice chants, waking them up with the prayer said immediately on arising. "I'm not ready to get up," Beth grumbles to herself. "It's only 7:00 A.M. and I was up talking until 3:00!" She turns over, but the voice on the loudspeaker persists: "Now it's time to wash *nagel vasser* [morning ritual washing]." Beth slowly pulls herself out of bed, beginning the morning routine that in the three weeks since she's been at Bais Chana, a Lubavitch Hasidic learning center for women, has become almost automatic. (The Lubavitch Hasidim are a sectarian group of ultra-Orthodox Jews.) She walks to the bowl of water in the center of the room, which is placed, according to the Lubavitch interpretation of this hand-washing ritual, so that everyone can reach it within three steps. Four of her six roommates are still in bed; the other two are at the bowl, one by one performing the morning ritual of pouring water over her hands from a large cup with handles. Beth waits her turn, washes, and says the blessing, which she already knows by heart. She then shuffles into the large bathroom across the hall. Meanwhile, Cindy, a nineteen-year-old *madricha* (counselor and teacher) from South Africa, is walking into the room on her morning wake-up rounds.

When Beth returns to her room she makes her bed and dresses in the three-quarter-length sleeved blouse and long skirt she'd asked her mother to send a week ago. She puts on nylon knee-high socks under her sandals, thereby leaving no skin bare, and proceeds upstairs for breakfast. She's still uncomfortable in so many clothes in July. Yet she finds herself smiling, looking forward to talking with her new friends at breakfast and taking the day's classes.

Beth, a twenty-nine-year-old woman, had spent most of her twenties in a community of "born-again" Christians she had met through a group of friends at junior college. She enjoyed belonging to that warm, close group of people who spent a lot of time talking, praying, and doing charity work together. She was also attracted to their idea that as believers they would play an important part in ushering in the kingdom of God, which was coming soon. Her parents—although not observant Jews themselves—had been quite upset about her involvement in Christianity. "Even though we don't follow all the laws like Grandma and Grandpa did," her mother said, "we are still Jews and are part of the chain of tradition that's gone on for thousands of years."

When her mother suggested she talk with a Lubavitch couple, a rabbi in a yeshiva and his wife, a *shadchan* (matchmaker), who were doing outreach work in a nearby town, Beth agreed to meet them. The Sternblooms were generous and accepting people, and Beth felt comfortable with them. Sarah, the rabbi's wife, invited Beth to accompany the family to an Orthodox girls' sleepaway camp they were going to for July Fourth weekend.

Beth went along and greatly enjoyed the weekend. The Shabbos rituals reminded her of those she'd enjoyed observing with her grandparents and occasionally even with her parents when she was a child: lighting Shabbos candles, eating a special meal, singing at the table, discussing Jewish subjects. Being there, she felt the same sense of belonging as with her Christian friends, but in the camp she also felt the stirring of comforting memories and the feeling that *this* was hers.

Seeing how happy Beth was at the camp, Sarah told her about Bais Chana. Sarah described it as a residential center run by the Lubavitch Hasidim where young women at all levels of knowledge could learn about Judaism. Because Beth had been struggling for six years to support herself on the meager wages of a computer operator and was currently unemployed, she immediately wondered how she could afford such a place. Sarah assured Beth that she shouldn't be concerned about the money: if she was interested she should attend, and if necessary, the expenses could be picked up by the Lubavitch. Sarah told her that by living and studying together, the girls (the Lubavitch term for unmarried women of all ages) at Bais Chana become close. Beth, who had begun to wonder—with her parents' assistance—if she belonged in her Christian community, liked the image Sarah was creating and thought, "Why not? I'm going to collect unemployment anyway this summer. I might as well find out what it's like. I have nothing to lose" (she could leave after a week if she didn't like Bais Chana). And now, three and a half weeks later, she occasionally stops to wonder at how quickly she has made friends and adapted to the routines. But she feels comfortable and at home.

On her way upstairs for breakfast she passes young women coming out of other rooms who are also heading to the dining room. Once upstairs, Beth enters a large lobby hung with the posters that were the first items she saw on her arrival. The largest sign, in colored letters, announces, "Welcome to Bais Chana." Other posters offer details about kosher foods, the mitzvot (commandments) that the women should do daily, an oak-tag sheet with all their names and a star next to their names for each of the mitzvot they perform each day, and a huge sign, changed daily, that announces the day's schedule. She glances at the list of today's classes and heads into the dining room.

The large dining room is furnished with three rows of long tables and chairs. A painting of the Rebbe, a bearded, white-haired, benevolent-looking man, smiles at them from over the mantle on the right wall. The Rebbe, she's learned, is the head of the Lubavitch movement and is adored by all members of his community. The Lubavitch Hasidim go to him for advice on every type of personal and religious question. Since she's been at Bais Chana she's seen the *madrichot* (plural of *madricha*) help a few of the women compose letters to the Rebbe. Perhaps she'll write one, too, she's been thinking. Pictures of the Rebbe are throughout the house, and some women have brought their own. Beth walks to the wall opposite the picture and from a large table helps herself to silverware, a napkin, and a plate. She joins a small group of young women at the middle table.

With Beth are both "BTs" and "lifers," the main types of women at the institute. BT, she's learned, is an abbreviation for *ba'alat teshuvah*, a woman not brought up Orthodox who as an adult chooses Orthodoxy, whereas lifer refers to a woman brought up in the Lubavitch community. (The main one is in Crown Heights in Brooklyn; there are many other Lubavitch communities around the world established where the Rebbe sent *shlichim* [representatives] to do so.) There are also potential BTs at the table—that is, women who are new to the Lubavitch and who, like Beth, have been sent to Bais Chana by a Lubavitch rabbi or *rebbetzin* (rabbi's wife) in their hometown. The woman sitting at Beth's right is a convert from Christianity. A couple of the women at the table are *madrichot*; the *madrichot* comprise BTs and lifers. Within the house, at least one *madricha* sleeps in each room with the other women.

Some of the women eat breakfast quietly, still groggy. Others

talk about the previous night's class, which, like all evening
classes, was taught by Rabbi Friedman. Cindy tells the group she
woke up this morning with the song "We Want Moshiach [the
Messiah] Now" running through her mind, which means the previous night's class must have been great. A couple of women talk
about the new campaign initiated by the Rebbe to get all Jews to
have a letter of the Sefer Torah (scrolls of the Torah) inscribed in
their names. One of the lifer *madrichot* explains the *mivtza* (project,
campaign) to Beth. The *madricha* says that Torah scrolls are all
written by hand by a trained scribe. When a new Torah is being
inscribed, Jews may donate a sum of money in order to have a
letter (usually the first letter of their Hebrew name) inscribed in
their name. The Lubavitch are interested in promoting the unity of
all Jews; by getting many different Jews to have letters in the Torah, their names will be together in the scrolls, thus bringing these
people closer together. Beth thinks, "This is what I love about this
group: the people all have so much energy and commitment, so
much *ahavas Yisroel* [love for fellow Jews]." Two others at the table
are also very excited about the *mivtza* and make plans to hand out
sign-up sheets to all the women that day.

After they eat breakfast, many of the women wander back to
their rooms to finish dressing. Beth hangs around in the lobby,
waiting for her beginners' prayer group. (Morning prayers are divided into beginners, intermediate, and advanced.) In this group,
which Cindy leads, most of the prayers are read in English, and
many explanations of the prayers and rituals are offered. Four
other women attend the group this morning, none of whom
knows Hebrew. Cindy encourages them to study Hebrew in the
afternoons in a *chavrusa*, a one-on-one study session in which the
madrichot teach the women whatever they're interested in.

After prayers, and before Rabbi Friedman's class begins at 10:00,
Beth has about fifteen minutes, so she wanders back down to her
room to write a letter. She finds three of her roommates getting
dressed. Malkie, who is eighteen, and Liz, who is nearly twenty,
chose to room together because they are close friends; they have
been involved with the Lubavitch for a couple of years. Beth enjoys
hearing their stories of the previous summer and winter sessions at
Bais Chana and asking them about Crown Heights, where they live
in the Lubavitch girls' dorm and attend classes at Bais Rivka, the
yeshiva there for women.

Beth listens to both women confer about Liz's outfit. Liz had dressed in sneakers and ankle socks, but Malkie tells Liz that she can't have bare legs showing below her skirt. Liz decides Malkie's right and puts on pantyhose. Rena, the third roomate, asks if they think her dress neckline is too low; she is concerned that her collarbone sticks out. The other women aren't sure, so to be safe Rena puts on a scarf.

Beth and Rena hurry upstairs to Rabbi Friedman's class. Neither one wants to miss his class because they, like the other women, find it, and him, fascinating. Beth had heard from the Sternblooms that the rabbi was a terrific teacher and that his twice-daily classes were the highlight of the institute. Now that she's been here a while, she understands what they meant—he's bright and insightful, and his knowledge is so wide ranging.

The class meets in the library one floor above the dining room. Walking in, Beth notices again the placard announcing that this room is dedicated to the deceased wife of the former Lubavitch Rebbe. This placard is a vivid reminder of the love and reverence the Lubavitch have for all their Rebbes,[4] past and present. In the library Beth sits down at one of the sixty or so student desks, arranged in rows in a loose semicircle. The rabbi's chair faces the group.

The women slowly assemble in the room. In the three weeks since they've been here, they've learned that class generally begins a few minutes late, on "Jewish standard time." While waiting, some women sit and read from their Tanyas—the main Lubavitch text, written by the first Lubavitcher Rebbe, the *alter* Rebbe, in the eighteenth century. The text provides the foundation for the Lubavitch Hasidic philosophy. Rabbi Friedman's classes are listed as classes in the Tanya, although, as Beth has learned, they often begin with a passage from the Tanya and then spin off into a wide variety of other topics, primarily relationships between women and men and mothers and daughters. Other women talk seriously among themselves; a few chat and giggle. Beth watches Jane, a nineteen-year-old potential BT from South Africa, walk into the room dressed in a V-necked, sleeveless blouse with long fringes hanging down. She overhears Gittl, a recent BT, call to her, "Cover up!" Beth can understand Gittl's zeal to do things correctly. Although Bais Chana does not have a dress code (except for Shabbos, when the women are expected to wear skirts or dresses),

Gittl's enthusiasm often spills over into corrections of the others' behavior.

When the rabbi walks in, he sits down in the nearly full room and opens his Tanya. Without any preliminaries, he begins to read a section on the *beinoni*, the man who is neither saint nor sinner and is the major subject of the Tanya. The rabbi says that in the *beinoni* the instinct to do good (*yetzer hatov*) and the instinct to do bad (*yetzer hara*) are evenly balanced.

> The *beinoni* is forever dealing with the competing tugs of his animal soul and his Godly soul. The animal soul starts in his heart, spreads to his mind. The Godly soul starts in his mind and spreads to his heart. Were it not for God helping the Godly soul, it would not be able to win the battle with the *yetzer hara*. When a person doesn't know what to do, he should ask what would God want, and that will help the good instinct win out. We must use the mind to control the heart: the heart is fleeting feelings; the mind, the will, must rule over them.

The women ask many questions and in so doing try to understand what these concepts mean and how they can apply in daily life. Beth is a bit lost—these are such complex ideas—but it is stimulating to listen and try to grapple with them. A woman asks, "But what about the emotions? Where do they fit in?" The rabbi answers:

> We have three kinds of emotions. One feels nice, good, but it isn't so intense, so you can easily give it up. That's a *chochma* type of emotion. Another one, *binah*, is a strong one—wild horses couldn't change your feelings—these don't come easily and they're harder to change. But a year later, of itself, the emotion dies. It's *only* heat. The third kind may come easily or hard, it may be intense or soft, but year after year it's there. That's the emotion coming from *da'as*, "wisdom." It's the only viable one. Emotions are the children of the intellect, so this one is viable. It's just like relationships—you may have casual ones, or very hot ones, but unless they come from *da'as*, from being with someone who's so similar to you that you can know him thoroughly, it will fade. That's why a relationship between a Jew and a non-Jew, even though it seems so exciting at first, is bound to cool down—it's not real because it doesn't come from *da'as*.

The women ask many more questions, this time from their own experiences. Beth wonders about the man she was engaged to at sixteen, who died in the Vietnam War. Would their relationship have been classified as *da'as?* They did feel very similar to each other. She frowns as she remembers the next man she got involved with, a non-Jew she met at junior college who dropped and hurt her. "Maybe what Rabbi Friedman said makes sense here: he and I were *very* attracted to each other, and perhaps that's why it couldn't last," she thinks.

After about three hours the rabbi abruptly closes his Tanya, and the women go downstairs for lunch. On their way into the dining room, they leaf through the day's mail, which is placed on a table in the lobby outside the dining room. Beth is excited to find a postcard from a friend vacationing in Florida who is responding to Beth's letter describing Bais Chana and her feelings about being there. The postcard is full of questions: Is Beth really serious? Is she planning to become a Lubavitch? Does that mean she'll have an arranged marriage? Beth smiles; she's not making all these leaps yet, but she really does enjoy being here and finds the closeness and security of the Lubavitch way of life very attractive.

Lunch, as always, is a multicourse feast. Today the meal consists of vegetable soup, a salad, macaroni and cheese, broccoli and carrots, apples, cookies, and juice, all made by Sophie, the full-time cook, who is herself a *ba'alat teshuvah.* As Beth begins to fill her plate, she is greeted by Esther, another roomate, who had not been to class that morning. Esther says, "Good morning. How're you doing?" and Beth answers, "Good, thanks." Esther corrects her: "*Baruch Hashem* [thank God]—that's what you're supposed to say. You're supposed to thank God for your health and that you're doing well." Beth nods and tries it. "*Baruch Hashem,*" she says. "How're you doing?" "*Baruch Hashem,*" Esther answers with a grin.

Beth then sits down at a table with several other women. "Hi, Batya," says Ruth, a twenty-year-old lifer *madricha* from Crown Heights. Last week, when Beth wrote home asking for "Lubavitch-style" clothing, she also asked what her Hebrew name is because many of the women here are called by their Hebrew names. Beth enjoys hearing "Batya" and visualizing her namesake—her great-grandmother, a strong Polish woman—just as she likes the sound of the women calling her by this name.

Conversation over lunch is animated. Two women declare how much they loved the rabbi's class this morning. Rena says that she was most connected to his discussion of relationships, particularly when he said that the relationship between opposites can be very exciting for a while but that it cannot be really deep or true. "That is exactly what happened to me and my non-Jewish boyfriend," she says. "My relationship with my husband is much less intense than my relationship with this other man had been, but he really was so different from me that in the end it couldn't have worked." Beth joins in and tells them about her two boyfriends and that she, too, had noticed how what the rabbi said was reflected in her own experiences.

Two other women discuss the conflicts one is having with her parents over her involvement with the Lubavitch. Her parents feel she is abandoning them and are insulted that she has chosen a lifestyle so different from the way they brought her up. She feels torn between respect for her parents, which is commanded by the Torah, and doing what she wants and knows to be right. The other woman, also a BT, says reassuringly, "Don't worry. They'll come around. My parents were upset, too, but now that they see how much happier I am, they're glad for me." Beth adds, "My mother has just been thrilled from the beginning. She was sick for years over my involvement with the Christians."

While they eat and talk, groups of women from other tables begin singing "We Want Moshiach Now" and other Lubavitch songs in English. As they sing they pound on the table energetically. Beth smiles broadly; she loves this singing and she happily joins in, pounding on the table herself.

When the women finish eating, several women from another table bang on their glasses with a piece of silverware to attract everyone's attention. Sarah, the head *madricha*, a twenty-nine-year-old woman who'd grown up in a non-Hasidic Orthodox family, stands up to announce the afternoon's schedule. She reminds the women that if anyone has a subject she would like to study that is not offered in a formal class, arrangements for study can be made. Sarah then introduces Naomi, a sixteen-year-old girl from California whose turn it is to deliver the *dvar torah* this meal. Beth has not yet had her turn to present a *dvar torah*—a brief talk about the Bible, *Hasidus* (Hasidic thought and lore), or the Rebbes—that the women share with each other over lunch and dinner. Her turn will be in two days, however, so she knows how nervous Naomi is and listens closely.

Naomi stands up and announces that her talk is about *lashon hara*, or "gossip." She says that before she met a Lubavitch rabbi in her hometown a few months ago, she loved to gossip and never thought twice about it. But then he told her a story about what one of the rabbis had said about *lashon hara* that really changed her attitude, so now she wants to share it with the other women.

> A man came to a rabbi, upset that something he had said to a close friend about another man in the community had come back to the man it was about in a distorted way and hurt him. The rabbi took the man outside and handed him a feather pillow and a knife. "Cut that open," the rabbi said. "But the feathers will blow all around," the man responded. "Exactly," said the rabbi. So the man cut the pillow, and the wind picked up the feathers, tossed them around, and blew them in many different directions. "This is what happens with what we say," said the rabbi. "Just as the feathers scatter about and blow away till it's not even clear anymore that they're from a pillow, so we idly make a comment to one person, but it gets picked up and passed around from person to person till it's no longer clear what the original statement even was."

Naomi breathes a sigh of relief and sits down. Several women including Beth call out to her, "*Yasher coach.*" Beth really enjoyed Naomi's talk and thinks, "That didn't seem so bad; I could do that, too."

After lunch the women scatter around the building for their afternoon classes. Beth goes to the screened-in porch off the dining room for her Chumash (Pentateuch) class. Just as with the prayer groups, Bible classes are offered at beginning, intermediate, and advanced levels. Beth attends the beginners' class, taught by Ruth, one of the lifer *madrichot*. They are studying *B'reishit*, the first chapter of the first book (also called *B'reishit*) of the Bible. Each day they get through only a few sentences because Ruth introduces them not only to the text but to various rabbinic commentaries on the text as well. Beth really enjoys this class: the approach is so different from the way she had been taught the Bible in her Christian community. There, they were never presented with different interpretations of the same passage but rather were taught one "truth." Beth finds the diverse interpretations of the rabbis the most fascinating part of the class.

Following the Chumash class, at 3:00, Beth goes back to the library for Sarah's class in Halacha (Jewish law), at which there are about twenty women. Sarah announces that to illustrate today's topic—*brachot*—she will go through a day's sequence and describe the *brachot* to be recited for each activity. Beth and several other women smile and nod their heads; they've picked up some of the *brachot* since they've been here, but there are so many that it's hard to keep them all straight. Sarah begins with the blessings said on arising and the morning hand washing and then proceeds to breakfast, to the *brachot* for food. She tells them that different categories of food require different *brachot*. Then, with a little laugh, she remarks, "This is where it gets complicated." For instance, because fruit salad is an assortment of foods, each requires a different blessing, and there are laws governing their order of priority—which Sarah begins to enumerate. Beth exchanges a look with the woman next to her. "This is overwhelming!" their eyes say. Class members ask many questions, and Sarah does her best to answer them. Beth feels a little uncomfortable and confused about all these blessings. Like everyone else, she wants to get them all right. The class ends at 4:00 with many questions still lingering. Sarah assures her students that in future classes they can spend as much time as necessary on *brachot*.

The women troop back downstairs for a snack. Today Sophie has baked brownies, which are heaped on trays on the table. Beth helps herself to brownies, juice, and an apple and sits down by herself, tired. Several women in a corner of the dining room are dancing in a circle and singing, "We Want Moshiach Now." Beth smiles. Many times in the past few weeks she's joined them, but today she's content to sit and let the day's events settle. "The daily routine here is so full," she thinks. "Even though it's so exciting, I get so tired. I'll have to go to bed early tonight, instead of staying up like I usually do."

At 4:20 the women meander out of the dining room for the next class. Beth stays; it's time for her *chavrusa* with Cindy on the daily prayers. For the past ten days Beth has been meeting with Cindy for lessons in the siddur. By way of introducing the Lubavitch siddur, Cindy has explained its history and compilation, telling Beth that it differs in some ways from the standard Orthodox prayer book. As they go through the siddur, Cindy, who has a wonderful voice, teaches Beth some of the songs that are part of the prayers. Because Beth can't read Hebrew yet she is eager to learn the songs; this way she can at least sing some of the prayers rather than reading all of them in English. The *chavrusa* passes quickly.

At 5:00, Beth thanks Cindy and goes to the last class of the afternoon—the *sichoth* (discussions, lectures) of the Rebbe—which is taught by Rachel, another lifer *madricha* from Crown Heights. The *sichoth* that the women have received are in Yiddish, so Rachel spends most of the class time translating the text, which focuses on the need for unity among all Jews. Rachel says that the Rebbe feels Jews shouldn't pay attention to superficial differences among themselves, such as Reform, Conservative, or Orthodox, but should realize that all Jews are the same and have but one mission: to follow God's law and thus hasten the coming of the Moshiach, after which time there will be peace and harmony among the Jews and between the Jews and other nations. This image appeals to Beth; it is similar to the messianic teachings she'd learned as a Christian, but here she is learning her distinct role *as a Jew* in bringing these changes about.

When this class ends at 6:00, the women have a free hour before dinner. Beth runs into Malkie and Liz and asks them if they want to walk to the convenience store a few blocks away. As they all walk Malkie and Liz tell stories about Bais Chana and about Crown Heights. Beth takes it all in hungrily. She wonders if she'll want to move to Crown Heights or perhaps just spend some time there. At the convenience store Liz plays a few rounds of a video game. Beth is surprised at first; she had thought that someone who was really involved in the Lubavitch wouldn't be so frivolous as to play video games. But she is also a bit relieved: at least these women haven't given up everything in the secular world. When Liz finishes, Beth plays a round herself. She buys batteries for her tape recorder and asks the other two which candies are kosher. She can buy peanut butter cups and a few other kinds of chocolate, they tell her, but she can bring back to Bais Chana only dark chocolate with no milk. At Bais Chana there is only *cholov Yisroel* (Israel milk), specially kosher milk and dairy products; ordinary milk chocolate cannot be brought in. The three women arrive back in their rooms in time to rest for fifteen minutes before dinner.

At dinner Beth sits at a table across from Ruth and Naomi. They have so much energy and enthusiasm, and they try to be so helpful to the newcomers. Janet, a twenty-year-old woman who had arrived from Florida the day before, sits down next to Beth. As usual, the conversation at dinner is lively. Janet recounts how she came to Bais Chana. She'd taken drugs and begun to get involved with the guru Maharaj ji by attending classes and meditations. She had really wanted to become a "premie" (the name for Maharaj ji's followers) and find higher truth. Then on the bus one day she met a young man who'd been a premie and then had got involved with Lubavitch. He said to her, "You can find the same thing in Judaism as in Maharaj ji's group, but this is really yours, where you belong." Their conversation sent her on a search about Lubavitch that brought her to Bais Chana. Ruth is wide-eyed at Janet's story and asks her what it was like taking drugs. "Well," Janet says, "I was trying to reach a higher state, but it didn't work." Ruth replies, "But drugs are so dangerous! Here, through singing, dancing, and prayer, we try to reach God."

At the end of dinner—another huge meal—there is a *dvar torah*, this one by Malkie. Beth is impressed with Malkie's presentation: she seems so self-confident and does a great job weaving together the sayings of the rabbis with her own personal experiences at Bais Chana. "That'd be a good way to do it," Beth thinks. Dinner over, the women sing the *bentching* and head upstairs for the evening class.

This evening Rabbi Friedman again starts with a section of the Tanya, continuing the early discussion of the *beinoni*. Tonight, however, the rabbi wanders into a discussion of the prophets and then into stories of the various Rebbes and the different miracles they performed. Beth loves these "Rebbe stories"; telling them is a favorite Lubavitch pastime. Tonight he tells them about the previous (*friedeker*) Rebbe's diaries and what can be learned from them about the making of a *zaddik* (holy man). Everyone in the room listens closely; other women, particularly the lifers, share other Rebbe stories they'd heard from their parents and grandparents. The class goes on till about 12:30; the rabbi is so "on" and the women so fascinated that they just stay in the library learning.

After class, although many of the women go to their bedrooms exhausted, activities in the house continue. Many of the women are still energetic, and they animatedly talk and plan the rest of their evening. A group walks down to the dining room looking for Sophie, who is a late-night person, to persuade her to give them some snacks. A couple of women decide to study together. A few others head out for a walk. Beth is tempted to join the women in the dining room; that's always such a spirited and interesting scene. She remembers her promise to herself, however, and realizes that if she doesn't get a good night's sleep, she won't be able to pay attention the next day. Reluctantly she says good night and goes downstairs.

2

Women, Judaism, and Modernity

Stephanie, Beth, and the other women I introduced in the last
chapter caught my attention because they were engaged in an
unusual enterprise: they and their companions at Lincoln Square
Synagogue and Bais Chana were modern secular women who
were choosing to explore Orthodox—that is, very strictly observant—religious communities. While any evidence of renewed interest in Orthodox Judaism (the most fundamentalist form) is surprising because it challenges some commonsense assumptions
about the fate of religion and Judaism in modern society, Orthodox
Judaism's appeal to this group of women is especially intriguing
because it runs counter to an additional set of assumptions concerning the liberalization of women's roles. In terms of religion,
the predictions of social scientists and laypersons, and much of the
evidence, have pointed to the secularization (decreasing influence
of religion) of modern Western societies. Judaism was expected to,
and in many ways did, follow this general trend. With reference to
women, it is well known in Jewish circles that Orthodox Judaism
delineates a role for women that is largely defined in terms of their
duties as wives and mothers in nuclear families. Therefore, Orthodoxy's appeal to young, middle-class, educated women, who
would appear to have a wide range of options, and at a time when
feminist critiques of women's traditional roles are so widely available, is even more surprising.

This book represents my attempt to grasp the meaning of these
women's attraction to Orthodoxy and the process of their transformation. This is an ethnographic study of the ways two groups
of Jewish women and the religious communities to which they are
drawn construct religious worlds in the context of modern society.
The anthropologist Clifford Geertz writes that the goal of ethnographic research is to

grasp concepts that, for another people, are experience-near [i.e., the language they themselves would use to talk about their experiences], and to do so well enough to place them in illuminating connection with experience-distant concepts theorists have fashioned to capture the general details of social life.[1]

Here I seek to present my analysis of the women's experiences as the women themselves represented them and to place these experiences in the context of general theoretical understandings about religion, religious conversion, and women's choices about their roles in contemporary U.S. society.

The underlying assumption of ethnographic research is that a case study that pays close attention to a specific experience—even an exceptional one—reveals patterns and designs that pervade the larger picture as well. The women's attraction to Orthodoxy does represent an exceptional choice: Orthodox Jews represent a tiny minority (9 percent) of all U.S. Jews,[2] members must follow strict and rigid guidelines in almost all of their daily activities, and women's roles are defined in conventional terms. Nevertheless, the story I tell of women's attraction to Orthodoxy must be seen as part of a general pattern of religious resurgence in late-twentieth-century societies around the world. The specific details of how these young women and the representatives of the religious institutions they enter interact to produce their "conversion"[3] into an Orthodox Jewish community may shed light on the more general question of the nature, status, and appeal of religion in modern society. Similarly, the choices these women make, and the ways in which they account for them, have implications for the larger issues of women's roles and self-definitions in the late-twentieth-century United States.

This book is about women and about religion. The intent is that each focus will illuminate the other: the fact that these women are choosing religious contexts in which to satisfy their needs can offer insights into what religion offers modern secular individuals. Similarly, an understanding of why women in particular are making this choice may suggest some insights into the more general question of the wants and needs of contemporary women. My attempt to understand these women's attraction to Orthodoxy leads me to several separate but equally relevant discourses. In order to tell their stories I will draw on the language, background knowledge, and central themes in three bodies of literature: the sociology of religion, Judaism and modernity, and women and religion. Here I provide a brief introduction to these fields.

RELIGION IN MODERN U.S. SOCIETY

THE SECULARIZATION THESIS

The question of the nature of religion in modern society has been a concern of sociologists since the beginnings of the discipline in the nineteenth century. Discussion of this question has largely been framed in terms of what is called "the secularization thesis." Although this thesis—which claimed that religion would inevitably decrease in influence in modern societies—was dominant in the field for more than a century, since 1970 it has been seriously challenged. The result is what we can now refer to as the "secularization debate."

Early sociologists, such as Emile Durkheim, had predicted that the forces of modernization—industrialization, the development of bureaucratic nation-states, the rationalization of the economy and the state, and the development of science—would result in the inevitable and irreversible erosion of religious commitments.[4] According to this thesis, the conditions of life in modern societies pose serious structural as well as cognitive challenges to the continued survival of religious institutions and beliefs. On the social structural level, institutions such as the state, the schools, medicine, and science have taken over the functions once performed by religious institutions. Religions have retreated to the private world, where they have authority only over their followers.[5] On the cognitive level, the conditions of daily life in a modern urban culture make religious beliefs and ways of life increasingly implausible.

Peter Berger, whose analysis of secularization focuses primarily on the cognitive level, asserts that in preindustrial societies people lived in small, tightly knit communities in which the entire society served as a "plausibility structure" (social base) for the legitimation of religious beliefs.[6] In contrast, modern society is highly differentiated, social institutions perform specialized functions, and individuals move among a variety of institutional spheres in the course of daily life. Therefore, individuals are confronted with a plurality of spheres of meaning within which they can define their world-views and construct their identities. This pluralism threatens the legitimacy of any one institutionally sanctioned way of life because competing alternatives are always present.

The implications for religion are obvious. If a person can try out the Moonies, Hare Krishna, and Fundamentalist Christianity all in the same week, then no one way of life can seem compelling. The constant presence of alternatives reminds recruits that they do not have to adopt this worldview: they can just as easily choose something else tomorrow. Thus, religion—which in Berger's view used to permeate all aspects of life, was legitimized by the entire society, and provided a coherent framework for order and meaning—is now relegated to a discrete and chosen entity. And if it can be chosen one day, it can easily be abandoned the next.[7] Additionally, he claims, the dominance of functional rationality makes the "leap of faith" required for religious belief difficult for modern individuals.

On the other side of this debate are an increasing number of social scientists who challenge the secularization thesis. They claim that the description of an inevitable, inexorable, unilinear process of religious decline presented by secularization theorists stems from a flawed understanding of religion, society, and human nature, both past and present. Mary Douglas, a contemporary anthropologist, argues that there is no good evidence that traditional societies were as uniformly "religious" and integrated as Berger has portrayed.[8] Nor is life in modern society quite as wide open to individual choice as he claims. "The strangest conceit of all," she writes, "is that modernization has endowed us with greater freedom of choice than our parents."[9] Structural factors still shape our lives to a great extent. Furthermore, "belief" is not impossible in a rational scientific era: religion in modern society is not significantly challenged by science and rationalization because "religious and scientific explanations apply to very different kinds of problems."[10]

In a similar vein, Mary Jo Neitz, author of a fine ethnographic study of Charismatic Catholics, challenges Berger's theory by arguing that awareness of choice does not necessarily weaken the convert's commitment to her or his new religious community. The people she has studied are aware of other belief systems yet feel that they have "tested" this belief system and are convinced of its superiority.[11] In addition, Neitz argues that modern society is not as rational as Berger claims: many people still accept most things on faith. Religious beliefs are thus no less plausible than any other set of assumptions on which people base their understanding of the world.[12]

Other social scientists argue that the unilinear process of religious decline described by secularization theorists can never take place because it contradicts some basic elements of "human nature." Rodney Stark and William Sims Bainbridge, for example, assert that "the vision of a religionless future is but illusion."[13] While they acknowledge that secularization is a major trend in modern times, they claim that it is not a modern development and that religious economies are always undergoing simultaneous processes of decline, revival, and innovation. Religion will never disappear because people need "compensators"—systems of belief promising that rewards presently unavailable to them "will be obtained in the distant future or in some other context which cannot be immediately verified."[14] Or, as Anson Shupe and David Bromley put it:

> everything we know about human relationships indicates that . . .
> transcendent symbol systems . . . are necessary to the sustenance of
> the most important forms of human interaction.[15]

Many of these writers cite the contemporary flourishing of "new" and fundamentalist religious forms around the globe as evidence that the unilinear process posited by secularization theorists has simply not taken place.[16]

BEYOND THE SECULARIZATION DEBATE

Recently, several students of religion have begun to acknowledge that the secularization debate as it is currently framed—whether religion will inevitably fade as the forces of modernization spread—is unresolvable. Anson Shupe and David Bromley assert that "social science lacks the capacity to forecast the ultimate course of secularization."[17] Furthermore, the debate cannot be resolved in its current terms because it is frequently carried out simultaneously on two different levels of analysis: secularization theorists focus on the structural features of modern society that will lead to the inevitable decline of religion, while antisecularization theorists present evidence of individual choices to resacralize as "proof" that there is nothing distinct in modern society that is particularly threatening to religion.

I agree with the critics who assert that on the individual level secularization is clearly not proceeding in the unilinear fashion predicted by the theory. Many people in modern society are indeed choosing to seek out religious sources of meaning and norms. But I also believe that certain structural features of modern society do indeed pose serious challenges both for the individuals and the institutions involved in the creation and sustenance of religious ways of life. Thus, we need an approach that takes seriously individual choices and understandings of religion and the structural and institutional factors that shape it. Studies of religion must examine individual and collective religious behavior—how people in religious groups create and maintain transcendent symbol systems—as it is shaped by the opportunities and pressures of the larger social context.[18] This is the task I have set out to accomplish in this book.

This book does not attempt to provide a resolution to the secularization debate; a case study of two communities cannot be generalized to global macrostructural processes. Instead, one central goal of this book is to explore how two very similar, yet distinct, Jewish religious groups construct their religious worlds in the modern context. The analysis will highlight the ways in which these groups respond to such pressures of modernity as pluralism, individualism, rationalization, and the changing of women's roles. This is a study of how these factors affect the choices of individual women to enter Orthodox religious communities and of the ways in which the religious institutions create transcendent meaning systems that will appeal to these modern secular individuals.

Recently, there have been several excellent ethnographic studies highlighting the ways in which particular religious communities, especially "new religions" and Fundamentalist, Charismatic, or Evangelical Christian groups, construct themselves in the modern context.[19] These works demonstrate that religious organizations may adopt a variety of strategies for creating religious worlds within secular society. One approach religious groups have taken is *accommodation*—that is, adapting certain features of the religion to make it more consonant with secular ways of life. James Davison Hunter's study of Evangelical Protestants illustrates how they have accommodated their theology to the subjectivism of modernity by incorporating in their teachings guidelines for achieving "mental health."[20] The Charismatic Catholics studied by Mary Jo Neitz similarly adapt their religious symbols so that they are attractive within the context of "the culture of narcissism": for example, "God—the stern, authoritarian Father-figure—has become a loving, permissive parent."[21]

A different strategy open to religious groups attempting to carve out a mode of existence in the modern context is *resistance*—establishing strong boundaries with the broader culture, resisting cultural encroachments as much as possible, and setting the group up as a radical alternative. The Fundamentalist Christians studied by Nancy Ammerman "do not accept either the cultural pluralism or the institutional differentiation that have come to be assumed in the modern world."[22] They vehemently reject the idea of accommodation and make no compromises with such elements of the modern worldview as subjectivism. Instead, they seek ways to withdraw and fight back against the encroachment of modernity. They insist on separatism, and, rejecting differentiation, they construct a religious way of life that seeks to encompass all aspects of members' lives within one religious framework.

It is important to note, however, that even those groups attempting to resist modernity and purporting to represent a "return" to "fundamentals" are in fact themselves products of and responses to modernity.[23] Ammerman writes that "Fundamentalism could not exist without modernity." Fundamentalism arose as a movement only when the old orthodoxy encountered the challenges of modern pluralism and critical scholarship, and Fundamentalism is most prevalent in those social locations "where tradition is meeting modernity, rather than where modernity is most remote."[24] Fundamentalist religious beliefs and practices are necessarily different in "traditional, rural, often southern" communities than in places where people encounter and deal with diversity every day. So a great deal of the Fundamentalists' current religious organizations and ideas are actually constructed anew—as responses to modernity—but are then legitimated in "traditional" theological terms.

The use of the adjective *traditional* requires further discussion. Modern society is fraught with ambivalence and confusion about the meaning and abiding value of tradition. While politicians, advertising agencies, and the mass media appeal to the nostalgic value of tradition, others reject the authority of established patterns and celebrate the increased freedoms available in a modern society. Nevertheless, it is not clear what people are referring to when they speak of traditional ways of life: for example, some scholars have recently pointed out that what individuals now refer to as the "traditional" family is in fact a product of nineteenth-century Victorian culture.[25] As the anthropologist James Clifford emphasizes, in the twentieth century there are no continuous cultures or traditions. "Everywhere individuals and groups improvise local performances from (re)collected pasts, drawing on foreign media, symbols, and languages."[26]

Similarly, the two Orthodox Jewish groups in this study do not represent unbroken traditions. Each is a relatively recent form of an ancient tradition,[27] even though the representatives and recruits of each group stake its validity on the form's long-standing value. Therefore, the particular uses and meanings of the term *tradition* in the language of the women and rabbis in the modern Orthodox and Lubavitch communities are a central underlying concern of this study. What the term means, how they choose to use it, the authority it represents, and the differences in how the term is used by the women and the rabbis are a major feature of the religious construction of meaning in these settings.

JUDAISM AND MODERNITY

Most ethnographic studies of the ways religious organizations and individuals interact to create religious worlds in the context of modern society have been about Christians and new religious movements. Although there have been many studies addressing the question of how modernity has affected Jews,[28] there are few ethnographies that detail the particular ways Jewish communities construct themselves in the face of the secularizing influence of modern society.[29] This book aims to contribute to an understanding of these issues.

Jews are particularly interesting to study because they represent a special case of the intersection of religion and modernity. Although I agree with critics of Berger that life in preindustrial societies was probably less cohesive and uniform than he portrays, Jews in premodern Europe, particularly Eastern Europe, did live in small, self-contained, highly integrated communities. In conformity with the requirements of their national governments, which limited where Jews could live and what occupations they could choose, Jewish communities formed their own internal governing bodies. Social life was relatively undifferentiated for premodern Jews: there was a great deal of interpenetration among religion, occupation, language, ethnicity, family, and government.[30] Identity was ascriptive, given at birth, rather than achieved. The religion legitimated the community's way of life, and the community in turn maintained and reinforced the religion, which was much more a matter of practice than of doctrine and belief. The internal governing body of each community, the *kehilla*, was able to enforce conformity to Halacha through the application of sanctions. Even though I am certain that violations of the rules occurred, the religious way of life was fairly well maintained by face-to-face interactions within the small communities. The entire community served as a plausibility structure for upholding the "sacred canopy" of the Jewish religion.[31]

The sweeping social structural changes that constituted "modernization" had a profound impact on the European Jewish communities, beginning in Western Europe. Following the French Revolution, male Jews were granted full citizenship in the French state, marking the beginning of the breakdown of the walls of the ghettos that had confined Jews since the Middle Ages. New opportunities for geographic and economic mobility emerged, and Jews, primarily men, began to enter the wider society in many of its various occupational, educational, social, and cultural spheres. Not surprisingly, changes in religion were soon to follow.

Even though Jews have to some extent always modified their religious practices in response to the influence of surrounding cultures, the opportunity for integration into the wider society presented Jews with new opportunities and challenges. One way they attempted to meet these challenges was by reconstructing their religion so that they could maintain their religious participation without attracting unwanted attention to their differences from their neighbors.

The first significant attempts at reform began in Germany in the early nineteenth century. Young, intellectual Jewish men, who had finally had the opportunity to receive university educations and had studied with philosophers such as Kant and Hegel, attempted to create a Judaism that would be more suitable for modern life.[32] Following the lead of the eighteenth-century German-Jewish philosopher Moses Mendelssohn, they sought to transform those aspects of synagogue worship and ritual observance that set Jews apart, thereby facilitating Jews' integration into the mainstream society.[33] The first Reform synagogue was founded in 1810 to establish a contemporary Jewish service in which rituals, customs, and prayers that were unenlightened or unaesthetic would be eliminated; this service would demonstrate that Judaism was "as progressive, modern, and enlightened an expression of the common religion of humanity as any other faith."[34] The Reform Judaism that began in the Jewish communities of Germany spread throughout Europe and in the 1820s took root in the United States as well.

This new variety of Judaism, created in response to the challenges of modernization and the Enlightenment, represented an extreme form of accommodation.[35] The founders of the Reform movement in the United States, like their European counterparts, attempted to fashion a brand of Judaism that would be more in tune with the sensibilities of their Christian neighbors. These reformers eliminated or modified the traditional practices and doctrines that had established and reinforced Jews' uniqueness, such as kashrut (the dietary laws), observance of the Sabbath, the idea of the divine origin of the Bible, the belief that Jews were "the chosen people," and Hebrew language services. Today Reform Judaism is the second largest denomination: 29 percent of U.S. Jews identify as Reform.

In the twentieth century, two additional forms of Judaism were developed in the United States: Conservative and Reconstructionist. The founders of Conservative Judaism were Reform rabbis who, while no longer committed to strict observance of every detail of traditional Jewish law, nevertheless reacted against the seeming disregard for tradition in Reform Judaism. These men sought to create a variety of Judaism that would attract Orthodox and Reform Jews by offering the perfect combination of tradition and change.[36] In the early 1900s a group of rabbis espousing this orientation founded their own rabbinical academy, the Jewish Theological Assembly, and then their own congregational organization, the United Synagogue of America.

In contrast with Reform rabbis, Conservative leaders generally agreed on the need to maintain such basic practices as the dietary laws and Sabbath observance and such essential doctrines as belief in Jewish nationalism and the importance of Hebrew in Jewish life.[37] They were also willing, however, to modify or discard some of the other laws, such as the traditional Jewish divorce laws, which relegated women to a passive role. Conservative Judaism is the largest U.S. denomination: 34 percent of U.S. Jews identify themselves as Conservative.

Reconstructionist Judaism, which claims only 2 percent of the U.S. Jewish population, represented yet another approach to constructing a Jewish religious alternative that suited the times. It was founded by Mordecai M. Kaplan, who in 1922 broke away from the Orthodox synagogue of which he had been rabbi to form a new congregation, the Society for the Advancement of Judaism. He felt that the other branches of Judaism were notoriously unsuccessful in attracting and keeping adherents. Therefore, Judaism needed a new approach. His major treatise outlining his vision of a "reconstructed" Judaism was published in 1922 under the title *Judaism as a Civilization: Toward a Reconstruction of American Jewish Life.*

Like the Reformers, Kaplan eliminated "outdated" doctrines such as supernatural revelation and divine "choosing" of the Jews. In contrast to the Reformers, however, he sought to maintain many of the traditional customs, rituals, ceremonies, and festivals. He specified that these were to be retained not because they were divinely ordained but because they provided rich opportunities for spiritual experience. Judaism, in this view, served primarily a social function: Jews were most centrally a people, not a religious group. Kaplan conceptualized Judaism in its broadest terms as including a variety of religious and secular components.[38]

Whereas Reform, Conservative, and Reconstructionist approaches have to varying degrees accommodated the secular society, Orthodox Judaism represents the other end of the continuum of responses to modernity and adheres most strictly to the tenets of Halacha.[39] Most Orthodox Jewish communities—which in premodern Europe represented the norm and thus did not need the special label *Orthodox*—attempt to resist modernization's encroachments on traditional religious ways of life. Orthodoxy's leaders and members share the belief that the Torah is of divine origin; therefore, all of its commandments must be obeyed. This acceptance of the obligatory nature of religious law is what distinguishes the Orthodox from the other branches.

Nevertheless, even within this seriously committed branch of the religion, there are enormous variations that reflect the myriad stances to the modern world adopted by Orthodoxy's many subgroups. The scope of this intragroup variation can be seen in the areas of training and governance: whereas Reform, Conservative, and Reconstructionist Jews each have one rabbinical academy that trains their leaders, and one religious assembly that governs the group, Orthodox Jews may be ordained in numerous different seminaries and yeshivas or even by individual rabbis, and the congregations may belong to one of several synagogue assemblies.[40]

Although these Jewish responses to modernity offer interesting possibilities for research, this study focuses on Orthodox Judaism because as the most fundamentalist form it seems to represent the most unlikely choice for individuals in modern society. By choosing the most unusual case I am able to see in high relief the various ways in which a group that is committed to tradition but nevertheless exists in a modern society can attract modern people and deal with the conflicts produced by the ongoing tensions between tradition and modernity.

For this study I purposely selected settings in which I could explore two distinct contemporary Orthodox approaches to constructing religious worlds in the modern context: a modern Orthodox synagogue and a Lubavitch Hasidic residential yeshiva. Conducting research in two similar, yet disparate, communities would, I expected, help make the belief sytems, worldviews, and religious ways of life in each community more apparent. Because newcomers to Orthodox Judaism (and to some other religions as well) generally learn behaviors and beliefs appropriate to the community in the context of institutions that specialize in resocialization, I chose for each type of Orthodoxy a setting widely known for its outreach work: Lincoln Square Synagogue for the modern Orthodox approach and Bais Chana for the Lubavitch Hasidic approach.

The most fundamental differences between these two groups of Orthodox Jews result from their distinct stances toward modern society. Modern Orthodox Jews differ from the sectarian Orthodox Jews (of whom the Lubavitch Hasidim are one subgroup) along the continuum of responses to modernity. Of course, all contemporary Orthodox Jewish groups, like their Fundamentalist Christian counterparts, are in fact new constructions representing different approaches to creating "traditional" religious worlds in the modern context. Nevertheless, modern Orthodox ideology explicitly advocates accommodation to the surrounding culture, whereas sectarian group ideology is committed to resistance.

Modern Orthodoxy, which emerged as a distinct approach in Germany in the middle of the nineteenth century, was founded by Rabbi Samson Raphael Hirsch. He believed that Jews did not have to choose between a commitment to tradition and life in the modern world because classical Judaism mandated a creative synthesis between Torah and secular knowledge.[41] Hirsch's guiding principle was *Torah im derech eretz*, combining "Torah with the ways of the people of the land." In the United States this approach was institutionalized in the early twentieth century by the founding of Yeshiva University (1915–1928), a center for rabbinical training that is also committed to educating its students in all fields of knowledge, secular and religious.

Modern Orthodoxy accommodates the pluralism and structural differentiation of the wider society: the synagogues have a loose social structure in which members come together for Sabbath and holiday observances but otherwise carry out most aspects of their lives within the secular society. Modern Orthodox Jews attend secular educational institutions, may have friends who are not Jewish, and generally have occupations outside of the Jewish community. Although institutions offer numerous opportunities for members to "Judaize" their daily lives by participating in Jewish activities throughout the week (such as prayer services for men, adult education programs, and social events), modern Orthodox

Jews live a bicultural existence characterized by a dual allegiance to the conflicting worlds of tradition and modernity.[42]

In contrast, the Lubavitch Hasidim attempt to preserve the ancient traditions by resisting accommodation with the secular society. Despite this commitment to resistance, however, the numerous sectarian Orthodox communities can themselves be divided along a continuum from accommodation to resistance. Those groups variously referred to as the "traditional" Orthodox—the *yeshivishe velt* (yeshiva world, a term that represents the organization of this community into subgroups that center around one rabbi from a yeshiva) or the "black hat" community (a reference to the black hats worn by men in this group)—are slightly more accommodating to the secular society than are the numerous Hasidic sects. Black hat Jews resist modernity by upholding extremely stringent levels of observance (such as drinking only *cholov Yisroel*), socializing mostly within the group, and generally avoiding higher secular education. But they may also participate in the secular society through their choice of occupation, pursuit of a secular education, and participation at cultural events such as sports, theater, and the movies.

Hasidim, in contrast, resist modernity in nearly every imaginable way. They are organized into tightly knit and highly insular subgroups that center around a particular rabbi, called a Rebbe, a spiritual leader to whom followers attribute extraordinary powers and whose advice they seek on all matters of personal and religious life. The names of the various Hasidic groups, such as Lubavitch, Belz, and Satmar, represent the towns in Europe in which the communities originated. In light of the stringency of observance among contemporary Hasidic sects, it is striking to note that Hasidism originally arose in Eastern Europe in the first half of the eighteenth century as a populist movement. Its leaders, responding to the disintegration and despair in the Jewish community that followed the pogroms of the seventeenth and early eighteenth centuries, tried to make Judaism accessible to the poverty-stricken masses whose lack of scriptural knowledge excluded them from the dominant rabbinic Judaism of the time. The Hasidim asserted that God could be approached through the heart far more than through the mind and that singing and dancing were appropriate means of worship.

In contrast, contemporary U.S. Hasidic communities—with the exception of the Lubavitch, whose primary goal is outreach to the assimilated Jewish masses—are strictly introversionist and exclusivist sects. They establish and maintain strong boundaries that shield members from the encroachments of the modern world, and the group exercises strict control over members' lives. The Hasidim resist the differentiation of modernity: the members' basic needs, such as obtaining jobs, residences, and even spouses, are met within the confines of the community. Secular education is completely shunned, members maintain a distinctive style of dress, and U.S. national holidays are not observed. These groups truly attempt to maintain an alternative to life in the secular world. Yet even while they resist modernity, the Hasidim adopt elements of the surrounding society—for example, the Lubavitch Hasidim broadcast some of the Rebbe's lectures in Yiddish on cable television.

WOMEN AND RELIGION IN
MODERN U.S. SOCIETY

A significant feature of contemporary social life to which religious communities must respond is the expansion of women's roles that has accompanied the various structural shifts of modernization. Established religious traditions such as Judaism and Christianity generally included guidelines for distinct gender roles and the organization of nuclear family life. These religious norms were a reflection of members' lives as well as models for how they should live.[43] As the ordered, patterned ways of life in premodern Western societies crumbled under the onslaught of industrialization, urbanization, and differentiation, many of the productive tasks women had performed in their homes were moved into the newly developing factories. Although some women followed their work into the factories, the majority did not. Mary Ryan, a feminist historian, reports that "as of 1860 only 10.2 percent of the women enumerated on the United States Census were said to be gainfully employed outside the home."[44] Thus, a question emerged about the nature of women's roles and the organization of family life in the new industrial era.[45]

In the early to mid-1800s, "the topic of womanhood was among the central preoccupations of the national culture."[46] Even though the nineteenth century did witness various movements for the expansion of women's roles beyond the home, the dominant ideology of the time separated "home" from "commerce" and divided these spheres by sex. The social, economic, and spatial differentiation of work from home and male from female contributed to a conception of male and female natures as essentially distinct. Women were presumed to have special personal qualities of warmth, piety, and purity that would enable them to set up homes that would be loving havens in the heartless world of modern industrial society.[47] Men would fill the complementary role of rugged individualists whose identity would be defined by their ability to succeed in the harsh, competitive world of work.

The religious and communitarian movements of the late nineteenth century articulated their own responses to this central concern. Some religious communities, such as spiritualism and Christian Science, supported women's empowerment and constructed religious ideologies that encouraged women to challenge the established order, both within religion and in the larger society.[48] Most religious groups of the time, however, adopted a conservative solution. They sought to resolve the questions of women's roles within their own communities as well as in the wider society by preaching that women and men had distinct natures that suited them for different roles in life.[49]

In the second half of the twentieth century, similar questions about gender, work, and family life have emerged, occasioned by the occupational, technological, educational, and social changes of the postwar United States. Women now marry and bear children at a later age than they did in the 1950s, and their participation in the paid labor force nearly doubled between 1950 and 1985 (from 33 percent to 56 percent). In addition, women now constitute a majority of undergraduate students in colleges and universities, and the percentage of women in all of the professions has increased.[50] In the late 1960s the sexual revolution overturned the Victorian morality that had reinforced a sexual double standard. Thus, many of the social restrictions and norms that had kept women "in their place" since the late nineteenth century have been eroding, resulting in the reemergence of the debate over woman's true nature and proper social role.

Just as in the nineteenth century many social, religious, and communitarian movements offered their own resolutions to the dilemma of "woman's place," so, too, contemporary religious groups all take a stance on the nature of women and men, their proper relations, and the dilemmas of family life. Some religious groups—especially some of the "new" ones that emerged in the late 1960s and 1970s—provide religious legitimation for current efforts to replace traditional roles with a wider variety of options for women and men.[51] Many mainstream groups accommodate their teachings and regulations concerning gender, marriage, and the family to the liberalization of options in the wider society. For example, by the mid-1980s, most religious denominations (including Reform and Conservative Judaism) that had previously barred women from ordination encouraged women to study to be ministers or rabbis.

A significant portion of contemporary religious groups, however—from Fundamentalist Christians to the Hare Krishna to Pentecostal Catholics—have resisted the liberalizing tendencies of the times and constructed ideologies and rules that create and maintain "traditional" definitions for female and male roles. Indeed, recent research on contemporary religious movements demonstrates that in the current climate of loose gender definitions and multiplication of options for family life, converts are often strongly attracted to a religious community's legitimation of reconstructed "traditional" gender roles as the basis for marriage and family life.[52] As Meredith McGuire writes in her book on Pentecostal Catholics:

> [Their] teachings reassert gender norms of chaste behavior and dress, traditional sexual morality, women's obedience to husbands and male superiors in the prayer community, and finding the satisfaction of one's "place."[53]

Newcomers are attracted to the certainty of specific guidelines for nuclear family life and comprehensively defined rules for gender behavior. In support of women's primary role in the home, religious leaders instruct their followers that being a housewife is very meaningful to the Lord. Pentecostal Catholics, for example, teach that liberation is to be found not in rejecting that role but in "discovering how beautifully and richly one can grow as a Christian by being the Lord's own dependable servant in that role."[54]

What is particularly interesting about the role definitions and family guidelines provided in these groups is that although the model for women is traditional, meaning home based, the communities actually offer men an alternative to the rugged individualist ideal of the broader culture. Many of these movements define a role for men that emphasizes the importance of their participation in family life. Thus, women members are benefited by the community's emphasis on the nuclear family because it provides legitimation of and clear instructions for men's greater involvement in the home.[55]

Most of the research on contemporary religious responses to the current social ferment about gender has focused on various Christian and new religious groups. (Two exceptions to this are Herbert Danzger's book and Debra Kaufman's articles on newly Orthodox Jews, both of which I discuss later.[56]) This book examines the processes by which leaders, new recruits, and members in two traditional *Jewish* groups construct solutions to the dilemmas of personal life in modern industrial society. In this book I explore the experiences of modern secular Jewish women who are choosing the branch of Judaism that maintains the strictest division of roles—in both the public and private spheres—by sex. Unlike the other branches of Judaism, which in keeping with their commitment to modernize the tradition have liberalized many laws concerning women's place in the religion (such as allowing women full and equal participation in the religious life of the community), Orthodox Jewish groups have largely resisted the encroachment of feminism. Orthodox Judaism does not ordain women as rabbis, allows women no public ritual roles or honors, and prescribes a home-centered role for women.

This book is an attempt to understand how and why young, educated, secular Jewish women are attracted to religious communities that offer such traditional definitions of gender and how these women are then resocialized into the community's norms and way of life. The newcomers' resocialization to Orthodoxy requires learning the role of the Orthodox Jewish woman. How do the rabbis and *ba'alot teshuvah* interact to create and transmit the community's definitions and norms? Because gender is such a central part of identity, the religious reconstruction of the women's ideas and behaviors in this realm constitutes a significant dimension of the creation of Orthodox Jewish religious worlds in the modern context.

Other researchers who have studied *ba'alei* and *ba'alot teshuvah* indicate that the Orthodox definitions of gender and clear guidelines for nuclear family life are a major factor in their appeal to modern individuals.[57] Debra Kaufman reports that her respondents all "affirm gender differentiation and celebrate traditional feminine qualities, particularly those associated with mothering."[58] Herbert Danzger's recent book on newly Orthodox men and women reports that the community's emphasis on the nuclear family is particularly attractive to the newly Orthodox women.[59]

Although this book shares concerns with these two studies, it differs from them in several important ways. Danzger's book resembles this one in its focus on new recruits and their resocialization in the various institutions representing a wide variety of Orthodox approaches. His book, however, is largely a study of men. Although he does include women in his sample, he was naturally granted access only to the men's resocializing institutions. Thus, his book is more successful in illuminating the world of the *ba'al teshuvah* than that of the *ba'alat teshuvah*. This book, in contrast, highlights the experiences of the women.

Kaufman's research, like mine, focuses exclusively on women. Nevertheless, our samples and research foci are quite different. Kaufman's study was based largely on interviews with *ba'alot teshuvah* who had completed the "conversion process" and were married, established members of Orthodox communities. Her book illuminates how these women understand their original attraction to Orthodoxy and the nature of their daily lives as members of Orthodox Jewish groups. Within this work she does not make comparisons between the recruits in the very different kinds of Orthodox Jewish communities she studied, such as the modern and the Hasidic. This book, in contrast, focuses on the experiences of new recruits—the majority of whom are single—in two very different types of Orthodox communities. It presents an analysis of the women's initial attraction to Orthodoxy and the processes of resocialization involved, highlighting the significant contrasts between the different types of Orthodoxy, the women attracted to each, and their distinct modes of constructing traditional Jewish worlds in the modern context. The two works can be seen as complementary: together they offer a fuller picture of the various stages in becoming a *ba'alat teshuvah* from initial attraction and resocialization to marriage, childbearing, and daily life as married women.

THE NATURE OF THIS BOOK

This book tells the story of two groups of secular Jewish women who were troubled by some of the characteristic dilemmas of modern life, such as feelings of isolation, rootlessness, and confusion about gender. These women sought solutions in an unusual way through participation in Orthodox Jewish resocialization programs. Comparisons between the two groups of women and the institutional ways of life at Lincoln Square Synagogue and Bais Chana allow us to appreciate the diverse ways modernity affects individuals and institutions. Although contemporary life poses some common stresses and strains for people, the particular nature of individuals' stresses and the ways they seek solutions are shaped by their actual position within modern society. Similarly, although contemporary life poses certain characteristic problems for religious institutions, they formulate distinct responses that are rooted in their characteristic stances toward modernity.

In this book I trace the processes through which these two groups of Jewish women, who were at different life stages and occupied different positions in society, were attracted to particular variants of Orthodox Judaism. The story follows them as they participated in the institutions' programs for religious resocialization and then looks at what happened as the women and the representatives of the religious institutions interacted to create distinct types of conversion experiences. The comparisons between the two groups of women and their diverse socialization experiences in these distinct Orthodox institutions are a central analytic focus here.

Looking from the outside, we may see these groups of women as doing the same thing: choosing to participate in fundamentalist

Jewish communities. In fact, however, they started out from very different positions, which affected what they were seeking when they explored membership in an Orthodox community. Similarly, the Orthodox Jewish groups they selected differed from each other in very significant ways. Thus, the comparisons between the two groups of women and the institutions allow us to see a range of individual and religious responses to modernity and how these shape the creation of two distinct Orthodox Jewish worlds.

Obviously there are many other secular Jewish women who are in social locations similar to those of the women in this study, find themselves with similar dilemmas in their lives, but do not choose to join Orthodox Jewish communities. Perhaps some of these women join health clubs, or social activist groups, or other religious groups in an attempt to find a "core" to their lives. Or, perhaps, like many in the United States, they are simply content to live their lives without any central overarching belief system and community base. The goal of this book is not to explain the women's choice of this unusual solution in terms of the factors that distinguish them from other secular Jewish women in similar circumstances. Instead, this ethnography focuses on the religious resocialization of women in two different Orthodox communities.

Contemporary ethnography is understood by its followers as a process of interpretation rather than explanation. Phenomenological approaches in social science, "in the tradition that leads from Wilhelm Dilthey, via Max Weber, to 'symbols and meanings' anthropologists like Clifford Geertz,"[60] cannot tell us why some people do one thing and others do not. Thus, rather than try to find the distinctive characteristics of joiners, ethnographers of religious communities instead try to portray the religious world as it is experienced by those inside or entering it. That is the goal of this book as well.

My research concentrated on the early stages of the women's attraction to Orthodoxy: their seeking out and beginning to learn the culture as it was presented to them by the rabbis and representatives of their chosen communities. This was a study of conversion as a process of interaction and mutual influence between the women and the religious organizations and spokespeople who reached out and attempted to recruit them. In this book I will describe in detail the initial interactions between the two groups of women and the religious communities they chose to enter and the beginnings of their process of transformation.

Although this book focuses on the experiences of two very small, unusual groups of women and the marginal religious groups they have chosen, I have engaged in a detailed analysis of their experiences as a way to illuminate more general social trends. As I will show throughout the book, the dilemmas and concerns of these women are those of other women as well and offer us a vivid and concrete image of how some people act out some of the central questions in our culture. That the *ba'alot teshuvah* have chosen this unusual solution puts them in a position of having to explain themselves—to their families and friends as well as to researchers—more than do women whose choices are not as radical.

Jill Matthews uses a similar strategy of selecting an unusual group as a way to explore more general social meanings.[61] She has examined the case records of women who were institutionalized in mental homes as a way of uncovering the normative definitions of femininity in Australian culture. By concentrating on those who "broke the rules" of femininity, she has been able to tease out the underlying, implicit rules for what it means to be a woman. Similarly, a detailed exploration of how the *ba'alot teshuvah* account for their unusual choices offers us a context in which to explore wide occurrences—how women make choices, understand their roles and feminism, and assign meaning to community and tradition.

I began in chapter 1 with an introduction to the women and the communities they entered. I continue the story in chapter 3 with an account of how I came to study and meet these groups of women and some of the ways in which I tried to learn about their experiences. Comparisons between the types of women attracted to each Orthodox community—the life circumstances surrounding their entry, their different social locations in modernity, and the distinct natures of their quests—are developed in chapters 4 and 5. In chapter 6, I present the religious teachings offered to the women in each community, highlight the differences in worldview and ways of life, and connect the institution's stance in modern society with the social characteristics of the women who were attracted to them. Chapter 7 shows how the different types of women and institutions interacted to produce a distinct process of religious resocialization. Chapter 8 reviews the main findings of the book and analyzes their broader significance for our understanding of trends in Judaism, religious institutions, and women's lives in the late-twentieth-century United States.

3

A Journey into Two Jewish Communities

Believing, with Max Weber, that [humans are] animal[s] suspended in webs of significance [they themselves have] spun, I take culture to be those webs, and the analysis of it to be therefore not an experimental science in search of laws but an interpretive one in search of meaning.

Clifford Geertz,
"Thick Description:
Toward an Interpretive
Theory of Culture"

BAIS CHANA

In late June 1983 I boarded an airplane in Boston that was headed to the Minneapolis/St. Paul airport. I was on my way to participate in and study the daily life at Bais Chana, a residential institute run by the Lubavitch Hasidim. Bais Chana serves to introduce young, mostly Jewish women to traditional, Lubavitch-style Judaism through an intensive program of classes and everyday living. I was twenty-eight years old, I had been married for four years, and I was doing research for my doctoral dissertation.

I had first learned about Bais Chana through the literature I had been reading on *ba'alei teshuvah*. In a sociology doctoral dissertation written by Malcolm Kovacs, a Jewish man who had done fieldwork in a Lubavitch residential study center for men and who had himself "converted" in the process, I found a short footnote referring to a similar institute for women in St. Paul, Minnesota.[1] As the goal of my study was to understand the experience of becoming a *ba'alat teshuvah* from the point of view of the women who do this—and taking into account that I was not becoming a *ba'alat teshuvah*—my research strategy was to immerse myself in two settings in which this transformation occurred. This research method, known as fieldwork or participant observation, would allow me to hear not only retrospective accounts of the process (information I would

49

obtain through in-depth interviewing) but to experience the contexts, ideas, and relationships that led the women to be converted. Hence, this footnote was a wonderful discovery. Here was a setting that could allow me to do exactly what I wanted: to observe and participate intensively in the ongoing process of the religious creation and transmission of meanings. I immediately sought more information about this institute.

By telephoning the Lubavitch center in Boston, I obtained the address and name of the director of Bais Chana. I wrote a letter presenting myself and my project to Rabbi Moses Feller, director of the Upper Midwest Lubavitch, whose offices were housed at the institute. Through a series of letters we arranged for me to spend a month at Bais Chana that summer, going through the program with the new recruits.

My interest in a project on secular women who become attracted to Orthodoxy emerged from personal experience as well as from the intellectual considerations described in chapter 2. I had been brought up Orthodox, although at the time of the study I had not been Orthodox for nine years. In fact, I was unaffiliated with any synagogue or denomination. Nevertheless, being Jewish was still an important part of my self-identity. Therefore, I was very curious about the people involved in what the Orthodox referred to as the *ba'al teshuvah* movement. What did they find in it that I had not seen? How did their experience of Orthodoxy differ from mine so that they were attracted to it whereas I had fallen away? In particular I was interested in the women: I had become a feminist and was uncomfortable with the largely domestic roles for women delineated in Orthodox Jewish conceptions of gender. Nevertheless, I knew that many educated professional women were attracted to Orthodoxy. How did they reconcile their professional identities with the more domestic definition of women's roles that prevailed in the Orthodox world?

Early on I learned that I had to struggle to separate my own assumptions and worldview from those of the women I was meeting. This was a self-selected group. They would not have continued participating at Bais Chana or Lincoln Square Synagogue if they had experienced cognitive dissonance there—that is, if the worldview being offered clashed with values they held dear. Thus, a central goal of this project was to understand their attraction to Orthodoxy from the perspective of their life experiences, not mine.

Through participating with the women in their worlds I came to appreciate the many attractive features they found in Orthodox Jewish life. As I will illustrate, the Orthodox world offered these women several important dimensions of life they felt were missing in secular society. The women I met in these two communities were acting constructively to seek solutions for problems many individuals experience in modern societies. Even though I did not "go native," in the end, I emerged from the study with more empathy for the Orthodox world, a deeper understanding of its appeal to modern individuals, and an increased interest in finding ways to express my own Jewish identity.

Because I knew that Lubavitch women followed a strict dress code, I inquired about it prior to my departure. Joanne, one of the secretaries, wrote that Bais Chana had no dress code except that on the Sabbath women were expected to wear skirts or dresses. Her response suggested to me that they were flexible and did not force observances on newcomers before they were ready. I also learned that although the tuition was $100 a week, I, like many of the other women, was granted a large scholarship and directed to "pay the balance when [my] financial situation improves."

I arrived in Minneapolis/St. Paul with no clear images of what the physical setting, the other women, or the daily routine at Bais Chana would be like. I was greeted at the airport by Joanne, who drove me to the institute, pointing out other Lubavitch buildings along the way and chatting about her own experiences with the Lubavitch (she was a convert from outside of Judaism). In response to my query about how women found out about Bais Chana (I had found out about it almost by accident), she explained that Lubavitch *shlichim* around the world sent Jewish women there to learn more about traditional Judaism. She told me that approximately two hundred women—from all over the world but mostly from the United States—stayed at the institute for one to eight weeks each summer. The women ranged in age from sixteen to sixty-five; most, however, were in their late teens and early twenties. She assured me that I'd get used to Bais Chana in no time and that I'd enjoy myself thoroughly: "All the girls do," she said with a grin.

I already knew a little about the history of the institute from an article in one of the publications I had been sent. In the mid-1960s, a young rabbi, Rabbi Feller, and his bride, Mindy, arrived in Minnesota at the direction of the Lubavitcher Rebbe for the purpose of *kiruv*—bringing assimilated Jews to traditional religious practice. In 1965 they bought a large house in the suburbs and named it the Merkos (center) Retreat House. They sponsored *Shabbatons*—weekend retreat programs in which participants learned about and experienced the Sabbath—and a variety of other educational and social activities. By 1970 this couple had been joined by another young Lubavitch couple, and they formulated the idea of a "Live and Learn Center, where girls of extremely limited background in *Yiddishkeit* [traditional Judaism] could pursue purely Torah studies. At that time, there was no such program anywhere in the country."[2] The first session—called the Women's Institute of Jewish Studies—was held in 1971 and had an enrollment of eleven women. Since then the program had grown. Now they ran a two-month program in the summer and a one-month program in the winter, both designed to coincide with college vacations.

Prior to my arrival, I had been anxious that some of the women might feel suspicious and threatened by a researcher in their midst. Yet when I introduced myself to two of my roommates and told them the purpose of my stay, both were actually pleased that someone "outside" thought they were worthy of study. One said, "Oh, what a fascinating project!" I was reassured by their responses that I would probably be well received by the other women. Relieved, I settled down to start my work.

As I began to meet the women and the leaders in this setting, I sketched for myself a picture of the major resocializing agents. These were the two rabbis, the dean of women, the *madrichot*, and, to some extent, all of the women. Rabbi Manis Friedman was the principal and taught two three-hour classes daily that were attended by nearly every woman. He also spent time privately counseling the women. He lived with his family several blocks from the institute. Rabbi Feller, Mindy, who was the dean of women, and their young son lived at Bais Chana for the summer and served as role models and "local parents." During Shabbat they sat at the head table and led the ritual prayers and singing.

This setting had only female participants, with the exception of the rabbis. About 80 percent of the women in the setting were *ba'alot teshuvah* at varying stages of the process, from those who had recently encountered the Lubavitch to those who had entered the community several years earlier. More than 95 percent of all the women, *madrichot* as well as *ba'alot teshuvah*, were single.

PARTICIPANT OBSERVATION

Participant observation, the principal form of data collection in ethnographic research, is a "process in which the [researcher] closely observes, records, and engages in the daily life of another culture."[3] The work involves a continuous attempt to "see" the researched community from the "inside" and from the "outside," to grasp nuance and detail and subtle meanings from within, but then to situate them in a wider social context.[4] The final product of this work, an ethnography, is an account of this culture emphasizing descriptive detail and offering an interpretive framework within which to understand the meaning of the details presented.[5]

A fundamental goal of my fieldwork was to understand the women's actions from their own points of view so that readers of my account could grasp the process and meaning of the turn to Orthodoxy. But as an "outsider," my experiences in the research settings were never identical to those of the women; I could never quite "think, feel, and perceive" as they did.[6] As the anthropologist James Clifford writes, this inability of field-workers to "inhabit indigenous minds . . . is a permanent, unresolved problem of ethnographic method."[7]

Instead of attempting the impossible, I strove to achieve a stance referred to as "detached involvement," which acknowledged the complexity of my position as "part of and distant from the community."[8] I strove to understand the women's experiences through my own engagement with them and involvement in their daily activities. I used myself as an instrument, realizing that my reactions to the setting were a valuable clue to what the other women might be experiencing. I also strove, however, to pay attention to what made their experiences distinct from mine. They, after all, were involved in a process of "conversion," while I was there to study this process. The sociological tasks I had set myself thus kept me rooted in a reality apart from that of Orthodox Judaism. My efforts to maintain a sociological perspective; analyze interactions, prayer services, and classes; record notes; and ask members lots of questions reinforced my marginality to the group.

I found maintaining these multiple roles to be enormously challenging.

Throughout this research I had to clarify for myself as well as for the members and leaders of the groups my own personal stance toward the religious teachings of the communities I was studying. I was always open with members about my research goals as determining my presence in the communities. When asked about my own personal religious commitments, I explained that although I had been raised Orthodox, I no longer was, although I was still deeply attached to Judaism and the Jewish people. From the very beginning of my study, however, members of the settings chose to reinterpret my project to suit their own frameworks and priorities. Thus, when contacted about this effort, the rabbi at Bais Chana wrote, "I'm sure that you'll find the results of your study most rewarding and that—successfully completed—it will benefit *klal Yisroel* [all of Israel]." Thus, he redefined a sociological study as a project that would strengthen his religous group.

Members and leaders of this setting treated me as another potential *ba'alat teshuvah*. It became clear to me that it would be exciting and reinforcing of their beliefs if even the researcher could be "converted." This experience resembled that of many other sociologists studying "conversionist" religious communities. For example, Nancy Ammerman; Mary Jo Neitz; James Richardson, Mary White Stewart, and Robert B. Simmonds; and R. Stephen Warner found similar processes in their studies of Pentecostal, Fundamentalist, or Evangelical Christian groups.[9] Researchers in these religious settings all found that they were classified as potential converts by members of the group and were proselytized, prayed over, had hands laid on them, and so on. Through these experiences in my settings I came to a better understanding of what it meant to be involved in a conversionist religious group: all outsiders were seen as potential converts, although in the case of Jews it was largely *Jewish* outsiders who were seen as potential recruits. These interactions were useful to my research; they gave me the opportunity to experience directly how attempts were made to recruit newcomers in these Orthodox Jewish groups.

As a participant observer I tried to take part in a wide range of events that were part of the socialization process. At Bais Chana this meant that I lived in the institute and participated fully in all aspects of the program. I ate all my meals with the women and thus had many opportunities for informal talks. Through these daily conversations I came to know, at least slightly, all sixty of the women who were there for all or part of the four weeks of my stay. I went for walks with some of them; I went jogging with one of my roommates; and I had exercise classes some mornings (to a Jane Fonda tape) with a small group. In addition, I occasionally stayed up late with some of the women, studying, gossiping, and eating midnight snacks provided by the cook. Many of the women remained awake until 3:00 or 4:00 A.M. nightly, a routine I found absolutely exhausting. I was careful to explain my research to each woman soon after we met and consistently found that each was receptive to me in that role. By participating in this intense daily routine for a month, I was able to get to know many of the women well and develop a strong sense of the resocialization process in this setting.

Throughout the research project I solicited the guidance of the women, rabbis, rabbis' wives, and teachers I met. I continually asked the members of the settings what concerns were primary for them, what they would want to know, and what questions they would ask if they were doing this study. This was one way of finding out what issues and themes they thought most important or at least those that they felt comfortable expressing to me.

During my stay at Bais Chana several of the women volunteered themselves to be my "guides" and spent time teaching me some of the ins and outs of the setting and the special terminology used within it. I developed a close relationship with Iris, a woman who had an advanced degree in psychology and who had been involved with the Lubavitch community for a couple of years. Because she was in the process of converting (from Christianity) but had not yet completed her conversion, she was in some ways a marginal member of the group. This drew us to each other, as did our social science backgrounds. Stephen Warner and Meredith McGuire similarly report that they were tempted to spend a great deal of research energy on the less dogmatic, exclusivist, and conversionist members because they were less threatening to the researchers.[10] Marginal members of a community often stick together; thus, researchers, who by definition are marginal to the group, are often drawn to the other marginal members.

A major tool of researchers engaged in fieldwork is the recording of field notes. I tried to record as much as I could because I did not know what themes in the notes would provide the crucial information for the developing analysis. I learned to jot down a few notes here and there and then as soon as possible record the details fully. Notes from the classes were easy to accomplish: nearly all of the students took notes in classes; thus, my attempts to quickly record everything that was being said earned me the reputation of a good note-taker. The women would often ask to see my class notes if they wanted to know what had gone on in a class they had missed.

Recording field notes on all other aspects of life at the institute, however, proved to be a difficult task. Because of the crowded conditions and the nearly absolute lack of privacy, I could not find a place in the building in which to type out my field notes. There was no desk or table on the premises on which I could set up a typewriter and sit in privacy and type. I tried writing notes by hand in my room on my bed, but my roommates would frequently wander in and casually look over my shoulder to see what I was writing. Early on I developed a routine of jotting down a few words every couple of hours to spark my memory and then leaving the premises every few days and walking to a nearby golf course, where I would sit on the lawn and talk my notes into a tape recorder. When I returned home from Bais Chana I made a detailed index of these recorded field notes.

At Bais Chana the living conditions made fieldwork difficult for me in other ways as well. I found the lack of private space and time trying; this was a clue to me that it was probably difficult for some of the other women, too. I also found the hours exhausting. I am a light sleeper and could not sleep through women wandering in and out of the room half the night. Frequently, I did not fall asleep until 3:00 and then had to begin the next day at 7:00. Midway through my stay I left the setting for one night and checked into a motel in downtown St. Paul. I reveled in having a room and a bathroom to myself, ate a very peaceful and relaxing dinner, and slept for twelve hours! Greatly refreshed, I returned to the setting the next morning.

The position of researcher set me apart from the women in some important ways. It became clear to me that attention was a valued commodity in these groups, as in most social settings, and that the desire for recognition and attention might even have been a factor in the women's attraction to these Orthodox communities. As a researcher I was a novelty and a special person in both communities. I was someone with whom people wanted to talk, and I was often introduced and had access to many of the leaders of the groups. Because part of the women's attraction to these groups was a desire to be welcomed into a community, my relative ease of entrée and the amount of attention I received distinguished my experience from that of most of the women I met.

At Bais Chana I received a disproportionate amount of attention. I was mentioned in every issue of the newsletter the women published and was singled out in other ways. An excerpt from my field notes makes this evident:

> Friday night [the first Shabbat dinner of the summer] the rabbi went around the room asking the women how they got to Bais Chana. When it was my turn I explained that I had come to do research for my doctoral dissertation, which was a study of the experiences of *ba'alot teshuvah*. He asked me how I found out about the institute. I responded laughingly, "Actually, you were a footnote in somebody else's doctoral dissertation."

Rabbi Feller was very amused and pleased with that response. After that, whenever important or famous people came to visit the institute (usually for fund-raising purposes), he would ask me to stand up and tell the guests how I had come to Bais Chana.

A common question for field-workers is, What is their impact on the setting they are studying? Alvin Gouldner and other reflexive sociologists recognize that researchers inevitably change others and are changed by them in the process of doing research. "Knowing and changing are distinguishable but not separable processes."[11] In the foregoing example from Bais Chana, for instance, I wondered what impact my account had on these distinguished visitors and ultimately on the setting itself. Might my account have made these guests more inclined to donate money? Less inclined? Rabbi Feller was somewhat aware of "using" me in this way: one day when he was expecting visitors for lunch he asked me, "Are you going to be here for lunch today? We're expecting some important visitors, and we want to show you off."

INTERVIEWING

Of the sixty women who were present at Bais Chana during my one-month stay, approximately fifty were *ba'alot teshuvah* (a few of these were also converts) at various stages of this journey, and the rest were *madrichot*. There were ten women who were my room-mates during the month (seven at any one time), and I got to know each of these women quite well.

Even though in this setting informal interviews predominated, I also conducted eleven formal interviews. I selected a group of women to interview who represented a range of the types of women attracted to Lubavitch (age, level of education, prior religious experience) and the various stages in the process of trans-formation. In addition, I interviewed the two rabbis, three *madri-chot*, and the dean of women.

Scheduling the interviews was difficult at Bais Chana. Only one hour of each day (the hour before dinner) was free of scheduled classes or activities, and the women were understandably hesitant to give up that free time. They were also reluctant to miss classes to be interviewed. In addition, no one in that setting had a private room, so there was nowhere we could go to be guaranteed privacy during an interview. Many of the interviews were therefore con-ducted out of doors, on the lawn of the institute. A few were conducted in bedrooms of the building during hours when most of the other women were in classes or otherwise engaged. The ad-ministration of Bais Chana also occasionally gave me access to an office on the premises to use after regular business hours.

Before going to Bais Chana I had prepared an interview guide consisting of thirty-six open-ended questions (see Appendix A). After assuring each woman of confidentiality and her anonymity in any published findings, I began each interview with the request, "Tell me how you came to be interested in Orthodox Judaism." With this approach each woman could tell me her story in her own terms, stressing those experiences that were most salient for her. Some women talked for nearly an hour in response to that question alone; other women were helped and encouraged with further questions.

This open-ended method of interviewing enabled me to learn more about the women's perceptions of their experiences than if I had asked forced-choice questions. But as a result, I could not always get uniform data from each woman, which made subsequent data analysis difficult. Nevertheless, the richness of the data gathered through open-ended questions outweighed the difficulties posed by data that were not always strictly comparable.

I tape-recorded each interview so that I could attend to the dialogue and maintain eye contact with each woman without having to worry about remembering later what she had said. I did make sure to cover all my questions, but beyond that I spoke as little as possible while the interview was going on. I was careful not to interrupt. Often my responses consisted of simply repeating a phrase as encouragement to the interviewee to continue and elaborate.

The interview schedule changed slightly over time. For example, shortly after I began I realized that one of my questions— "How do you feel about women's roles in Judaism?"—might betray my egalitarian bias. Instead, I changed the question to, "What do you think are the most important issues for women in Judaism?" Although I had designed the interview guide and it reflected the concerns I thought central, I tried to follow the women's leads as well. For example, my first interviewee at Bais Chana enthusiastically described her early involvement in recruiting other *ba'alot teshuvah* as a major attraction of the Lubavitch recruitment methods. Consequently, I added a question about the women's interest in helping others to become Orthodox. (Because the large majority of the women were asked the revised set of questions, this is the version that appears in the appendix.) At the end of each interview I asked whether there were any other important aspects of this experience that the woman wished to report. Some women did, but most said that the questions were exhaustive.

These interviews lasted an average of two hours, although one lasted eight hours (over two meetings), and one lasted less than an hour. I was generally impressed by the women's openness to me, although in retrospect I suspect that perhaps the group's norms concerning female modesty caused the women to edit their accounts and leave out certain types of details, such as those relating to sexuality, a topic I found the women at Lincoln Square Synagogue to be more open about discussing. A few of the women I interviewed seemed very troubled emotionally. One of these women had difficulty expressing herself in the interview—she was in too much turmoil and confusion to be comfortable talking about herself.

This raises a more general question about the wisdom of interviewing people who are at a transitional stage in their lives. For people whose identities are in a state of flux, being questioned in great detail about the changes they are going through, and how these changes affect other areas of their lives, could lead them to raise questions that they otherwise might not have considered or could in some other way affect the course of the process. One rabbi in the Boston area whom I had contacted to ask for referrals to *ba'alot teshuvah* refused to give me names for this reason. He asserted that women who were becoming Orthodox were in a vulnerable position and that my questioning them might lead them to question themselves.

Nevertheless, interviewing someone during such a time could give her the opportunity to focus and articulate her thoughts and feelings about the transformations she was going through. Many of the women I interviewed told me that they experienced the interview process as helpful and clarifying. At a time when their identities were fluid, they found it useful to be asked to reflect on their experiences. It helped them to become aware for themselves what they were thinking and feeling about the process.

QUESTIONNAIRE

In my last week at Bais Chana I realized that I would not have a chance to formally interview even half of the women present. Therefore, I prepared a questionnaire to distribute to the women so I would have some information from all of them (see Appendix C). The institute was fully supportive of this effort: I was allowed to use office equipment to photocopy my questionnaire, and several women volunteered to help me collate and staple the pages. Rabbi Feller agreed to set aside an hour and a half of class time for filling out the questionnaire. Of the sixty women present in the setting at the time, fifty filled it out. Thus, this study relies on data obtained through several methods: participant observation, interviewing, and questionnaires.

DOCUMENTS

To further familiarize myself with the culture of the setting, I perused the available institutional documents. Prior to my arrival at Bais Chana I carefully read the copies of newspaper and other media articles describing the institute that Rabbi Feller had sent to me. While I was there, I also read the brief weekly newsletter the women produced, their song sheets, some Lubavitch publications on topics such as keeping kosher, marriage, the laws of family purity, and other reprints of mass media articles about the institute. Because my research was based primarily on participant observation and interviews, I do not present in this book a systematic analysis of the contents of these documents; rather, they provided a background that informed my understanding and analysis of the settings.

LINCOLN SQUARE SYNAGOGUE

In early January 1984 I loaded my clothes, typewriter, books, and papers into the car of friends who were driving from Boston to New York City. I was on my way to begin research at my second setting, Lincoln Square Synagogue, a large modern Orthodox synagogue on the Upper West Side of Manhattan. I had known about this synagogue for years; it was famous within religious Jewish circles for its charismatic rabbi, its very activist and extensive outreach programs, and its highly educated and professional membership. Thus, I felt that this setting would be an exciting place to observe the processes of religious resocialization among an interesting group of women.

In the fall of 1983 I had received permission from Rabbi Ephraim Buchwald, a man I had known for many years who was then educational director of the synagogue, to conduct my research there in the winter and spring of 1984. He made it clear that I would be welcome to attend whatever events I chose and further offered to help me select women to interview. I understood that my long-standing friendship with this rabbi (we had known each other since meeting at a summer camp as children) facilitated my entry into this setting and helped my research. Nevertheless, he let me know right away that he, too, was reinterpreting my research goals to suit his own priorities. In response to my description of my research questions, he claimed that I was conducting this study because it represented a choice (returning to Orthodoxy) that I actually wished to make for myself but didn't "have the guts to— *yet!*"

Lincoln Square Synagogue was founded in 1963 by a small group of unaffiliated Jews. They had put up a notice in the laundry room of a large apartment complex asking for people interested in forming a congregation for the High Holy Days. About twenty families responded, and they hired a rabbi to lead the services. The following year, a newly hired rabbi, Shlomo Riskin, made such an impression on the small congregation with his warmth, vitality, and obvious love for teaching Judaism that they asked him to stay beyond the holidays. At that point, the congregation defined itself as Conservative and did not have a *mehitzah,* the physical separation between women and men required in Orthodox synagogues. An Orthodox rabbi himself, Riskin told them that he would stay for six months and if in that time he could not convince them to put up a *mehitzah,* he would have to leave. Within six months the *mehitzah* was up. Riskin's mission to reach out to unaffiliated Jews and bring them closer to traditional Jewish observance was successfully under way.

From its inception, Lincoln Square differed from other Orthodox synagogues because its rabbi was interested not only in preaching to the "already converted" but in reaching out, inspiring, and educating assimilated Jews to adopt the traditional Jewish way of life. He strove to create a synagogue community that would attract the large numbers of professional, assimilated Jews in the neighborhood. He began offering classes that were open to the entire community—Wednesday night Bible classes and a Wednesday night lecture series. The lectures dealt with contemporary themes; the intention was to demonstrate that traditional Judaism offered insights into modern issues superior to those available in the secular culture. These classes, particularly the lecture series, brought Jewish adults into the shul. The character of the synagogue, a center where uncommitted Jews could learn more about their tradition, began to take shape.

Over the years additional classes and programs were added, all with the explicit purpose of reaching out to secular Jews and teaching them the texts, laws, and practices that formed the basis of an observant Jewish life. The adult education program grew and in 1971 was formally incorporated as the Joseph Shapiro Institute for Jewish Studies. This institute offered many evening courses for novices: basic Judaism, introduction to the Bible, Jewish living laboratory, several beginning-level Hebrew classes, and a wide variety of other courses in Jewish philosophy, history, texts, and ritual. Synagogue representatives estimated at the time of my research that between twelve and fifteen hundred students from all over the city attended classes each year. Many of the adults who learned to become *ba'alot* and *ba'alei teshuvah* within this community first found their way into the synagogue through these classes.

In addition to the adult education program, the synagogue sponsored several other innovative programs for beginners. In 1975 it innovated a beginners' minyan, described in a handout given to newcomers as "a special service for those with little or no background [that] is meant to serve as a learning experience for people who wish to gain proficiency . . . in the standard traditional minyan." Many of the women I interviewed in this community had initiated their contact with Orthodox Judaism through this Beginners' Service, which was founded and led by Rabbi Buchwald. Approximately seventy people attended each Saturday. The services were very lively—traditional tunes were taught and sung, and the energy level got quite high. Rabbi Buchwald offered many explanations of the service and other aspects of traditional Jewish observance and encouraged the participants to ask questions. According to the rabbi, between two hundred fifty and three hundred new people came to the Beginners' Service each year. Of these, he estimated that about one hundred twenty-five became traditionally observant, as indicated by their strict observance of Shabbat, holidays, and kashrut. Altogether approximately twelve hundred people attended one of the four different services (beginners', main, early, and late) held at this synagogue every Saturday. In addition, several hundred people attended weekday classes in the adult education program.

The synagogue offered several other programs that were intended to expose newcomers to traditional Jewish practices and beliefs. Three times a year it sponsored a *Shabbaton:* an intensive, retreatlike weekend of services, Shabbat meals complete with traditional foods, and lecture and discussion sessions. Established members of the community were encouraged to share meals with beginners, reach out to them, and follow up with an invitation for a Shabbat meal at their home. The synagogue also sponsored a hospitality program in which arrangements were made for newcomers to have Shabbat meals and even sleep over (if they were observant and did not want to travel on the Sabbath) in the homes of families in the community. This program was important to the resocialization process because it helped newcomers get to know families in the community and see how the religious norms affect family life. Once a year the synagogue had a "Turn Friday Night into Shabbos" dinner, which was publicized in the neighborhood and was intended to introduce the synagogue and its programs as well as offer a taste of traditional Jewish observance.

The synagogue sponsored several other programs and activities for beginners, including a beginners' schmooze (rap session), a beginners' newsletter, and programs for various Jewish holidays. The beginners' schmooze was a monthly meeting facilitated by a former "beginner" (meaning someone who was not brought up Orthodox) that provided a forum for newcomers to discuss some of the personal issues that came up as they began to become more observant. During the sessions I attended, discussions focused on the reactions (generally negative) of family members and friends to the participants' new religious practices; how to avoid "beginners' burnout," the result of taking on too much too soon; and an overview of the major Jewish texts (Torah, Mishnah, and Talmud) and their history and interrelationships. The beginners' newsletter was published monthly (or so) and included articles by the beginners' rabbi (Buchwald) and by various beginners, who wrote about different aspects of becoming a *ba'al* or *ba'alat teshuvah*. The newsletter was mailed to the several hundred people on the beginners' mailing list. For several of the Jewish holidays the synagogue sponsored various outreach activities: for Passover the beginners' rabbi and others held a model seder on the street, and for Purim the youth director and several members went out on the streets of the city and handed out packets containing *shalach manos* (edible treats distributed on Purim) and some information about the holiday.

The major resocializing agents in this community were the rab-

bis of the synagogue, the teachers of the various classes, and the
other members of the community. The synagogue had three rabbis—a main rabbi, an associate rabbi, and the educational director.
All three rabbis were involved in outreach and educational activities. They taught classes, did counseling, and invited newcomers
home for Shabbat meals. Adult education classes were taught by
the rabbis as well as by other religious and secular people.

The Lincoln Square Synagogue community as a whole had a
high proportion of *ba'alei* and *ba'alot teshuvah* (about 50 percent) and
a high proportion of singles (also about 50 percent). Among the
ba'alei and *ba'alot teshuvah* about 90 percent were single and between the ages of twenty-six and forty. The synagogue was well
known for its high proportion of single members; on Shabbos after
services they could be seen socializing on the street in front of the
synagogue. People found out about the synagogue through various means: talking to friends, relatives, and acquaintances; passing
by the synagogue on the street in their neighborhood; and reading
synagogue publicity, such as fliers announcing events. Almost all
the members were college educated and highly successful professionally. Women outnumbered men by five to three.

PARTICIPANT OBSERVATION

As at Bais Chana, I began my research with participant observation and conducted interviews only when I felt familiar with the
setting and with the range of people in it. During the five months
I was in the Lincoln Square community, I participated in all synagogue events regularly attended by beginners in the process of
their resocialization to Orthodoxy. I attended Beginners' Service
every Saturday, weekly evening classes in basic Judaism and introduction to the Bible, and the Wednesday night lecture series. I
often phoned the synagogue hospitality committee to be placed in
a family's home for Shabbat meals. Thus, I had many Friday night
dinners and Shabbat lunches in the homes of members of the community. As I got to know people, I was invited on my own to their
homes for Shabbat meals. I always found people in the community
to be warm, open, and interested in my project. I returned to some
of these families a few times during my stay in this setting. I also
befriended a few of the other "students" and spent time with them

informally. Through such personal contacts and attendance at a variety of synagogue events I developed an appreciation of the process of becoming a *ba'alat teshuvah* in this setting, which was very different from the intensive Bais Chana approach.

After attending any synagogue event or sharing a meal at someone's home, I returned to my apartment to type up field notes about what I had seen or heard. Keeping up with field notes on Shabbat was challenging because members of the community do not write or use electronic devices on the Sabbath. In an Orthodox community, Saturday involves many special activities: services in the morning, Shabbat lunch (often with company), sometimes a brief nap, then (for the men and some of the women) return to synagogue for evening services. I always went to services and then to lunch at the home of a member of the community. A typical Saturday consisted of three hours of services in the morning; then a meal at a family's home, which often lasted until 3:00 or 4:00 P.M.; and occasional attendance at evening services. By the time it was dark and I returned home to write field notes, I had been participating in and observing events since 9:00 in the morning. During my five months in the community I worked on training my memory to remember details from the entire day and reconstruct them in my notes. Yet despite this difficulty, field notes at Lincoln Square Synagogue were much easier to keep up with than they had been at Bais Chana. I lived in an apartment that was completely removed from the community and thus had the privacy to type my field notes as needed. During the week, I would sometimes simply "hang out" at the synagogue and chat with the staff, attend classes, and conduct interviews.

In both settings I found that my familiarity with Orthodox Jewish tradition made it simultaneously easier and harder to be an effective field-worker than it would have been for someone with little or no Jewish background. On the one hand, my familiarity with Hebrew and with Orthodox rituals meant I did not have to be afraid of making mistakes or behaving inappropriately. Rather than attending to my own self-consciousness, I could attend to the events and people. Yet fear of making mistakes is one of the hallmarks of someone new to a culture. Many of the women told me how difficult it was to come into this setting as adults who felt competent in other spheres of life and suddenly have to start all over again. They described feeling "dumb" when faced with services in a language they could not understand and said they were frequently afraid of making mistakes and offending people. Because I did not have this experience in these settings, I strove to think of situations in which I was a newcomer and afraid of feeling dumb and apply that feeling to my understanding of their situation.

As at Bais Chana, the position of researcher set me apart from the women, particularly in terms of the amount of attention and ease of entrée I experienced in the setting. For example, I received a fair amount of attention from Rabbi Buchwald: I was invited to schmooze in his office before or after evening classes, it was easy for me to obtain appointments with him, and I was more than occasionally singled out or referred to in Beginners' Services or in classes. The rabbi's attention helped me get into the setting and gain legitimation in the eyes of the community because of his obviously high regard for me. But this attention distanced me from the experience of coming into the community unknown and perhaps waiting several months for an invitation from the rabbi or outreach from someone else.

The question of my possible impact on this setting was raised by some of the ways the beginners' rabbi would refer in classes to what I had said to him privately. During my stay in the community he devoted a great deal of energy to trying to convince me that I would find Orthodox Judaism a most satisfying way to live. He claimed that he remembered me as the child who wrote "beautiful" Hebrew poetry for the camp journal; therefore, he wanted to harness my talents in the service of the Jewish community. These discussions with him were an important source of data because his attempts to bring me into the fold were probably similar to his attempts to reach out to other women. In these talks I responded to his assertions, stating my own view of Orthodoxy. In Bible class on two different occasions he referred to some of these remarks, saying, "Lynn Davidman has convinced me . . ." Because I was trying to be relatively unobtrusive and trying not to impose my point of view, I was uncomfortable with his singling me out in this way.

INTERVIEWING

I had decided prior to my arrival at Lincoln Square Synagogue that I would conduct between thirty and forty interviews in this setting.

This amount would allow me to speak with a range of women at various stages of the process and provide me with a reasonable sample on which to base my analysis. After I had been in the setting for more than a month I began deciding which women to interview. Several of the women I interviewed were people I had come to know through events at the synagogue, especially the Beginners' Service. Because these particular women were at nearly every synagogue event I attended, they were at the time a core group actively engaged in the process of becoming *ba'alot teshuvah.* In addition, Rabbi Buchwald gave me brief summaries of all of the women on the beginners' mailing list (which had more than two hundred names on it) so I could select a sample that would include a range of ages and length and intensity of religious involvement.

Next I sent a letter to sixty women selected from the list in a stratified random sample to ensure that I would reach women who were at all stages in the process of becoming a *ba'alat teshuvah:* women who were just beginning to become interested, women who had been involved for one year, women who had been Orthodox for several years, and women who had tried Orthodoxy and decided it was not for them. I introduced myself, explained my project, asked whether they would be willing to be interviewed, and stated that I would be phoning them to set up an appointment. Rabbi Buchwald wrote a message on my letter encouraging the women to cooperate. Several women later told me that his note was crucial in their agreeing to be interviewed. With my letter I enclosed a stamped, self-addressed postcard on which the women could check whether they were willing to participate. Forty-nine women wrote back saying they would like to be interviewed; one woman refused. Regarding the other ten women, a few of the letters were returned to me undelivered by the post office; the others simply did not respond. One woman who did not respond told me in synagogue that she was too confused at the time to be interviewed. As I received these responses, I began interviewing the women. I also interviewed Rabbi Ephraim Buchwald, his wife, Aidel (who got to know many beginners because with her husband she hosted large meals for newcomers every Friday night and Shabbat lunch), and another rabbi and his wife who worked intensively with *ba'alei* and *ba'alot teshuvah.* I continued interviewing until I felt I had saturated each category: the themes were repeating, and I felt I had found patterns and understood what it was like to be at that stage.[12] Altogether I conducted thirty-five interviews in this setting.

The interviews were conducted at a place of the woman's choosing, usually her home. Several of these interviews took place in the kitchen, the rest in the living room. Because the majority of the women lived alone, we generally were alone in their apartments during the interview. The few married women usually set up times when their husbands would not be home; one, who could schedule only an evening appointment, spoke with me in the living room of their small apartment while her husband hid in the bedroom watching television. I met one woman on her lunch hour and interviewed her in a Y near her job. Many of the women had bought treats for the interview. I was offered Stella D'Oro cookies (a brand that has rabbinical supervision, thereby ensuring its kashrut), frozen pizza, bagels, grapes, coffee, and tea and was invited back for meals. Several of the women expressed some nervousness about being interviewed; many said that they had been thinking about the interview and had been attempting to pull together what they would say.

I used the same interview guide I had used at Bais Chana. These interviews lasted an average of two and a half hours. A few of the women who were articulate and reflective, and who greatly enjoyed the opportunity to talk about these experiences, were open to a second and even a third meeting. Several of these women became friends, and we continued to meet over tea and meals.

When I began this research, I had reservations about interviewing, about walking into people's homes with my tape recorder and asking them to tell me about their lives. The more conflict-ridden the women were, particularly about women's issues, the more interested I was. The whole enterprise seemed parasitic, and I was unclear about what I was offering in return. As Judith Stacey highlights in a feminist analysis of the new ethnographic literature, there is a constant threat of exploitation of research "subjects" in ethnographic studies.[13] Nevertheless, the women I spoke with all let me know that I offered them a valuable opportunity to share their thoughts and feelings about a crucial matter in their lives. Undergoing religious transformation as an adult is an intense process, and most women felt they did not have people with whom to talk about this profound experience. My readiness to listen was thus welcome and sometimes even helpful.

In addition to these thirty-five formal interviews, I conducted numerous informal interviews with women I came to know through the synagogue. I chatted with women after services, before and after classes, and at other synagogue events. This allowed me to become acquainted with a wider range of women than I was able to interview formally and to hear more about the women's experiences and concerns.

In this setting, too, I sought to engage members of the community in assisting me with my research. Rabbi Buchwald was a helpful collaborator. A few of the women undertook to spend time as my informants. They called my attention to certain features of the setting I might otherwise have overlooked.

DOCUMENTS

At Lincoln Square Synagogue I examined current and back issues of *Bereshith*, the beginners' newsletter, and *Echod*, the newsletter of the main congregation. I looked at the course catalogues and various other outreach and publicity material put out by the synagogue. In addition, I read and continued to follow the numerous articles about this synagogue in mass media such as the *New York Times*, *Newsweek*, and other national publications.

THE EMERGING ANALYSIS

Leaving the field was both a welcome relief and a sad time in both settings. I found fieldwork to be all-consuming and exhausting, particularly at Bais Chana where the number of roommates made privacy impossible and the very late hours made sleep problematic. Yet despite my difficulty with the living conditions at Bais Chana, I found myself suffering from a bit of culture shock when I returned home. I found it disorienting to be alone all day and not have my activities scheduled for me. This was a clue to the power of the setting and to some of the factors that draw the women into the community.

By the time I had finished my fieldwork in both settings, I had a total of three thousand pages of interview transcripts and field notes. These written "texts" were but a one-dimensional (verbal) representation of the "unruly experience"[14] of life in these Orthodox communities. As James Clifford points out, field-workers' data are constituted in situations in which multiple forms of communication are going on simultaneously, and competing interpretations of the same events are always present. These "multivocal," "polyphonic," and multilayered data are necessarily reduced when they are taken out of the settings in textualized forms.[15] My notes and transcripts thus represented a muted and abbreviated version of the research events and encounters. Nevertheless, together with my memories, images, and ongoing relationships with some members of the communities, these texts constituted the material I had to rely on in constructing my final analysis and writing up my findings. I analyzed these transcripts and field notes by looking for common themes, use of language, signs of affect, inconsistencies, repetition, key characters, dynamics, and connections between events.

It is important to note that this book represents the experiences of the particular women and rabbis I met, and the processes of their religious resocialization, in the context of the communities to which they were attracted. This book does not claim to represent the viewpoints of all modern Orthodox or Lubavitch Hasidic rabbis or the experiences of all *ba'alot teshuvah*, modern Orthodox, Lubavitch, or otherwise. Nevertheless, it is my belief that well-done case studies of particular communities highlight trends and patterns that can be found in the larger society as well. My aim has been to present a vivid, detailed account of the two communities studied and to locate the women's descriptions of their lives and the rabbis' attempts to reach these women in the context of patterns in the larger Jewish and secular worlds.

Like all ethnographic accounts, this one is necessarily partial and incomplete.[16] Although I have sought to let my research participants speak for themselves as much as possible, so that the reader will have some basis for assessing my analysis, in the end it is I who have staged their quotations.[17] As researcher I developed a particular interpretation of their experiences, and as author I have included those findings and quotations that substantiate my analysis.

How reliable, then, is this analysis or any ethnographic analysis when all are "fictions" in the sense of "something made and fashioned"?[18] How can the researcher or the reader know whether any ethnography accurately captures the settings and is not simply a product of the researcher's initial biases and presuppositions? After all, the researcher is obviously an instrument in the study, and her data collection reflects those features of the setting she attends to.

As a writer of an ethnography, I must acknowledge the constructed nature of this particular account of the communities I studied. Another researcher, or indeed the members of these groups, might indeed pay attention to different aspects of the settings and thus come up with analyses that differ from mine. For example, someone interested in charismatic leadership could come into Lincoln Square Synagogue and Bais Chana and engage in a close analysis of the rabbis' and recruits' ways of creating a particular kind of rabbinical authority within the community. That person would obviously emerge with a different ethnographic study from mine. But would that person find material that generally *disconfirmed* my analysis? I feel fairly confident that the answer would be "no" because I employed several types of checks on the accuracy of my interpretations.

First, I frequently tested my interpretations by trying them out on my respondents while I was in the field. Second, as I wrote papers and chapters developing my ideas, I gave them to leaders and members of these communities to read; on the whole, they recognized themselves and their experiences in my representation, which endorsed my interpretations. Third, I sought endorsement from outside the community. I presented my newly developing ideas to colleagues in the form of articles and conference papers; their responses affirmed the plausibility and usefulness of my interpretations. Fourth, I continually read the literature on similar religious communities and was reassured to discover that the themes I was finding at Lincoln Square and Bais Chana were present in the similar communities other sociologists were writing about. These various forms of confirmation provided some reassurance about the validity of my research. Nevertheless, the intention of this book is not to provide final, definitive answers but to keep the analysis and dialogue open.

4

Order, Belonging,
and Identity

At both Lincoln Square and Bais Chana the impetus to join an Orthodox community was clearly related to each woman's perception of her place in her life course. More than 90 percent of the women I met in both communities were in a transitional phase of adulthood that was shaped by their increasing desire to create and establish families of their own. For the Lincoln Square women the critical age was generally when they reached their early to mid-thirties. In contrast, the college years, especially the first year at college or the year following graduation from high school, were critical stages for the women attracted to Bais Chana. The death of a parent was a significant turning point for a few of the women in both communities, as was the need, for a small group of the women (less than 5 percent), for a context in which to socialize their children as Jews. As a result of these life circumstances, the women were faced with a need for new approaches to the ongoing creation of order and meaning in their lives.

A significant characteristic of the new *ba'alot teshuvah* was that most were single. Other studies of *ba'alei* and *ba'alot teshuvah* have confirmed this pattern, as did the rabbis I interviewed: a much higher proportion of people become newly Orthodox when they are single than when they are already married.[1] One possible explanation for this phenomenon is that becoming Orthodox involves such major changes in a person's life that she or he is less likely to embark on such a journey when already in a committed relationship and therefore "settled" in some important ways.

MEET THE WOMEN

THE WOMEN AT
LINCOLN SQUARE SYNAGOGUE

The *ba'alot teshuvah* I met at Lincoln Square Synagogue ranged in age from twenty-four to fifty-two, with the large majority between twenty-nine and forty. As a group, these women had a great deal of formal education. Of the thirty women I interviewed in this community, only three had not completed college. The majority had B.A.s and about a third had advanced degrees beyond the B.A.: several women had M.A.s (in communications, social work, library science, education), two had M.B.A.s, two had Ph.D.s, and one had an M.D. Nearly all of these women worked in a variety of well-paid positions in business or the professions, including public relations, managerial or sales positions, teaching, film producing, medicine, writing, acting, and the arts. They all had their own apartments and had been living on their own for an average of ten years.

Madeleine Ostrow was a very tall, single woman in her early thirties at the time we met. She had been coming to the synagogue for about a year and a half. She described herself as a spiritual person who had been taught to think about God at an early age. Although her family barely practiced any Jewish rituals at home, she was sent for a couple of years to Reform Sunday School, which she "hated." She had a B.A., had traveled a great deal throughout Europe, and had been working as a writer in an advertising agency for several years. She lived in a brownstone apartment that she had decorated in a bright and casual way. She was one of the few women I met in either community who described herself as a feminist.

Deborah Wechsler, a twenty-eight-year-old single woman with a B.A. from an Ivy League school and a job in publishing, asked many direct questions and had an air of restlessness and intensity about her. She had been attending synagogue for nearly a year at the time of our interview. She was very involved in the Beginners' Service and was quite friendly with the beginners' rabbi and his wife and family. She described her Jewish background as "nothing": her parents conducted a ten-minute Passover seder with their relatives and did not observe the High Holidays.

Nancy Hanover had been attending Lincoln Square Synagogue for nearly eleven years when we were introduced at the beginners' rabbi's home. At thirty-eight, she had two children and was a successful academic. She had met her husband at the synagogue in the early days of her attendance. Nancy was a careful, articulate woman who shared with me her thoughts about the *ba'alot teshuvah* she had known over the years. She had been raised a combination of Conservative and Reform, depending, as she said, on the available synagogues in the various communities in which her family had lived.

Sharon Greenberg was a single woman for whom spiritual concerns were central: prior to coming to Lincoln Square Synagogue a year and a half before we met, she had spent several years on the West Coast intensively studying Eastern religion. Her style, mannerisms, and modes of speech were reminiscent of the devoted students of Eastern religion I had known in the mid-1970s. She was a serious woman who had long, dark, frizzy hair; wore wire-rimmed glasses; and dressed in peasant blouses and skirts. Although her family had been only minimally observant, as a child she had insisted on attending an Orthodox Hebrew School for several years.

Ellen Reiss, a thirty-seven-year-old divorcée, had been involved in the synagogue for about two and a half years prior to our meeting. She had grown up in a non-Jewish community and was taught very little as a child about the meaning of being Jewish, even though she had attended Hebrew School for a couple of years and her family had observed, albeit minimally, the major Jewish holidays. At the time of our interview, she was moving away from her career as a social worker and into a career in computers.

Janet Machtiger, a vibrant journalist in her early fifties when I first met her, had been attending classes and services at the synagogue for a few years. A divorced woman with a teenage son, she was fully committed to Orthodoxy and enthusiastic about its impact on her life. She felt that she had always had a strong religious impulse, although she had grown up in a "very assimilated" Jewish family that celebrated Christmas and Easter. She was also concerned with social causes and was deeply involved in a campaign to provide relief to Ethiopian Jews.

Elizabeth Bloom, the daughter of Holocaust survivors, had grown up in a rural area totally removed from any Jewish community. Her parents had arranged tutors for her in Jewish subjects, however, and the family observed the major Jewish holidays. She was a single woman of twenty-eight at the time of our interview, which took place at her office, where she maintained a private practice as a physician. (She had graduated from an Ivy League college and medical school.) She was thoughtful, articulate, and self-reflexive. At that time she had been coming to the synagogue on and off for a few years.

Stephanie Moore, the woman first mentioned in chapter 1, was an artist working in advertising who had been attending services and classes at Lincoln Square for a year and a half when we met at the Beginners' Service. She was a strikingly beautiful single woman who was used to attracting men at social gatherings. She was lively and fun to spend time with, even though at forty-two she had a slight air of sadness about her.

THE WOMEN AT BAIS CHANA

The sixty women I met during my stay at Bais Chana were nearly all younger than thirty; about a third were teenagers, and nearly half were between the ages of twenty and twenty-five. One woman was as young as sixteen; another was fifty. Only three of the women were married. Two-thirds came from families in which at least some Jewish rituals—such as Passover seder and High Holiday synagogue attendance—were observed. The large majority of women had completed twelfth grade. A few had completed college, several were in college, and three had advanced degrees beyond the B.A. Of those who worked, their experiences included general office work, computer operations, and day care. Only four had professional positions (lawyer, social worker, school psychologist, and nurse).

Lisa Shapiro, a twenty-four-year-old woman with curly reddish hair, had just recently dropped out of college and moved back to her parents' home when we met. She was an intense woman, who, although she was still unsettled, was seriously concerned with finding the "truth." She had been raised as a Conservative Jew but had become quite involved with a Fundamentalist Christian group at college. Six weeks prior to her arrival at Bais Chana, her parents had introduced her to a Lubavitch couple in her hometown who had attempted to "deprogram" her. Sending her to Bais Chana was part of this agenda.

Tamar Friedman was thirty-two when I first met her. She had been involved with the Lubavitch since the last year of her under-graduate education at a state university in California and had at-tended a summer session at Bais Chana ten years earlier. She was married to a man she had met at a Lubavitch party in California, where she lived, and they had a daughter who was seven years old at the time of my study. Tamar had a nursing degree and worked part-time in a local hospital. She often tried to assist the other, mostly younger women at Bais Chana, where she had returned that summer, as she said, to rekindle her enthusiasm and love of God. Although she had been brought up Reform and had felt discomfort with her Judaism as a child, when I knew her her reli-gious devotion was strong. For example, she always kept her hair covered, a tradition followed by very Orthodox women, and even wore a scarf over her head while she slept.

Rachel Stein had had minimal exposure to Jewish religious ob-servance as a child. When we met, she was a very distressed twenty-three-year-old who had attempted suicide a year earlier. She lived in a major Midwestern city with her alcoholic mother. Rachel's unhappiness had resulted in her experimenting with a wide variety of contemporary religious groups, such as the Hare Krishna and Fundamentalist Christianity. A friend sug-gested that she might find what she was seeking among the Lubavitch.

Naomi Weinstein, a sixteen-year-old high school student from the West Coast, had been involved with the Lubavitch for about a year before coming to Bais Chana. She first encountered the Lubavitch when the rabbi at the Lubavitch center in her hometown ap-proached her on the street and offered to teach her more about being Jewish (such an approach on the street is a well-known Lubavitch tactic). She was an earnest, somewhat sophisticated, but confused young woman whom some of the older women took under their wings. She had come from a family with little Jewish observance and had not had any Hebrew school training.

Rivka Goldbloom, a twenty-one-year-old, single, redheaded speech major at a state university in the Northeast, was the most enthusiastic woman I met in either community. Our interviews lasted for hours at a time, for days in a row; she had an abundance of energy for speaking of her newfound love for the Lubavitch and their way of life. At the time we met she had been involved with the Lubavitch for three years and was attending Bais Chana for the second summer in a row. She was a bright, articulate woman who enjoyed the more challenging classes offered. Although her family occasionally celebrated the major Jewish holidays, she felt she had received little substantial knowledge of Judaism.

Layah Fromm came from a troubled family. Her mother had spent years in and out of mental institutions, and her father had given Layah to her Orthodox grandparents to raise. She had strayed far from her Orthodox upbringing as a teenager and young adult. At the time we met she was a thirty-year-old social worker who managed a group home. She had been involved with the Lubavitch for three years and had taken an apartment on her own in Crown Heights a year earlier.

Beth Lieberman, the Lubavitch recruit discussed in chapter 1, was a heavyset, short, dark-haired computer programmer who was twenty-nine at the time we met. She had briefly attended a community college but was unemployed and living with her parents in a small city in the Northeast. She conveyed a sense of a person who wanted to belong. She tried hard with the other women and was eager to please and be liked.

These brief descriptions suggest several initial differences, particularly in terms of social location, between the two groups of women that shaped their choice of religious community. Compared to those who came to Bais Chana, the women who joined Lincoln Square Synagogue tended to be older, more highly educated, and better established in their lives. Because the Lubavitch residential center is more sectarian and encapsulating than the modern Orthodox synagogue community, it makes sense that it would appeal to women less firmly rooted in the world and less invested in an established pattern of life.

PATHWAYS TO LINCOLN SQUARE AND
BAIS CHANA

LINCOLN SQUARE SYNAGOGUE

For the women who were attracted to Lincoln Square, a neighbor-hood synagogue, contingency factors such as proximity, personal contacts, and reputation were key influences in the choice of this particular synagogue. Half of the women had a personal contact at the synagogue or a friend or relative who had had some experience with it. As Ellen told me:

> Over the years my sister became involved with Lincoln Square Syn-agogue, and when she first started it was rather strange to me and originally it probably created some distance. . . . Then two years ago from last Rosh Hashanah [the Jewish New Year] I was with my sister at *tashlich* [a ritual that takes place on the afternoon of the first day of Rosh Hashanah] and she introduced me to Rabbi Buchwald, and he said, "Why don't you go to beginners' minyan?" I went and I just really liked it, and that was really the beginning of my involvement at Lincoln Square Synagogue.

The prevalence in the women's accounts of a personal connec-tion that drew them into the synagogue is consistent with the literature on recruitment to other religious groups. For example, John Lofland's well-known study of the Moonies, as well as many other studies of religious resocialization, found that interpersonal bonds between members and potential recruits played an impor-tant role in bringing new members into religious organizations.[2]

Nearly a third of the women specified proximity in their ac-counts of how they came to this synagogue. Five of these women lived in the huge apartment complex right near the synagogue, and the others lived within five blocks. In fact, nearly all of the women interviewed lived within ten blocks of the synagogue. Ac-cording to several women who had frequently walked by this syn-agogue, at a time when they were in need of some support or feeling religiously inspired, they realized the synagogue might be available to them. One woman recounted her experience in this way:

> Well, one day I was walking along and it was around Chanukah time and for some reason I was thinking about the candles and when do you light them, and I've lived in this apartment for about twelve

years, and Lincoln Square Synagogue has been there all this time, and it just suddenly dawned on me, "Oh, there's a synagogue down the road. Why don't I go in and ask?" So I did.

In addition to proximity and personal contacts, the reputation of the congregation and its rabbis was another important factor in directing the women to this particular synagogue. Lincoln Square Synagogue is well known in the New York Jewish community for innovative beginners' programs and a large singles population. Madeleine related how she had made up her mind to go to a synagogue, and on a Friday night she walked into the very small synagogue (*shtiebl*) down the block from her apartment, where she mostly found old people. The sexton approached her and welcomed her, asking if she was new in the neighborhood. She said:

> "No, I've been living here for about a year, but I thought I would come." He said, "Listen, you don't want to come here. It's only old people. Go to Lincoln Square Synagogue. They have lectures; they have young people. You'll find a *chassan* [husband]; you'll find a man." And he said, "Just go. I know you'll find something."

The factors highlighted in the *ba'alot teshuvah*'s accounts of their entrance into the community are rooted in contingencies, rather than in the women's personal characteristics. This is a common finding in recent studies of religious recruitment and resocialization.[3]

BAIS CHANA

Even though the location of Bais Chana in suburban St. Paul precluded proximity as a central factor in the women's entry into this community, personal contacts and the institute's reputation did play a key role. Most recruits were introduced to Lubavitch Hasidism through a Lubavitch *shaliach* (emissary) in their hometown. If a woman showed sufficient interest, the *shaliach* then suggested she go to Bais Chana to learn in a more intensive environment. If she could not afford it, the Lubavitch movement would often pay her way, footing the bill for airfare as well as room and board. Some of the women found out about the Lubavitch through relatives or friends, some of whom were themselves *ba'alei* or *ba'alot teshuvah*.

The women reported that everyone who told them about Bais Chana had recommended it highly. Rivka had heard about it through the *rebbetzin* at the Lubavitch center in her college town:

> She said, "You must go. You really must go. You're going to love it. There is nobody who goes there that doesn't like it. And Rabbi Friedman, oh, Rabbi Friedman, everyone loves him."

Many of the women reported that Bais Chana was recommended to them as a place where women from all over the world who were at different stages in their discovery of Judaism came together in a religious atmosphere to learn more about Judaism.

STRUCTURE OF THE
CONVERSION STORIES

THE WOMEN AT
LINCOLN SQUARE SYNAGOGUE

Humans are always engaged in an ongoing process of ordering and making sense of their experience. The language people use to talk about their experiences and the sequence of their stories "reveal the world that they see and in which they act."[4] Because everyday life encompasses an ongoing process of constructing the meanings of our experience, the ways in which people talk about their experiences are as important as the content of the experiences themselves.

The large majority of the women I met at Lincoln Square Synagogue used the rhetoric of *choice* to describe how they came to Orthodoxy.[5] Their stories reflected a self-perception as rational actors who consciously decided to learn about and become involved in their ascribed religious tradition. They were aware that this was one among many other possible options—religious and secular belief systems, ideologies, and lifestyles—available in contemporary society. Their accounts were constructed to reflect this modernist notion of individual self-determination. As Sharon remarked, "I made a *decision* to go to the Eastern religion center. I made a *decision* to come to Lincoln Square Synagogue. I made a decision to learn and explore it." Madeleine expressed the same idea when she said:

Ba'alei teshuvah have so much enthusiasm about it. I think that I know the things that *I am choosing* to change in my life or to give up. Whereas the women that have been brought up with it wonder what it might be like, and they're sort of always wanting to taste forbidden fruit, so to speak, I feel I've tasted it and it's not worth it.

These two women's expression of a commitment to Orthodoxy *and* an awareness of choice corroborates Mary Jo Neitz's assertion (in her study of Charismatic Catholics) that contrary to the assumptions of many secularization theorists, the awareness of choice does not necessarily weaken the plausibility of any religious worldview.[6] These women's sense of having chosen Orthodoxy actually validated their choice. As Neitz describes the Charismatic Catholics she studied, their awareness of choice "did not seem to undermine their own beliefs. Rather, they felt that they had 'tested' the belief system and had been convinced of its superiority."[7]

While the women were aware that they were choosing this religious way of life as one option among others, they affirmed and legitimated this choice by claiming that Orthodox Judaism was in fact "theirs." A thirty-five-year-old woman who had been a *ba'alat teshuvah* for several years expressed this idea clearly:

I couldn't feel metaphysical certainty in the Halacha but I have no metaphysical certainty in a secular way of life either. . . . And you can maintain a skepticism intellectually, but you can't maintain it in your life. On your level of action, you're either doing one thing or doing another. Living one way and not another. You're voting with your feet. And if I was not religious I was giving secular, or the non-Jewish, patterns of life a certain metaphysical normativeness. Why should I have? If I don't know, why not choose my own? Why make a non-Jewish way of life the standard or norm from which I have deviated more or less?

Janet articulated her sense of the correctness of her involvement in this way:

It seems to me to be right. It seems to me to be mine. One of the things I used to keep saying to myself when I left those early classes at Lincoln Square Synagogue, going home four feet off the ground, was I can't believe this is mine. I didn't earn this. It's just all sitting here. This huge thing gift wrapped, for me, because I happen to be born to a Jewish mother. If I were Gentile and I wanted this, I would have to earn it in the most agonizing way and prove my worthiness for it. It's just being handed to me. It's like going home. It's like a cup of hot tea on a cold night. It's just appropriate. That's a cold word, but I mean it in the warmest possible sense.

The women who came to Lincoln Square Synagogue were choosing to identify with their inherited religious tradition. Although they spoke of the Orthodox approach to presenting the tradition as "their own," their use of this phrase was not very clear because none of them had grown up in Orthodox homes. Nevertheless, the fact that nearly all of them as children had gone to Sunday School for at least a few years and had observed some rituals and holidays with their families was surely important in their adult attraction to Orthodoxy.

These findings are consistent with Janet Aviad's and Herbert Danzger's studies of newly Orthodox Jews; most of their respondents had had at least some Jewish background.[8] Likewise, studies of people who join Fundamentalist Christian groups have found that the adults who joined these groups were likely to have had some previous background within the religion.[9] Their earlier exposure perhaps made these adults more likely to search in a religious direction for a new mode of ordering their lives.

Yet despite this sense of prior claim on Orthodoxy, the predominance of rhetorics of choice in the women's accounts reveals that they nevertheless shared in the white middle-class view that the self is constructed by picking and choosing from available options. This attitude was found by Robert N. Bellah, Richard Madsen, William M. Sullivan, Ann Swidler, and Steven M. Tipton in their study *Habits of the Heart.*[10] Members of the white middle class in the United States, the authors found, assume that individuals are free to define their own selves, choose their own values, and thus become their "own person[s]."[11] In a culture in which the dominant sense of self among the white middle class is radically individualistic, these women described their choice of roots and community in the language of individual self-fulfillment.

These women's freedom to choose Orthodoxy illustrates that Jewish life in the contemporary United States offers Jews alternatives that were previously unavailable within the Jewish communities of Europe. For Jews the transformation "from fate to choice" has been swift and dramatic in the last one hundred fifty years.[12] In Eastern Europe membership in the Jewish *kehilla* was required of all Jews; the traditional Jewish way of life was thus maintained in tightly knit communities in which people were born and spent their entire lives.[13] Emancipation and immigration to the United States have led to a pluralism on the institutional level (Jews participate in a wide variety of institutions and communities, both Jewish and non-Jewish) and on the level of action (a Jew can now choose whether and how to "express" her or his Jewishness in daily life).

One way a person can affirm the rightness of her or his choice in becoming Orthodox is to present it as the logical progression of everything in life up to that point. This "consolidation" of identity is often found in conversion accounts.[14] Approximately a third of the Lincoln Square Synagogue women highlighted the degree of consonance between their turn to Orthodoxy and their previous lives. Because I began my interview with an open-ended request—"Tell me how you came to be interested in Orthodox Judaism"—the women's responses reflected what they thought was worth mentioning first. Several began by saying that they had "always" been involved with Judaism. As Ellen told me, "Putting dates and times on it is very hard because the more, the longer I'm in it, the more it seems that it was always there before." Sharon expressed the same sense of continuity:

> How did I get interested? Well, I guess I feel that when people ask me that question they kind of expect to hear some story, well, a year or two ago, two years ago. And I really kind of feel that the story goes back much longer than that. The Judaism goes back to infancy.

Emphasizing the similarity between the choice of Orthodoxy and other aspects of their lives was a device similar to claiming Orthodoxy as their own. Through these narrative strategies the women affirmed the integrity of their biography and by implication the "rightness" of their choice.

The new worldview they learned and the language of the community they were entering were then used to reinterpret past events, to "reconstruct" their biographies.[15] Janet said:

> How did I get involved? Well to put it another way, on a very different level, there is this *pintele yid* [Jewish spark] and it operates, and that is something that draws you, that draws many of us.

Nancy, too, adopted the religious terminology in presenting her story: "Coincidentally at that time, and I think it really was almost *bashert* [ordained by God], I got myself a job teaching at [a Jewish school]."

Nearly half of the women in this community began their accounts with their childhood experiences, going back to the families in which they were brought up and the level of religious observance in their households. These women felt that the deep sense of themselves as Jewish that was offered in the Orthodox community provided them with a better understanding of their own personal roots. A thirty-year-old artist who had grown up in a Conservative home recalled:

> We always had Shabbat in that my father wouldn't work Friday night and my mother would clean house all day and make a special dinner and light candles and very often we would go to shul on Friday night and come home. I remember that one of the very special things about growing up in my house—there weren't all that many—but one of the things that I really enjoyed was coming home from shul Friday night, walking home, and seeing the candles still in the dining room as we walked in the door and all the lights would be off.

Several of the women went as far back as their grandparents' religious observance and associated their present interest in Orthodoxy with fond memories of their grandparents. According to Stephanie:

> I learned where I came from. I learned to appreciate the fact that the greatest source of wisdom and kindness that I knew, which was my grandmother, was not hatched from an egg, without a background. That Grandma, who I thought was just unique, was, in fact, a product of a culture I knew nothing about. And the things that Grandma was came directly from this Jewish world. So the thing that I loved most in the world, which was my grandmother, was a product of something, and I'm a product of it, too.

Perhaps this tendency to frame their adult involvement in Judaism in the context of their family backgrounds was another way of integrating their biographies in the telling of the story. Their current Jewish involvement was understood to be such an important aspect of their lives, such a fundamental block in their identity, that it had to be seen not only in terms of the immediate circumstances of their lives but also in the context of the broader patterns of their biographies.

Unlike the women who came to Lincoln Square Synagogue, who adopted a rhetoric of choice in their accounts, the Lubavitch women used a rhetoric of compulsion. Rather than presenting their attraction to Orthodoxy as a conscious choice made after an examination and weighing of alternatives, their accounts emphasized that their selection of Lubavitch Hasidism was directed by God. Their narratives embodied the idea emphasized by the rabbi at Bais Chana that they had no choice about joining the community or following the dictates of Halacha, two activities that the Lincoln Square Synagogue women separated in their accounts; rather, their actions were predestined and necessary if they were to be true to their own inner natures. Tamar described her sudden realization of her true path:

> When I began to go to Chabad house [a Lubavitch outreach center that can be found in many cities around the world, often near a college campus], I met people who were similar to myself and a whole world opened up. And in a span of about a week this was where I had to be. This was it. There was no option of walking away.

The women incorporated the Lubavitch concept of *hashgocha protis* (divine providence, the idea that God controls a person's fate) in order to reconstruct their biographies and explain their attraction to the Lubavitch community. Rivka, in describing how on her return from Israel she became involved with the Lubavitch community in her college town, said, "*Hashgocha protis* and *bashert*—it was meant I should come home and be Lubavitch." Naomi wrote on her questionnaire:

> I feel that I belong to the religious world because Hashem gave us a precious gift, "TORAH," and Hashem has made me to become Lubavitcher—"*hashgocha protis*." I believe every Jewish soul should be religious, and we should follow the Torah because Hashem gives us everything such as air, water, soil for food, living creatures, woods and many others. . . . People steal G-d's property because they do not open their pure mind and heart.

Tamar, in describing her religious evolution, emphasized that in becoming a Lubavitcher she was simply becoming herself:

> When someone is clear about himself and is exposed to Torah in its true form, then by and large a Jew is attracted to it. By coming more in touch with their Jewishness, a person comes more in touch with themselves.

Nevertheless, a few of the women in the Lubavitch setting who were very new to the group and not yet socialized into its worldview did not use this rhetoric of compulsion and instead articulated more sense of choice and control in their accounts of joining the community. These women's accounts were more similar to those of the modern Orthodox women. Yet the majority of women in this setting either *were* already committed to the worldview of the community or were fairly prepared to accept it; otherwise they would not have flown out to the institute. Given that traveling to Bais Chana already required more commitment than simply walking into a neighborhood synagogue, it was not surprising that the women were prepared to quickly adopt the language and worldview of the community.

As did some of the women at Lincoln Square Synagogue, many of the women at Bais Chana affirmed the rightness of taking this path by seeing it as a consolidation of their identity, as the next logical step in their lives. They highlighted the similarity between this transition and their earlier lives. Beth thus described her experience of spending a Shabbos at an Orthodox summer camp with a Lubavitch couple who were influential in her "conversion":

> It reminded me of all the things I liked as a young child. That I used to do, like observing the Shabbos. It just reminded me of an earlier childhood. . . . I remembered all these things my grandfather instilled in me and how much peace I had at an early age, and then to come here and see it all over again it was like—I don't know the word for it—but I'm getting a lot out of being here; I'm learning a lot.

Another woman, in accounting for her rapid adoption of the Lubavitch way of life, said:

> It's not going from one extreme to another; it's going back to where I started from. . . . It's how I was raised as a very young child. It's what Judaism is all about. . . . I just want to reinstate that childhood.

In fact, this woman had *not* been raised as an Orthodox Jew, although she described celebrating traditional Jewish rituals with her grandparents. Her reconstruction of her biography to emphasize the similarity between her present experience and past life was a way of integrating her biography and thus affirming the validity of this choice. Note, also, her desire to "reinstate" her childhood, a theme that emerged for several other Lubavitch women as well.

As the women derived a new sense of themselves as Jews, they fleshed out this conception of their identities by relating themselves to their families' and communities' roots. As did the women at Lincoln Square Synagogue, many of the women at Bais Chana associated their present observance with their grandparents. They recounted fond and warm memories of traditionally observant grandparents, particularly grandmothers. Layah expressed this feeling:

> I feel that what's happening to me is really a symbol, not just a symbol, but a fulfillment; it's something very spiritual that's like the fulfillment of my whole family. Who we all are. It's like I look at myself in the mirror and I see my grandmother and I know that this is who she is.

Rivka, too, spoke movingly about her grandparents:

> You know how they say that your *bobbe* [grandmother] and *zaide* [grandfather] are often the causes of your *teshuvah* [return]? . . . They say, how could a person who is not brought up *frum* [traditionally observant] make *teshuvah*? How could they get so close to want to do such a thing that they should be put in a situation where they should be exposed to it? They often say that's 'cause they have a *bobbe* or *zaide* up there still looking after them. In my case that is very true, especially after I saw my grandmother's old house still standing in Crown Heights. For about two weeks I had very strong feelings of spiritual conversations with her, which were very meaningful.

The women's associations with their grandparents are reminiscent of Hansen's law of third-generation return, as discussed by Will Herberg in *Protestant, Catholic, Jew.*[16] This thesis states that the third generation born in an immigrant community will reinstate those traditional ethnic practices abandoned by the second generation in its attempts to "make it" in the new society. The women's belief that they were fulfilling the path laid out by their grandparents provided a sense of identity, a connection with a larger order and with their roots.

A RESTLESS DISCONTENT

THE WOMEN AT
LINCOLN SQUARE SYNAGOGUE

The large majority of the women I met at Lincoln Square Synagogue began their involvement with the synagogue as single adults who had been living and working in New York City for several years. Their accounts described a sense of discontent, a search for a more meaningful context in which to understand their lives. This sense of discontent was not surprising; after all, these were individuals seeking to make changes in their lives. Many of the people who joined other contemporary religious movements also expressed dissatisfaction with their lives prior to joining the group.[17]

For nearly half of the women, walking into the synagogue was at least partly a response to a crisis of a practical nature—a death in the family, the ending of a long-term relationship, a career change. Their accounts included such stressful experiences as being battered by a spouse, getting divorced or ending a long-term relationship, being raped, experiencing a death in the family, reaching a crisis point at work, or suffering a serious injury. Several women highlighted the feelings of loss and crisis that resulted from these events as important stimuli in their initial entry into the religious community. When asked how she became involved in Orthodox Judaism, Stephanie recounted this painful story:

> At the time when I first wandered into Lincoln Square Synagogue [I was at] an emotional moment in my life. . . . Someone that I had been with for six and a half years and I decided to separate. It was three days before Yom Kippur and it had been a very tough year—a death in the family and my job was not going well. Everything was no good, and I was feeling *very sorry for myself* and . . . someone said, "Well, why don't you go into the synagogue?"

Another woman said, "My father had died, we had just got up from *shivah* [period of mourning], and I wanted to say kaddish for him."

These remarks illustrate that when faced with the sorts of events that threatened to shatter their established systems of ordering and making sense of their lives, these women sought out the comfort of an established religious tradition. These quotations also suggest that a sense of broken connections, of the loss of important relationships, was another important factor in the women's turning to the synagogue.

In talking about the quality of their lives prior to joining the synagogue, the women expressed some sense of dissatisfaction, a growing realization that something was "not quite right" with the way they were going about their lives. Materially, they were not in want, but their lives seemed to lack a focus.

The majority of these women did not find the central meaning of their lives in their work. Less than a third felt that they were invested in their careers. Most felt that their work was a job but not a very central aspect of their identities.[18] Even the women who seemed to me to have fascinating jobs expressed this sentiment. Cynthia, a thirty-three-year-old woman who worked as an executive in the fashion industry, told me:

> I would leave my job in two minutes. I do not feel like I'm in a career. I happen to have a job that I love and I'm thrilled that I'm successful at it, but it is in no way my life. I do not look at this job as being *the* career that I've been building for all my life. It's absolutely secondary in my life.

Similarly, Stephanie emphasized the relative lack of importance of her work in defining her sense of identity:

> The synagogue and the experience that I'm having and the friends that I've made there have given me a kind of core to my life that I would not have had now. The core used to be a man, a particular man. The core might at some point be work. At this moment, because the work that I do is not really of interest to me—it's just a way to pay the rent—the core is not work.

Several of the women said that although they enjoyed their work, it was not a central part of their identities (as it often is for middle-class men).

Many of these women felt sated with the goods of the material world. They had engaged in all the glamorous activities that were supposed to be the stuff of an interesting life. And yet these fell short, as Madeleine described:

> I really felt like I had done Manhattan. I mean, I had been in the advertising business. I had an expense account. I went to all the top restaurants, you know. I went to the opera and the New York City Ballet when they were at their height. It's like Manhattan didn't hold any more lure for me. I had had it in a way. I was bored. I was bored with the idea of new movies; City Ballet wasn't even as good as it was anymore. You know, George Ballanchine had passed away—it's just like, it lost its thralldom for me. And I could see this whole other avenue opening up that seemed to be what I really wanted at that time in my life.

Despite their professional success, many women said they had come to a point where they realized "that there is much more to life than Lutèce [a leading French restaurant] or Saks Fifth Avenue or honors at work can offer you."

These women found it difficult to construct lives that were completely fulfilling. Even though many aspects of their lives were in order—their living situations were stable, they had achieved some measure of professional success, for example—they nevertheless felt that some key element was missing. This led to a sense of transience, of an unrooted life, that left them ultimately hungry. And many of the people they were meeting were in similar situations. This sense of anomie was illustrated in accounts of vacationing in the summer resorts surrounding New York, where sophisticated singles came to relax and meet each other. Nancy Hanover vividly depicted a scene that had been described by several of the women:

> What happened to me essentially was that I was living on the East Side and I was living a single's life, and I had a short-lived relationship with a man at work who was Orthodox. And he sort of started me on a road of thinking about my Jewish identity. And one of the things I began to realize was that there had to be a better way to live. I was living this existence that was very anomic. I spent a summer after I went out with him at a summer house in the Hamptons, which was a very alienating experience. Because people were, they weren't even having one-night stands; they were just sort of looking around at each other and seeing what was there. Everybody was in a big candy store and nobody wanted to buy anything . . . so there was this sort of relevant eight-month pre–Lincoln Square Syn-

agogue period in which there was a certain amount of thinking going on. This fellow introduced me to these ideas. I started thinking, I started reading, I went to the Hamptons.

The new recruits felt they were missing a "core" to their lives, a sense of being rooted in some firm, stable, and clearly defined way of being. Despite their basic middle-class success, they felt that some circumstance in their lives was always open to flux and that the society around them did not provide a stable system of values and meaning. As Ellen put it:

> This is something that gives a stable meaning to your life. I think it might be, particularly for a single person, it might even be a more serious issue. You know, different people pass through your life. Jobs pass through your life. All types of things come and go, apartments, all the basics, interests. Sometimes they come and they go. . . . Having something like the Jewish people is a real strength.

Within the Orthodox community they found affirmation for their feeling that there must be more to life than the work-a-day world struggle. The community offered them a sense of connection to a people and to their own roots and the realization that they had a place in the world and in history.

The feeling of being connected to something larger than themselves was frequently generated in the prayer services. Two-thirds of the women had entered the religious world through the services, most frequently the Beginners' Service. All found the services fascinating, exciting, and compelling. As one woman said, "Once I started going I really liked the services. I just loved the singing." The enormous energy in the room, as the rabbi enthusiastically conducted the services, was attractive. There was a fullness of life, a feeling of partaking of something rich and enduring. Another woman, in describing her initial reactions to the services, got teary-eyed as she was talking:

> It's a very emotional topic for me; the whole thing is very emotional. I used to stand there in the beginners' minyan and get choked up and not understand why. It's like, when I used to—when Rabbi Buchwald used to sing, you know, and make us sing, it was like, it was like it used to catch in my throat. It was like I could feel, and I talked to other people who also had that experience, standing there and just being very choked up. And they're usually people that are

very cut off from *Yiddishkeit*. They come back and they hear these melodies, and it has a very profound effect on them.

What they found so moving and attractive about the service was that through these songs they were put in touch with the Jewish people, past and present. The service offered the opportunity to engage in a ritual action that both reflected and created a sense of belonging to a people and a community. Once their sense of longing was satisfied through religious participation, the women could experience a capacity for joy (which little else in our culture calls forth). In contrast to the individualism of the general culture, the prayers invited the worshippers to participate in what Robert Bellah and his coauthors of *Habits of the Heart* refer to as a "community of memory . . . constituted by its past," involved in retelling its story, and thus creating a "context of meaning" that allows individuals to connect their individual aspirations with those of a larger whole.[19] The songs conveyed a sense of a rooted and ancient way of life that the women were encouraged to claim as their own. Through participation in the service, the women were exposed to an order that cast their individual lives in the broader framework of history. Their conceptions of their lives were thus expanded and given direction.

Sharon, the woman who had given up her study of Eastern religion to pursue Judaism, succinctly expressed this idea:

> What I loved about Orthodox Judaism is the sense that I was simply part of a three-thousand-year-old continuum that happened to skip a couple of generations. You can look at my parents' or grandparents' nonobservance as a little bloop out of three thousand years. So I like this sense of where I stand in history.

Janet, too, emphasized the appeal of the Orthodox sense of place: "I have a sense of history, that I'm part of a continuum. I really feel that I am continuing a tradition that goes way back, and I'm just more of it."

The women derived a sense of who they were and what their lives were about by tracing their connections with others—by understanding that they were part of a people whose life span extended way back in time and forward into the future. This realization lent a feeling of metaphysical certainty to their lives. At a time, and in a city, in which many aspects of life were frequently in flux and in which many people felt cut off from enduring human connections, it made sense that the feeling of belonging to a people would be so appealing.[20]

The *ba'alot teshuvah*'s awareness of their connections with their religious and communal roots helped shape and define the parameters of their lives and also provided some assurance of collective continuity, if not their own personal future. As Ellen said:

> I loved going to the services and singing the songs and they're really nice melodies and it's sort of ritual and you're singing them with other people and they're songs that have been sung for so many years and it just feels good. I really like the Hebrew language. It's the strength and the consistency and the stability of the institution in a chaotic world like ours, living in a city like New York, which can be so scattered and alienating.

Deborah also emphasized the importance of the sense of roots:

> And to know that I'm part of a community that has lasted for centuries—I think it's a special bond because you could be related to people, to Jews all over the world, without actually having any kinship. You get such a strong sense of responsibility and community and the feeling that no person's alone 'cause you're tied to all other Jewish families in the world. You have a link to the past and especially to the future.

The women's special emphasis on the durability of the Orthodox way of life was a clue to the particular appeal of Orthodox Judaism as a solution to some of the issues that brought them into the synagogue in the first place. Orthodoxy was appealing precisely because it was presented as an "ancient" way of life whose survival over the millennia was evidence of its abiding value. The women who came to Lincoln Square Synagogue did not choose Conservative or Reform Judaism, whose obvious relative newness and openness to innovation made them suspect to those in search of moorings and roots. Several of the women told me that they had explored Reform or Reconstructionist synagogues, but they were not attracted to the English liturgy or to the Americanization of the religion.

Clifford Geertz, a noted anthropologist and student of religion, writes that one of the most powerful characteristics of religion is that it conveys a sense of the "really real" by placing the proximate details of our lives in an ultimate framework of significance.[21] Contemporary U.S. society features a "marketplace of religious alternatives" in which "new religions," ancient traditions, and a wide variety of psychotherapies peddle peace, truth, and a meaningful way to live. Orthodoxy was compelling because it claimed the authority of tradition; in contrast to many of the other options available to the women, Orthodox Judaism did not appear to be a recent human construct subject to change with the changing cultural climate. Several women expressed this sentiment, as we can hear in this remark from Elizabeth:

> So about Conservatism, the reason I came to religion is I wanted some order out of the disorder of contemporary life. I wanted a guide, a moral guide, and if people don't go by the Bible or don't go by the oral code, then it's all relative and it's based on the belief of one person, the rabbi of that shul or whoever is the religious leader, and I don't find that satisfying. I wanted to find an order that's been maintained for centuries, throughout many generations all across the world.

Another woman also emphasized that the deep roots of the Jewish tradition were compelling to her:

> What's so exciting about Judaism is that it's something that's been going on for a long time. There aren't too many things like that nowadays; they're all here today and gone. And the values—the things that they said years ago feel so fresh. . . . All those therapies, the human potential movement, gurus, I've never been into anything like that; I never felt like it was mine. And I'm glad. This is something that is really mine and I want to know about it. There is something so reassuring, or valid, in something that goes on for so long and in basically the same way. I look around and think about what's going on today and I really don't think these weekend self-help seminars are going to be here two thousand years from now. . . . I don't think there are too many things in this world that have lasted so intact, rituals and prayer. So to me that's very convincing when I hear something like that and it was something I was born into.

Because Orthodoxy's attraction for *ba'alot teshuvah* was this ability to convey a sense of an ancient, unchanging, and therefore compelling order of existence, the women who chose this synagogue would not have found their needs met by an egalitarian or nontraditional service. Elizabeth, a physician in private practice, told me she recognized that it doesn't make sense that someone like me would be going to an Orthodox service and tolerating the passivity that's involved in it, but the psychological need which Judaism has played for me has been a sense of order and a sense of tradition. I'm not drawn to the nontraditional, even though theoretically I certainly believe in it.

Although this group of women used a language of modern self-determination to describe their entry into Orthodoxy, they also used a rhetoric that emphasized the abiding value of something that was not newly constructed, not relative, and capable of representation through rituals as ancient and unchanging. There was an interesting tension in their accounts between their valuing of freedom of choice and then using it to choose a religious practice whose authority was based on tradition.

THE WOMEN AT BAIS CHANA

For both groups of women, joining a religious community was an expression of a search for order, meaning, and belonging. For a small minority of the women at Bais Chana, their attraction to Hasidism was precipitated by the same kinds of immediate crisis described by the women at Lincoln Square Synagogue—deaths in the family, fractured relationships, and so on. Tamar, for example, told me of how she had been traveling with her non-Jewish boyfriend—her "passionate pasha," as she called him—when she received a message that her father had died. She returned from her travels and shortly thereafter began to attend Lubavitch activities in her hometown. About a third of the women, however, described crises that greatly differed from those of the Lincoln Square women in that they suggested a more serious disruption in the women's ability to function in daily life.

For example, Layah, a gentle woman who worked as a social worker and whose mother had been hospitalized for mental illness on and off throughout Layah's life, described the period preceding her joining the Lubavitch as follows:

Ever since I broke up with this guy—the last one who wasn't Jewish, that was about five months before I came to Crown Heights— ever since that breakup I had been very unhappy and I hadn't been able to sleep well at night. I was constantly crying and felt totally out of control. I kept feeling this tug back to him, but I

knew it wasn't the thing I wanted. I really thought I must be crack-
ing up. I'm going the way of my mother before me or whatever. It
runs in the family. It must be.

In her questionnaire Rachel described the suicide attempt that precipitated her seeking out the Lubavitch:

> It started when I was twenty going on twenty-one. I was doing
> drugs and with not-nice people. It was bad. I wanted to kill myself
> because I was non happy and I try to and I call for help and my
> friend could take no more of it and call my friend from the police and
> he came and went to the doctor that thought I was crazy and want
> to put me away for good and try to one day my police friend said
> there was a Jewish JDL [Jewish Defense League] meeting so I went
> to it and said I want to help and I did it was fun and met a *frum* guy
> told me about being Jewish and went back to my friend and told him
> and he made me call the rabbi and I did he was not so whatever.
> And I wait for his call and he call told me to come over to talk to me
> and he told me about the Rebbe and he told me to come for Shabbos
> and I did and it was nice and we learn a lot and he told me about
> going to Bais Chana so I went there.

Similarly, Naomi described to me the profound chaos in her life
prior to her encounter with the Lubavitch:

> I was getting into so much trouble, and each thing would lead to
> worse. Drugs and things like that. I was very much involved, like in
> ninth grade I started, I smoked pot a lot, very much, and then I
> started with coke and it got worse and worse as it went along, guys,
> more drugs, my period was late. . . . Everything you could think of
> was going wrong.

A few of these women seemed to have fairly serious problems
adjusting to daily life. One woman was hostile and frequently
fought with the other women at the institute. Another woman
repeatedly asked whomever would listen, "Hallo, do you know
about the sun?" Another woman tried to leave the institute in
midsession to hitchhike to New York City, where she planned to
set sail for Africa in her eight-foot boat.

Many of the women at Bais Chana described the same sense of
void, of a missing dimension to their lives, that I heard from the
women at Lincoln Square Synagogue. But for the Bais Chana
women the sense of dissatisfaction and searching had been present
for a long time, unlike the Lincoln Square women's description of
a more recent sense of dissatisfaction. For example, Tamar de-

scribed to me the difficulties she experienced growing up Jewish in a non-Jewish town and culture and her continual feeling of emptiness:

> I think in high school I never really belonged, never really fit in, and that was in the late 60s early 70s and I gradually went on to university and I guess there was always this need to fill a void. Some notion that that which was just apparent to the naked eye wasn't an end in itself . . . I always felt that there had to be something more that was happening, more than I could touch or see, smell, taste, or feel.

Similarly, Rivka described her sense of unease in the world:

> I felt lost as a person. I did not know how I felt about such things as morality, marriage, premarital sex, G-d. I was advised that this school [Bais Chana] was dedicated to helping women understand themselves better.

More than half of the women at Bais Chana expressed a generalized, ongoing sense of being lost and disoriented. They were searching for an identity, for a clear definition of who they were as people. As we know, identity within modern societies has become problematic because many of the sources of order, meaning, and community that people had relied on prior to industrialization have been undermined.[22] In the contemporary United States, middle-class individuals are expected to construct their own identities and lives by choosing from among the various institutional arenas those that will become the primary source of identity. The women who came to Bais Chana felt they had no clear sense of identity. As children they had not been given a strong sense of Jewish identity, be it ethnic or religious. As most of them did not have careers or jobs they found interesting, they did not derive a sense of identity from their work. Nor did they find an adequate sense of self elsewhere, such as in family, community, or political organization. Sandy, a woman who had trouble getting along with the other women, said:

> I've been lost for awhile in a spiritual way, I've been lost. I haven't been able to focus myself on any type of meaningful work. And work is very important to me, so it's been very frustrating because nothing's really fit. . . . A lot of it has to do with the fact that I'm over the age of twenty-five and I haven't settled yet. I'm not married. I'm interested in a lot of different things in life, but nothing

has really just grabbed me to the point where I'd really want to totally dive into something and really devote myself to it.

In contrast to the women who were attracted to Lincoln Square Synagogue, nearly all of whom had *not* tried other religious groups before, many of the women who came to Bais Chana had been searchers. They had been feeling a strong sense of disorder in their lives for a long time and had become involved in cults or Fundamentalist Christian groups as a way of securing a stable identity and a sense of belonging. As one woman told me:

> I've been very confused over the past several years. I've been reading a lot of philosophy, psychology, hoping to find some kind of answer to why I'm confused. I've tried EST, ESP, and TM and still didn't find what I was looking for.

Even though some of the women had found a place in these other religious communities for a while, they had sought out the Lubavitch community because ultimately they felt alienated from the other groups. They felt that only Judaism was truly "their own," as Lisa, who had been involved in Fundamentalist Christianity for several years, expressed eloquently:

> I feel comfortable with myself because I'm not trying to fake it anymore. I'm me now. I have so much time for other things because I'm not apologizing for who I am. My Jewishness isn't a burden anymore. My religious feelings are not misplaced onto other religions now; they're really where they belong, and it takes me deep down into who I am, how I was brought up, where I belong. I have a sense of where I belong in the order of things.

Layah had explored Sufism as a young adult as part of her quest to find a coherent identity and worldview. "I thought with the Sufis I would find a way to live, but the Sufis said, 'You're Jewish; go find out about your own religion.'" Within the Lubavitch world she saw the possibility of deriving a firmer sense of self, a more appropriate identity:

> I felt more comfortable being myself in the home of this family. . . . I don't have a problem that needs analyzing; I need to learn to live in a way that's going to work for me. . . . This has given me a whole context to understand my life, the past, and it's given me a way to move into the present and the future. It's a way of living and a sense of who I am.

Coming into the Hasidic community offered the women an axis around which to center their sense of selves and a clear definition of who they were. This was a major aspect of what they found attractive about the Lubavitch. As Naomi explained:

> I continued to be involved because the people I met impressed me so much—they seemed fulfilled and really knew what path they were taking in life. They knew who they were. I wanted this, too.

As I will later show, the rabbi at Bais Chana repeatedly told the women that they did not have a choice about whether to "become observant" because it was essential to their own inner natures as Jews. The women used a similar language when they affirmed the rightness of this choice by presenting it as the path to their own true selves. Rivka clearly articulated this feeling, which had been expressed by many of the others:

> It's like you say, when you find something that works and you keep doing it, you become more yourself. That's all. More of you shows. You weren't yourself before; you had to use masks. Now I'm myself.

Beth, too, emphasized the importance of the sense of self offered within the Lubavitch community:

> You know the Crosby, Stills, and Nash song, "You, who are on the road, must have a code that you can live by." This is a code for me to live by. Here it's easy; you can face practically anything. The people are so inspiring and so strong and so true to values that are real basic Jewish values. They are not afraid to teach you who you are. I don't have to hide anymore; it's very special.

Here let me highlight the distinction between these women's sense of finding *themselves* through their involvement with the Lubavitch and the emphasis in the Lincoln Square women's accounts on Orthodoxy as a path to finding *their places* in the larger order. The women I met at Lincoln Square Synagogue emphasized that they were attracted by the sense of roots and belonging offered by the long history and seeming permanence of Orthodoxy. These women basically had stable lives and a reasonable sense of who they were; their quest was for a sense of a larger purpose in life. Although a few of the Lubavitch women expressed the same idea—Layah said, "When they said the *Shema* in shul, I really felt tied into something bigger than myself"—this mode of expression was generally not part of the language of the women at Bais Chana. Their accounts instead highlighted the basic sense of identity they found in the Lubavitch way of life.

Part of this distinction is a reflection of the different language spoken by the rabbis in these settings. The rabbis at Lincoln Square always emphasized the profound value of Orthodoxy as a way of life steeped in an ancient tradition and history. The rabbis at Bais Chana, in contrast, repeatedly told the women that the Lubavitch system was the only path to their true selves. But the rabbis did not simply offer worldviews in a vacuum; their particular approaches and emphases were formulated at least partly as responses to the needs of newcomers. Thus, the rabbis at Lincoln Square addressed themselves to stable professional adults who were looking for meaning and a sense of being connected to something larger than themselves, whereas the rabbis at Bais Chana pitched their appeal to women who felt lost and were in search of a complete definition of self.

GOD AND SPIRITUAL EXPERIENCE

THE WOMEN AT
LINCOLN SQUARE SYNAGOGUE

This group of women, who had not been religious seekers, minimized the spiritual aspect of their attraction to Orthodoxy. In fact, half of the women I interviewed were not certain about their belief in God. Deborah responded to my question about belief by saying:

> Do I believe in God? I, I don't know. I mean, I wouldn't say no, I don't believe in God, but I can't say yes, I do believe in God. I don't *disbelieve* in God. I just can't say I *believe* in God.

Stephanie expressed the same ambivalence:

> I don't ask myself all of the questions, and I don't say, If there isn't a God, what are we all doing here jumping up and down and all of this foolishness? Because my connection to it, the reason that I'm enjoying getting into the observant mode, doesn't have to do with belief in God. It has to do with foundation, tradition, a kind of structure that I do believe is practical. And the rabbi often says, "Even if you could prove there was no God, I'd probably live my life

the same way." That's the precepts, that if one lived them life would be better on earth whether or not there was a God.

(I initiated the discussion about God in two-thirds of the interviews. In only ten of the interviews did the women themselves spontaneously talk about God.)

Two-thirds of the women I interviewed in this community reported that they had never had a religious experience. Several of the women said they did not even know what a religious experience was. Two of the women answered the question of whether they had ever had a religious experience in somewhat humorous terms. Such a response could indicate that they felt some tension or discomfort about being in a religious setting without having had a religious experience. Janet said:

> No, I never did have a religious experience. Would that I had! If I could have on my best day the kind of experience that I think my friend Jane has every time she opens a prayer book, it would be terrific. Once I loved God for about thirty seconds.

Deborah, too, offered a disclaimer:

> No. And the other thing is, I don't know what a religious experience would be. . . . I think when I meet the man I'm going to marry, that will be a religious experience. Because, you think, how on this planet can two people meet each other? That will probably be a religious experience. But you see, my whole thing about religion is, people say to me, "Deborah, you're becoming religious." Well, I don't connect religion to any of this, necessarily. I mean I like the community, I like to learn about Judaism, but I don't know what religious means.

Instead of talking about God and spiritual concerns, these women emphasized the powerful feelings of belonging and of being part of an ongoing community that they were afforded through participating in an Orthodox group. But these feelings can nevertheless be a path to a spiritual dimension, to a feeling of transcendence. This idea, expounded by the classical sociologist Emile Durkheim in *The Elementary Forms of the Religious Life*, was expressed by many of the women.[23] Stephanie vividly described the powerful feelings evoked in her by the prayer services:

> I do get an experience that is very, kind of overwhelming, but I don't think it's so much religious. Which is when we're standing in

that little room [where Beginners' Service is held] and it's wall-to-wall people, and it's standing room only and the rabbi is standing at the front. Toward the end of the service when we do the repeat of the Amidah and he is singing and he is bobbing back and forth like this and he's pounding on the book and there's this full energy in the room. Everybody singing and we have just all shared two hours of singing and learning and arguing and I just look and I say, I never even knew these people and now we're all here and this is what has brought us together and this little man [the rabbi] has galvanized us into a little community. And this song that was sung by Moses, this is a miracle. . . . And it makes me cry almost every single time. That's not really a religious experience—it's more like a cultural experience or something like that—and the feeling I had this last Shabbos, I finally put together what it was. It was yet again a family.

The powerful feeling of community Stephanie experienced during Beginners' Service was quintessentially religious, according to Durkheim. Nevertheless, Stephanie, like the majority of women within this community, explicitly denied the "religious" or "spiritual" dimension of her turn to Orthodoxy.

Even though the majority of the women I interviewed did not consider themselves spiritual, a quarter of the women did feel that they had been on a spiritual search or religious quest. As Sharon said:

For the past five years I've been on a very spiritual path anyway. I mean, I came to a true belief in God. I feel very spiritual, I have a very spiritual nature, and this sort of gave me a direction to plant it.

Four of the women felt God's active guidance in directing their path to Orthodoxy. Madeleine described the feeling thus:

I wanted to do what God wanted me to do most of all. I really felt, I've had experiences where I just have been pushed along this path. I really feel there's some kind of—it's not just me. I don't want to sound "out there" or anything, but I really do feel a sense of God in my life and that He wants me to be on this path.

She noted that she had opened a Bible on several occasions and had found a message there that spoke to her situation and gave her direction.

Only three of the women I interviewed had tried other religious groups, or any of the various contemporary forms of self-help movements such as transcendental meditation and sensitivity training. Eleven of the women I interviewed, however, spontaneously mentioned that they were in therapy: this was truly a modern, urbane group.

The finding that belief in God and spiritual experiences were relatively absent among this group of women differs strikingly from the findings reported in Janet Aviad's study of mostly U.S. *ba'alei* and *ba'alot teshuvah* in the live-in yeshivas in Jerusalem. In her book *Return to Judaism* she reports that 63 percent of her respondents described spiritual experiences associated with their turning to Orthodoxy.[24] One possible explanation for our contrasting findings may be the difference in settings and decades of our studies. Her research was conducted in the 1970s, and her respondents were spiritual seekers traveling around with backpacks who were available to be recruited into a setting where they could live and study Judaism full-time. These seekers of the 1970s were likely to have been differently motivated and to have spoken a different idiom from the Lincoln Square "yuppies" of the 1980s. Because God and spiritual experiences were probably emphasized more in these yeshivas than in the liberal modern Orthodox synagogue, this might also account for the differences in our findings.

Alternatively, our contrasting results could be a product of gender differences. Two-thirds of Aviad's respondents were male, and her analysis does not differentiate the women's experiences from the men's. Because men were the majority, their voices were the loudest, obscuring any possible differences in the men's and women's accounts. To further explore this possibility, I returned to Lincoln Square Synagogue and interviewed thirty *ba'alei teshuvah*, 90 percent of whom did report a belief in God.[25] This finding—that the men at Lincoln Square were much more likely to claim belief in God than the women were—corresponds with Danzger's report that the men in his study more frequently reported spiritual experiences than did the women.[26]

These gender differences, which contrast with the data on Christians—wherein women were found to have higher levels of belief in God[27]—might result from the gender distinctions in Judaism. Orthodox Judaism mandates that men have greater obligations in prayer and study, while women's primary role is in the family. Therefore, women do not participate as much in those ongoing rituals that create a relationship to God. Further research is needed in this area to understand how differences in religious

beliefs, ritual, and law within different religious traditions shape
the gendered nature of members' religious experiences.

The women in the Lubavitch setting, like the women at Lincoln
Square Synagogue, did not engage in lengthy theological discourses in accounting for their attraction to Orthodoxy. Nevertheless, belief in God was either explicit or implicit in many of their
accounts. For example, Beth, in describing her path from born-
again Christian to resident at Bais Chana, said:

> I came to a crossroads, a four-way intersection. When you come to
> a crossroads, you have a choice of three ways to go. So you make a
> right-hand turn. If it's a Godly path, you will have no obstacles in
> that path as you walk. And if you take an un-Godly path, you'll
> come to a dead end. I feel that that's where my life was at.

Another woman, an eighteen-year-old who had been involved
with the Lubavitch for a year, wrote that she would describe herself as a *ba'alat teshuvah*, "someone who is coming closer to God by
doing His will." A Russian woman wrote that she was "beginning
to realize that there is no truth in the world but Hashem and no
pleasures in the world but serving God through Torah."

The ease with which these women referred to God and the clear
convictions of faith they expressed presented a striking contrast to
the accounts of the women at Lincoln Square Synagogue. Indeed,
many of the women at Bais Chana described their turning to the
Lubavitch in spiritual terms. Layah said:

> I needed a spiritual community. There is a whole other level of
> spiritual reality, which I've always felt in my life very strongly, as
> giving me strength. There are certain experiences which people call
> religious experiences. I've had many of them, not on drugs, just
> naturally . . . so it's very fulfilling for me to be a part of the spiritual
> community where that part of me can really get exercise. It's not
> enough for me to be without it.

Sandy, in describing how she came to the Lubavitch, recounted a
recent powerful experience:

> I had this very strong inclination to contact a rabbi. I hadn't spoken
> to a rabbi in over ten years, but I had this very overwhelming

feeling that it was just something I had to do. This came about three weeks ago and it lasted for about three days, and then I remember on the third day, I just woke up and I looked in the Yellow Pages—I had an instinct that it should be an Orthodox rabbi—and called. I said, "I'd like to talk to you." And he said, "Okay, fine. When can you come down? . . . How about now?" And I went. It was at the Chabad house and I had some spiritual questions. . . . I had been seeing a picture in my mind of a Hasidic rabbi, very old, with a long grayish white beard. . . . This picture had been in my mind telling me to see a rabbi. Well, when I went into this rabbi's office there was a little picture on his wall of the man I'd seen in my mind. The rabbi was telling me about the Rebbe. I said, "Who is the Rebbe?" And he pointed to the picture on the wall. I was almost afraid to tell him that I had seen his face in my mind. And then I did tell him. And he kind of shook his head and said, "Well, sometimes he sends messages to certain people."

In contrast to the Lincoln Square women, some of whom claimed not to know what a "spiritual experience" was, the women at Bais Chana eagerly described these experiences.

Although the two groups of women who came into Lincoln Square and Bais Chana were in some ways dealing with a similar set of problems—the well-known sense of rootlessness, alienation, and anomie of modern life—their different social locations within modern society shaped their attraction to distinct religious communities. Different women have an "elective affinity" with the various approaches to Judaism.[28] In general, the women who were attracted to the Lubavitch community were those who were feeling more lost and troubled and in search of a radical antidote. Thus, they were more willing to join a community that constructed relatively impermeable boundaries with the wider society—which had proven to be difficult and, in their view, even harmful to them—and had strong internal social control mechanisms. The Lincoln Square women, in contrast, were rather firmly rooted in society; theirs was more a search for a larger order and sense of meaning. Both groups of women, however, had additional goals when they entered the religious communities: the fulfillment of their private, intimate lives.

5

Women into Wives and Mothers

The women coming into the modern Orthodox and Lubavitch communities were seeking a sense of self rooted in a larger, continually existing community with a past and a future. They were also seeking an ordered sense of self on a personal level: they were troubled by the confusion over gender in the wider society and by the lack of comfortable, established patterns for forming nuclear families. Critics of contemporary culture see the "deinstitutionalization" of the private realm—the transformations in society's norms for courtship, marriage, sexuality, and childrearing—as leading to a sense of anomie and discomfort that proves fertile ground for the growth of spiritual movements.[1]

In her extensive study of religious and secular communes, Angela Aidala found that at times of social dislocations and disjuncture, people seek clear guidelines for how to live their lives. A central aspect of the sense of self they seek is an understanding of how to be a person of a particular gender—how to live out a "masculine" or "feminine" identity. Times of social change also breed various forms of political, social, and spiritual activism, including the growth of communal movements. The religious communal groups studied by Angela Aidala all offered a "definition and implementation of a particular vision of male/female" that was a major attraction to potential converts.[2] The "sex and gender certainties" offered by these groups were among their most "useful truths."[3]

Many ethnographies of contemporary religious movements have found that the delineation of distinct roles for men and women and the provision of clear norms for family life were primary elements in their attractiveness to potential converts. In studies of such diverse communities as the Hare Krishna, Evangelical and Fundamentalist Christian groups, Pentecostal Catholics, and Orthodox Jews, sociologists have found that the norms for nuclear family life were central in the religious construction of reality and in its appeal to new members.[4] For the most part the communities generally spelled out conventional definitions of masculinity and femininity. Nevertheless, the community's emphasis on nuclear family had the consequence of involving men in family life to a greater extent than was the norm in secular society.

The women who came to Lincoln Square Synagogue and Bais Chana were on a quest for a clear articulation of their role as women, one that would place them in the center of nuclear families. The women's desires coincided with the centrality of the nuclear family in the world of Orthodox Judaism. The institutions thus spent a great deal of time on precisely these issues, and the differences between the two groups of women shaped their expression of this particular quest.

ORDERING A WOMAN'S LIFE:
THE SEARCH FOR FAMILY

THE WOMEN AT
LINCOLN SQUARE SYNAGOGUE

About half of the women I met in this setting specifically mentioned a longing for family and a committed relationship as an important factor in their choosing to enter the synagogue. Ellen expressed this feeling clearly: "Probably at this point in my life I would prefer to be married, and that may be part of the reason why I'm in this kind of community. Family is a value here." These women were at a stage in their life cycles in which the majority of their contemporaries were already married and having children. The desire to form families was often on these women's minds when they decided to explore the synagogue. As one woman in the community said:

> I'm more interested in family. It might be my age [thirty-seven]. I never wanted to get married. I would like to get married now. I didn't want to get married until I was maybe thirty-five. . . . I guess I just feel in the last few years that maybe I would like to get married and *maybe* have a family.

Another woman spontaneously told me (several times) about an attractive non-Jewish black man she had met that morning and agonized about whether she should go out with him. The weight with which this issue pressed on her mind was apparent:

> The fact of the matter is, I'm thirty-two. My friends who are married, they're very lucky. You know, I don't go out anymore just for kicks. I very much want a relationship with a man right now, but it just doesn't seem to be in the cards. And love seems so important, and yet it just seems so hard to come by. I want someone to come home to and put my arms around at night.

Many of the women I interviewed lived alone in studio apartments in high-rise buildings. They had moved into these apartments several years previously, when they were in their twenties, expecting to get married soon and move out. And yet six or eight or ten years later they found themselves still single and still living alone in small apartments. There weren't that many opportunities in their lives to meet compatible men, and they had given up on, or never even considered, Manhattan's renowned singles bars. Deborah expressed precisely the experience of many of the others: "I would really like to meet someone, but New York City is an island, a desolate island of singles."

A large part of these women's problems in meeting men is demographic: within New York City, as well as within the Jewish community in general and the United States altogether, there are more available women than men in every age group. Laurel Richardson writes in her study of women in long-term relationships with married men, "For a single woman over the age of 25 there is a serious undersupply of available men. One out of every five females does not have a potential mate."[5] And in each ascending age bracket, the proportion of available men to women goes down, largely because men prefer to marry women younger than themselves, and the women of the baby-boom generation do not have as large a cohort of "older" men from which to choose. As people age, the pool of eligible partners shrinks for women but expands for men.

Before coming to the synagogue, many of the women had had relationships with non-Jewish men. One woman told me:

> I always observed the High Holidays, I always found my way to synagogue, I'd always observed Pesach [Passover], I even had a

seder at my house once, but I was very mixed up. I was dating guys who weren't Jewish like crazy, and I guess I really didn't have a sense of direction.

Deborah described her past relationships in a similar fashion:

I haven't had any really Jewish boyfriends; I have never had an appropriate Jewish boyfriend. Thank God, I never married anybody I went out with because I have never had basically a Jewish boyfriend. But it never really occurred to me about marrying a Jewish person. I wasn't looking for a Jewish person. And now I wouldn't think of doing it any other way.

At a stage when they felt ready to begin the next phase of their lives—settling down and having families—joining a synagogue with such a high proportion of professional singles (the rabbi estimated that singles made up about 50 percent of the membership, with the ratio of women to men approximately five to three) increases the likelihood that they will meet a Jewish man. Several of the women expressed clearly that an attractive aspect of this synagogue was just this possibility. One thirty-year-old successful businesswoman described this feeling:

I liked the . . . sense of community and the support. And Lincoln Square Synagogue seemed like a great place to meet people and men. It seemed like a ready-made social life that I could climb into easily. I've never done the singles bar scene.

Ellen had had the same idea: "I remember one or two friends of my sister's saying, 'Oh, go to the synagogue. There are all these men there.'" The businesswoman told me that she had hoped that because the synagogue was a religious institution, the context might be more conducive (than the secular Manhattan singles world) to forming stable relationships. "Meeting men has not been easy in New York. You know, the same old shtick—they don't want to get married. I thought the men here would be different." A recent *New York Times* article entitled "Singles Seek Social Life at Houses of Worship" quoted a woman who was a newcomer to this synagogue: "It's a much more civilized place to meet than in a singles bar. . . . How bad can a place be where every guy's opening line is 'Good Shabbos'?"[6]

The women expressed not only the desire to get married; they also wanted children. And this wish was even more urgent as they felt their biological clocks ticking rapidly. One woman said:

> The older I get I keep thinking, well, when am I going to get married and have a child? Maybe I'll never have children and it really starts to become a concern and I really see how wonderful it is to be a mother and it starts to look more and more inviting. . . . Most women, especially women who are in their thirties, are finding that it's extremely important to be a mother or to at least be married and to try and build a family.

Sharon described how she had been out West intensively studying an Eastern religion. When she reached her mid-twenties she decided to move back to New York in order to give priority to her Jewish identity. This decision was sparked by thoughts about getting married and having a family.

> At the end of my stay at the center I was beginning to think about marriage. I was realizing, well, something about the biological karma of it, and that also definitely had something to do with my coming back to New York because I wanted my marriage to grow out of the Jewish community. So for me, it started at like twenty-five, and now I very much want a traditional family.

Several of the women revealed that they were inspired to live a more Jewish life so as to have something positive to pass on to their children. So strong were their desires for a loving, intimate family life that their accounts of their decisions to join an Orthodox community included children they did not yet have. For example, Deborah, in response to the question "How would you articulate what being Jewish means to you?" replied:

> Raising my children Jewish. Keeping these traditions alive for my children. For me Judaism means I will raise my children to be a little more Jewish than I was, so that at least I'll know for them that Judaism won't die out.

Another woman, in describing how she became interested in Orthodoxy, declared:

> I hadn't been in a synagogue or a temple for years. And recently, I've become more interested in learning more about the religion and just finding out. I think in my older age I value tradition and ritual more and I realize it's important to me, and when and if I have children I want to be able to pass along more of it than I got.

The idea of coming to the synagogue to meet men and possibly start families, however, was not entirely a comfortable one for many of the women. Ellen expressed her ambivalence in this way:

There are a lot of women who get into this, a lot of women in my age group; there's a particular age group, from thirty-five to forty, who are interested in getting married. So I think that the synagogue has a social function. But also, I know, a lot of us have talked about it, it's kind of awkward, too, because you don't want to get distracted, because you really are interested in the services, too. So you know, you have a conflict about it.

Sharon was uncomfortable with what she perceived as the social pressure at the synagogue:

Once I remember being at a *shalosh seudos* [Saturday late afternoon meal at the synagogue], and Rabbi Buchwald was having a really wonderful time. He was going around and saying, "You should all get married." And I remember feeling very uncomfortable because I did not come to Lincoln Square Synagogue to get married. I understand that some people do come to Lincoln Square Synagogue for that reason. I didn't come for that reason. In fact, I didn't even want to get married when I came to Lincoln Square Synagogue.

Curiously, Sharon was the same woman who told me that she had moved to New York from the West Coast at the age of twenty-five when she began thinking about having a family. There must be something uncomfortable for a number of these women about the idea of coming to the synagogue to meet men—it seems like such an areligious motivation, and it calls to mind the cultural stereotype of women desperate to "hook their men." Yet this was an important aspect of synagogue life at Lincoln Square and one acknowledged by the participants in this setting—the members as well as the rabbis. Indeed, the *New York Times* article cited earlier referred to this synagogue as "one house of worship in Manhattan that places a heavy emphasis on attracting single people." In fact, the synagogue has the nickname "Wink and Stare," an appellation used proudly even by the beginners' rabbi. Given that the rabbi was aware that the desire to find a partner was often a concern of the new recruits, he felt that anything that enhanced the synagogue's reputation in this area might help to bring in new people.

THE WOMEN AT BAIS CHANA

Like the women at Lincoln Square, the desire to form nuclear families of their own was on the minds of the women at Bais Chana, no matter what their age. Here, too, the women thought that an Orthodox Jewish community might provide them with the opportunity to do so. But as we saw earlier, some of the women who came to Lincoln Square Synagogue denied that they were there to look for a husband. In contrast, many of the Lubavitch *ba'alot teshuvah* explicitly stated that this was part of their agenda in participating in the Lubavitch community and in coming to Bais Chana. Layah said:

> I want to have a husband. I think I'm ready for it now, whereas before it wouldn't have been right. I do want to get married, and I think coming here to Bais Chana helps prepare myself emotionally for that.

Rivka was equally explicit about her goal:

> I came to Bais Chana because here's the place where I can get what I want to learn. The stuff that helps put myself together just in terms of the fact that marriage is one of my main goals now. At Bais Chana you learn about what it is. That's what goes on here. Everything, like Rabbi Friedman said, the first day, the very first day, everything that you learn here has to and must apply to your *Yiddishkeit* and to marriage.

Rachel, a very troubled young woman, nevertheless had the same idea: "The rabbi told me that in Lubavitch I could be married to a nice guy, and they would straighten me out first. I very much want to get married."

These women's explicit desire to get married fit in with the agenda of the Lubavitch community, which in its zeal to promote the proliferation of Jewish religious families actually arranged marriages for its members.[7] The women's desire also fit in nicely with the curriculum at Bais Chana; teachings concerning marriage were an essential component of the resocialization process.

A central factor in the attraction of these women to the Lubavitch mode of organizing relations between the sexes—eliminating dating, prohibiting all premarital physical contact, and substituting arranged marriages—was that many of them had had sexual relationships in which they had been hurt and which they now regretted. Beth described her experiences thus:

> I was never very good at playing the dating game, but I tried like anything to make it work. It didn't work and it isn't working. . . . I went to college and I met this guy at college and we started dating

and I started to care about him and then I got screwed, literally screwed by him. If I could go back to being sixteen years old again I'd do it all over . . . but I'd make a lot of changes.

Rivka expressed the same feelings:

> I had such a lousy experience with relationships when I was in college. . . . There was something wrong there 'cause you know what? I got into this thing. My mother was always concerned with my social life. She still is so concerned. Why don't you have a boyfriend? She would always ask me. So it was at the point where I would go out and I'd go to a party and sleep with someone . . . that's against my grain . . . well obviously I'm Jewish, it's got something to do with it . . . but even then when I didn't recognize my Jewishness, that was not me. And I went along.

These women's stories presented a striking contrast to the words of Malkie, one of the *madrichot*, a young woman who had grown up within the Lubavitch community and who was engaged to be married. Because the *madrichot* served as role models for the recruits, and interacted with them regularly, their expressions of satisfaction about not having been sexually active stood out against the recruits' difficult experiences. She wrote the following on her questionnaire:

> I didn't miss a thing. . . . I had the same amount of fun as a normal girl. . . . I didn't go through all the hell of competition of who gets that boy . . . and after talking with *so* many girls who went through it, they tell me I'm right. I saved *everything*, and he for me, and it's *beautiful*.

In having had negative sexual experiences, the Lubavitch recruits were probably no different from the large majority of contemporary single women, and women at Lincoln Square, who had probably also been hurt at some point in their relationships with men. Nevertheless, because I asked open-ended questions in the interviews, the women had the opportunity to expound on those themes and experiences that *they* understood as most relevant to their attraction to Orthodoxy. The absence of such stories among the women who joined Lincoln Square Synagogue suggests that they did not construe these experiences as so decisive in their decision to join an Orthodox synagogue. Perhaps because they had been on their own much longer, they had learned how to deal with and integrate these experiences. In fact, once they began going to

Lincoln Square, this group continued to be sexually active. In contrast, the prominence of such accounts from the women who came to Bais Chana indicates that these experiences played a major role in their attraction to an Orthodox religious community. These women, therefore, were willing to get involved with a community that demanded they surrender control over their sexuality and be completely chaste until marriage. They actually seemed relieved to follow the community's norms and to be given external reasons for not being sexually active.

Because the women who joined the Lubavitch community felt so hurt by their past sexual experiences, they were no longer interested in dating and were glad to follow the Lubavitch pattern of *shidduchim* (dates arranged by a third party for the explicit purpose of marriage). Layah expressed her preference for the Lubavitch system:

> I like this sytem because I was never very comfortable—you see, in this way there's a certain screening that happens before the first date and then afterward. It's totally different from hit or miss. I feel much more comfortable with this system. You don't have to say anything. You can get back to the people who got you together and say, I thought this about him and he can do the same. . . . Also within this system if you really want to get married, you know you're not going out with guys who just want to play around and stuff. I don't want to play around. So this is how I want it to be. It's honest and simple and direct and there's no games.

Her words were similar to those of the woman from Lincoln Square who said she thought the men at the synagogue would be different from the men in the secular world who didn't want to make commitments. The Lubavitch system actively helped the women find marriage partners, which was an important goal of the women who came to these communities.

THE ATTRACTION OF THE
RELIGIOUS FAMILIES

THE WOMEN AT
LINCOLN SQUARE SYNAGOGUE

As they were seeking models and guidance for forming families of their own, the women were attracted by the positive value attached to family in the community and by the happy families they saw as role models. The newcomers were exposed to some of the most prominent and "special" families in the community because they were generally the ones that opened their homes for hospitality. The contrast between these bustling households, as they prepared for Sabbath and holiday meals, and the women's own quiet and solitary lives made the Orthodox way of life very attractive. They talked about the families they saw in glowing terms, as Ellen's remarks illustrate:

> It's nice being with the families. I've met some really wonderful people and the relationships are so nice, between the husband and the wife and the kids. It's really very different from what I see in the secular world. They're closer and there's more substance to the relationships. It just seems like closer families. Kids seem to look after each other. And it's a very warm, nice feeling, a lot more togetherness.

Deborah's description echoed the same feeling:

> I love what I've seen in these observant homes, the respect that the adults have for children as people, that I don't necessarily see in non-Jewish or secular homes. The goal of the husband and wife on very spiritual levels is very important to me—that there's a sense of life, of direction, of why we are here, and of where we're going that I never had.

Interestingly, one of the aspects of family life in this Orthodox community that was highlighted by several women was that the men seemed to be involved in child care, both within the synagogue and outside of it. Because the religion places such a high value on nuclear family life, the men are encouraged to dedicate themselves to caring for their children. The religion offers men a source of identity beyond work and offers women the possibility of finding mates who will actually be supportive and responsible within the home. Within some other contemporary religious communities, too, members, particularly women, feel that men's involvement in the family is a significant benefit of the religious life.[8]

Within the synagogue itself, the men's involvement with child care can be understood at least partly as an unexpected consequence of the religious division of roles. The presence of the *mehitzah* means that most of the "action" in the synagogue—the cantor's singing, the rabbi's sermon, and the procession with the

Torah scrolls—takes place on the men's side, making it a more interesting place for children to be. In addition, women are not obligated to pray communally, so mothers may occasionally opt to stay home on Saturday morning and send their children to shul with their fathers. Several of the women spoke elatedly of this aspect of Orthodox Jewish life. Janet declared:

> One of the most remarkable things about the synagogue is not only is it full of babies and little children, but that the men are looking after them. I can't tell you how many of my friends who come in there for one time have been absolutely knocked out by that to the point where they decide that maybe the *mehitzah* and the separation aren't such a horror. They're seeing something so beautiful and so lovely that they think there must be something to this.

Stephanie admiringly expressed the same idea:

> Because of this structure, I see men more involved with their children and interacting more with their children than other men. The natural structure of the man takes the kids to shul and they all run in, you know, in between the rabbi's legs while he's talking and it seems that when there's a home and a family and they sit down for Shabbos meals, there's a lot more family togetherness and atmosphere than if they're just sitting down with TV dinners on Friday night.

Part of the women's descriptions of these families were accurate, but part might also have been idealizations born of some sense of deprivation. After all, the women saw these families at most once a week and only at the most special times. Few families could live up to the images painted by these women. Some women saw the happy, warm Orthodox families as a welcome contrast to the families they had had. Madeleine articulated this longing thus:

> Judaism provides a connection with way back. It's a sense of family. I like the concentration on the home. I really do. I think it's very important. I guess because the things that you never had become very important. Not that I didn't have a home—I had a home, but not in the traditional sense. It wasn't a typical home life. My family was so scattered and split up. And my father once had a boat, a big boat. And I always felt very good when we would take the boat out for a long trip because we'd all have to be in one place together. Everybody would be there all the time, for two or three days or whatever. And I felt very wonderful about that. And I think Judaism has been a place that concretizes that feeling, that says, yes, the

family is important. You should have a family and you should make it so that on Friday nights everybody comes home and spends Shabbos together. I think that that's a very important aspect of Judaism— that sense of family that I never really got as a child.

Sarah, too, contrasted the Orthodox families in the community with her own experience:

The families are so much nicer, more together than what I had or what I see or I just read of the typical Upper West Side upper-middle-class family. Everybody kind of goes their own way. I like the idea of Shabbos where people are together and you have to spend time with your family. It's real nice, and I didn't have much of that at home. It's very appealing as something I would like.

For many of the women, the close traditional families in the community provided a model for the kind of family they longed for. Several of the women said they believed this was an important part of why women became *ba'alot teshuvah*. Elizabeth offered the following analysis:

I firmly believe this, and I'll stand by this, that most people who get involved have some sort of sentiment of a lack of closeness and belonging and that's what draws them into the group. They go to a couple of meals at families' houses and that's what draws them in. The warmth, family closeness, the singing—that is what hooks them in; that is it.

Madeleine provided this interpretation:

They have come here because they're looking, they're looking for the right way, and they've come here for some answers. They've come here because their life is just not there; whatever they have been doing has just not made it. You know, there's a vacuum and they've come there to fill it. And I think that Jewish households and the dream of the family around the candles Friday night and the Shabbos dinner and the singing and the holidays . . . all that warmth just draws them in.

This point of view was echoed by one of the "experts" I interviewed, a therapist who in her role as rabbi's wife had a lot of opportunity to interact with *ba'alei* and *ba'alot teshuvah* at her Shabbat table:

[Joining an Orthodox community] gives them a family that they felt they never had, or it gives them a chance to have a family. I had a student like that this week, who became a *ba'alat teshuvah* in ninth or tenth grade. Her parents had felt that the yeshiva would give her a little bit better education, and her parents had been divorced just before she started yeshiva. And she told me that this [becoming Orthodox] was a way of acquiring a family, the family that she never really had. And an emphasis on family—she had no role model for this. This allowed her a role model to say this is okay, it's real good, and you can have it.

THE WOMEN AT BAIS CHANA

As at the modern Orthodox synagogue, an attractive feature of the Hasidic community was that it provided numerous models of caring nuclear families and affirmed the value of family, thus validating the women's desires. The women expressed enormous admiration for the families they met within the religious community and saw them as prototypes for the families they would like to create. Rivka voiced her longing in this way:

> God willing, I will have a large family. I see the families I've been with around Crown Heights. A family that I mostly stay with when I'm there—she just had her ninth child *k'neina hara* [without an evil eye] last week. Two weeks ago. There's such a beauty to a large family that was missing in my own.

Naomi was also exuberant about the Lubavitch families:

> What else turned me on? The family life. I loved it. I mean, they had bunches of kids and there were like so neat. The kids, I love; I mean, that's really what got me. How they raise their children and they never get into problems. You know, 'cause look at all these things. The problems that I had. I know that if I was brought up in a family like that I would never have those kind of problems. So it's very good. It makes the kids grow up really healthy. And they're close to each other and they have a sense of community or whatever and it's nice. Family life in Lubavitch keeps you out of trouble. . . . The Lubavitch families seem so perfect.

As in the accounts of the women at Lincoln Square Synagogue, these descriptions of family life within the religious community were at least partly idealizations based on deprivation. Many of the women's families contrasted starkly with the Lubavitch families. These women were generally young enough to still define themselves as children relative to their parents; they had not yet worked out their relationships with their parents or established separate lives. Whereas the Lincoln Square women spoke nostalgically about the warm families in that community, here the women sounded as if they wished they could still be kids and have these wonderful families to look after them. This is reminiscent of Beth's words, quoted earlier: "I wish I could reinstitute that childhood." The women fantasized that they would have been spared a great deal of hardship and pain if they had been brought up in a traditionally observant family. Layah described a conversation with a Lubavitch couple with whom she had become close:

> I could see that this [a Lubavitch rabbi] was a person that if faced with problems similar to those of my family would have found different solutions. And that input was very welcome to me. He seemed to think that he might have some answers and I didn't know. I was reduced to tears.

It is striking that the women at Bais Chana spoke a great deal more about troubled family backgrounds than did the women at Lincoln Square Synagogue. Several women at Bais Chana had grown up in homes without their natural parents. Rachel said, "I never had a steady home." Layah told me that one of her parents had been institutionalized since Layah was a child. Beth spoke bitterly about her father's "cruelty" and "heavy hand when it came to punishment." Another woman's mother had committed suicide. Several women told me that their parents had been through a difficult divorce.

Again, it is likely that at least some of the women who joined Lincoln Square Synagogue also had divorced parents or otherwise troubled family backgrounds. Yet that almost none of these women spontaneously spoke about these experiences in accounting for their attraction to Orthodoxy suggests that it was less salient in their understanding of how they came to join the community. Because many of the Bais Chana women still lived with their parents, their difficult familial experiences were important factors in their readiness to join a religious community that assumed such strong control over its members' lives. The community provided the closeness, guidance, firm boundaries, and foundations for identity the women believed they had not received from their own families.

COMMUNITY AS SURROGATE FAMILY

THE WOMEN AT
LINCOLN SQUARE SYNAGOGUE

As the women attended the synagogue and began to claim their heritage, they were affirming not only their connections with Jews of the past and future but were also afforded the opportunity to become part of an ongoing, vibrant, and tightly knit community. Almost every woman mentioned the lure of the strong community that the synagogue represented and offered. Living relatively isolated existences in Manhattan away from their families of origin and not yet having formed families of their own, they felt the need to associate with a community. As a friend of Ellen's said, "I think I just felt a growing need to be attached to a community and it's beyond like a neighborhood or a town." Ellen, herself, echoed this feeling:

> What I like most about it is the sense of community, as being a single woman in New York, that the support systems, the network of friends, and with everyone having a common binder, is extremely important to me today.

Being noticed and feeling valued are major benefits of community. A thirty-two-year-old graduate student described how important these feelings were to her:

> I guess I just do have a community up here now, and people are always happy to see me when I come and invite me over. I just like the feeling of being included and having this be a day when they are going to think of me and they are going to include me.

Ernest Becker writes in *Escape from Evil* that in human societies, not only are material goods scarce but so, too, are recognition and validation. The desire to feel special is "just as deep a problem in securing life" as is the search for food. "Importance equals durability equals life."[9] Joining the religious community puts people in a context laden with opportunities for recognition in face-to-face situations. Membership is also a means to a sense of metaphysical or cosmic validation: the synagogue rituals affirm the participants' significance as human beings through the creation and celebration of a community with a special destiny, a "chosen people."

Many of the women said that they had found in the religious community a substitute or extended family. As Janet remarked, "Well, there is a very nice communal extended family feeling expressed in the structure of Orthodox Judaism." Another woman announced, "They have become my surrogate family. I have a close family, but they're in California, and I have to create my own surrogate family here." Deborah, too, articulated the same feeling:

> One of the reasons for my involvement in a place like Lincoln Square Synagogue is a substitute for a family. I have used something like Lincoln Square Synagogue, which is all-encompassing and very supportive and warm and all, as a substitute family, and I got involved with religious Judaism for that reason.

The language the women used when they described the feeling of community was replete with metaphors associated with family, particularly with mothering—such terms as *warm, nurturing, loving,* and *closeness* were frequently used. The rabbis and directors of this synagogue and other programs for *ba'alei* and *ba'alot teshuvah* were aware that associations with warmth and family themes were attractive. Rabbi Buchwald emphasized to me that newcomers felt "embraced" by the warmth of the community when they were invited to someone's house for a Shabbos meal. One woman told me about an advertisement she had seen in the *Jerusalem Post* for a program in Israel called the Center for Jewish Living and Values: "The ad said, 'Do you know little about your Jewish past? Do you want to be more connected? Come live with us as a family.' I thought this is just for me." This particular woman had responded to the ad within a year after her father's death. I suspect that the choice of words in the ad—presenting the program as an opportunity to live "as a family"—was not coincidental. Many of these programs used fairly sophisticated marketing techniques—they knew what sorts of images were likely to attract their potential audience.[10]

That the synagogue did operate as a responsive community was attested to by the numerous stories I heard of how in time of need, such as the death of a parent, the birth or death of a child, or an illness, people in the community all rallied around the person in need and provided practical as well as moral support. One woman described the events surrounding her marriage to another *ba'al teshuvah*, who was a popular member of the community:

> What neither of us got from our families we got from this community. Richard and Noreen made us a wedding party. My friend spent a week with me in our apartment because I wasn't supposed to see Bob for a week before the wedding. I don't really know why; it's supposed to be bad luck, I think. It's just a *bubbe meisa* [old wives' tale] [laughter]. And my friend Barbara spent most of those days with me and slept here because the bride isn't supposed to be alone lest something happen to her. It was very wonderful. It was really very wonderful. Everybody was very supportive.

Many of the women exclaimed about how remarkable it was to find such a community in New York City. As Janet declared, "It's like creating a small village in the middle of New York. You know, it's what small-town living would be like. But it's New York City!" Stephanie described how the beginners' rabbi had called her on the phone one Tuesday evening after noticing in services on Saturday that her eyes were brimming with tears:

> He said, "You're in trouble, come in here, I want to talk to you." That this could happen in New York City is just incredible. This man had seen me maybe half a dozen times in his life. You know, he's not my church pastor, he doesn't know my family, he hasn't known me for years. This is New York City and this man called me on the phone to talk to me when he noticed I was down! He's got me, just for that!

The care and attention from the rabbi meant a great deal to this woman and made her feel noticed and special. This sort of support is a rare and precious commodity in modern urban life. In a large and alienating city the synagogue offers its members the opportunity to participate in the ongoing construction of a community in which individuals are cared for.

THE WOMEN AT BAIS CHANA

At Lincoln Square Synagogue the community functioned as an extended family for many of the women. Within the Lubavitch community, however, the women were actually given substitute families. Until the Lubavitch *ba'alot teshuvah* marry and form their own families, the community provides for each recruit a *mashpiah*, a "sponsor," who in some ways acts as a substitute parent. For these women, who were still deeply troubled by their difficult familial relationships, the Lubavitch system gave them an opportunity to have another chance, with a different, hopefully more understanding, set of parents. Layah said, "The Lefkowitzes became the family I never had." The *mashpiah* plays a very important role in the resocialization and incorporation of the novices into the community. One young woman told of how the rabbi's wife took her to the supermarket to teach her to shop for kosher food. In doing so, the *rebbetzin* was resocializing the novice in a fundamental aspect of her being: how and what she ate. Rivka described how the couple who acted as her *mashpiim* would help her find a *shidduch*:

> I trust the Druckers very much. They know me very well. . . . For me, when I'm ready to start going out, I'm going to talk with the Druckers to arrange something. They know who I am in some ways, sometimes better than my parents do. You know, a lot of times with *frum* people, people who have grown up *frum*, their parents are really the ones that sort of arrange this. 'Cause who knows you better than your parents? So in a sense in that way in this position the Druckers would be like my parents.

Here Rivka made a profound distinction between biological and spiritual parenthood. In having a new set of spiritual parents, whom, she claimed, knew her better than did her biological ones, she fulfilled the childhood and adolescent fantasy of substituting her real-life parents, with whom she got into conflicts, with an idealized set that would help her set up her life in the proper direction. Layah, similarly, was touched by the extent of her *mashpiim*'s concern:

> The Lefkowitzes called me every day. . . . They were tremendously fond of me. I was very lucky. They saw what a tremendous impact they had on me and they were terribly concerned about me. They felt terribly responsible; in a sense having opened me up, they didn't want me to be hurt. They saw I'd gone through something very deep and I'm telling you they called me every day. "How are you? What's doing?" After I really expressed interest, it wasn't that they were pushing me or anything. When they did see how I responded and there was a big response from me, they responded in turn. They didn't leave me cold, and that was a big help.

The Lubavitch *ba'alot teshuvah* were greatly assisted in their resocialization to Orthodoxy by establishing these "familial" relationships.

Additionally, like the women at Lincoln Square, the women at
Bais Chana were enthusiastic about the strength of the community.
Naomi, in describing how much she enjoyed the Lubavitch fami-
lies, also expressed admiration for the community structure:

> They're close to each other and they have a sense of community and
> it's nice. They all grow up together. They go to the same school. It
> is nice. I like little town–type settings.

The women at Bais Chana, however, placed less explicit emphasis on the benefits of "community" than did the women at Lincoln
Square Synagogue. Perhaps the availability of an immediate family
that "adopted" the Lubavitch women meant that the community
was somewhat less needed as a substitute family. Additionally,
many of the women at Bais Chana had not yet been to the main
Lubavitch community in Crown Heights, so they probably had
much less sense of the community as it functioned there.

ORDERING A WOMAN'S LIFE: DEFINING
A GENDER IDENTITY

THE WOMEN AT
LINCOLN SQUARE SYNAGOGUE

The women attracted to this religious community were not only
seeking assistance in forming families; they were also in search of
a clear and comfortable sense of themselves as women. Many
stated explicitly that the community's clear delineation of separate
roles for men and women was a welcome contrast to the blurring
and confusion about these roles in secular society. Ellen strongly
expressed this sentiment:

> As far as values, as far as certain values go, I mean, in a lot of
> ways I feel that there are a lot of values in the Orthodox community
> that I really believe in. . . . I find that in a lot of ways I agree much
> more with some of the views within Orthodoxy which are very
> traditional and that have to do with male-female roles and certain
> things that are important. . . . In modern urban society the idea of
> the family, or the idea of children, and certain basic ideas about why
> there are men and women, is considered really old hat and ridicu-

lous, and in a lot of ways I really think the traditional values are much more important.

Another woman also highlighted the religion's gender distinctions as an attractive feature of Orthodoxy:

> I am glad to see sexual differentiation in the area of ritual. People come in two flavors, and it's nice to see this emphasized sometimes. People need a gender identity; every society has one. But the contemporary view is men and women are exactly the same, with various gonads and apparatus sort of stuck on as an afterthought. And I have come to share the religious view that sexual identity is something that begins at the center and goes out. That we're men and women in every cell of our body.

Given that nearly all of these women had for years been active participants in the world of work, successfully competing with men for professional positions, I wondered how they felt about the sexual division of roles in the synagogue. The religion defined the public domain as the sphere of the men and assigned women primary responsibility for the private domain. Thus, women were excluded from full participation in public ritual life. Yet nearly all of the women I interviewed stated that they did not mind the traditional gender differentiation that undergirded these definitions of male and female roles. Nevertheless, these women's acceptance of traditional roles was not found in other areas of their lives: although they did not object to their lack of access to full participation in the synagogue, they would strongly object to the same lack in the workplace. According to Stephanie:

> Now if you said to me, "Stephanie, you can't work on this project because you're a woman," I wouldn't like that. Work seems to be an area where it doesn't seem fair to me, and I do feel I want to be an equal, but outside of work I don't feel that way.[11]

Stephanie, like most of the women I met at Lincoln Square Synagogue, never intended to be a "career woman." Rather, she and many of the others had graduated from college before 1972, the year in which the Senate passed the Equal Rights Amendment. Nearly all of these women were not feminists, or visionaries, who had intended to pursue brilliant careers.[12] This was an important factor in accounting for their readiness to join an Orthodox synagogue. As Ellen said, "I would not call myself a feminist. I would say that I'm more traditionally oriented." Deborah told me that she was not a feminist because "women don't need to be such glaring feminists in 1984 to achieve what they want to achieve in the secular world."

These women had hoped to achieve fulfillment in the conventional mode—through marriage and childbearing—and planned to work for a few years until that happened. But because they had not yet been successful in meeting their mates, they continued working, often doing well and receiving promotions. Yet they still sought their main fulfillment in the private sphere. The possibility of finally achieving that goal in the synagogue community was therefore much more important for them than was the struggle for equal roles in that sphere. Because work was not central for them, they felt they did not risk much by insisting on fair treatment. In contrast, the synagogue seemed to offer true fulfillment. Therefore, they did not want to jeopardize their chances by objecting to the system and struggling with it.

Although they claimed not to be feminists, half of these women did express concern with issues of equality in the workplace such as equal opportunity and equal pay. The woman who worked in the fashion industry expressed this feeling:

> I've never truly identified with the women's movement. I have to say that I agree with equal pay and equal time, but beyond that I have always been very comfortable in my role as a woman, in men's role as men.

Elizabeth told me that in fact because of her professionalism she did not identify with feminism:

> After making such a big statement by going to medical school and doing all this thing, I really had never been that interested in feminist politics or rhetoric or organizations outside the demands of my own career. This is very true that a lot of women doctors don't get involved in women's organizations. They just say, "Enough already, I've done my thing and I don't want to be bothered."

Part of the reason for not wanting to be vocal as a feminist after having asserted herself to establish her career was her fear that by doing so she might alienate men.

> There are a certain number of hazards in being a smart, successful woman. Many men are not tolerant of professional women. They don't seem to want what I have to offer.

Her feeling, which was articulated by several other women in the group, seemed to be that it was hard enough to find a mate having become a very modern woman in one sense; there was no need to risk alienating men further by wearing feminist politics as a badge.

Some of the women's responses to my questions about feminism, such as the use of the phrase *glaring feminists* in one remark, reflected images of feminism shaped by media stereotypes: for example, feminists were angry and aggressive. These were images from which the women wanted to disassociate themselves. Madeleine spoke of a women's minyan she attended once: "It was really awful. It was very, very angry women—we're going to do it, and we're going to, you know, they had some chip on their shoulder." A couple of the women said they had been feminists but were no longer. As Madeleine put it, she had definitely been an "angry feminist" but was now "just not so angry anymore."

In the late 1960s and early 1970s a popular media presentation of feminists was as bra burners. This image was cited by several of the women to show that feminism was concerned with trivial issues and empty symbols. One woman said, "I don't feel the kind of hunger for feminist things, the bra burning, and what have you, because, as I said, my grandmothers were strong." Another woman expressed the same disdain for feminism and feminist women:

> I didn't like the women who were involved in feminist politics in those days. I mean it was really the day when, there were so many issues to struggle about personally about growing up, that somehow, the issue of whether or not to become the stereotype of a female role was kind of out anyway in the 1960s—you know, setting your hair and shaving your legs, that was out anyway. Those issues were silly anyway, the kind of ban your bra, burn your bra whatever, was silly.

And feminists were perceived as antifamily, as Deborah expressed:

> I'm not a feminist in that I want very traditional things. My mother calls me a throwback to her grandmother. I think of family as very important, and I guess, even in this day and age, a really militant feminist would say that a family is not so important, and I think maybe it's the *most* important thing still.

The women who came to Lincoln Square Synagogue had professions. Yet clearly all professional women are not feminists, nor do they all derive a sense of identity through their work. These women were adults in a society in which the scripts for how to live as a woman were less clear than those their mothers had followed. They did not identify with the glamorized image of independent career women. Joining the religious community gave them a context that legitimated their desires for a role within a nuclear family and tried to assist them in meeting their needs.

THE WOMEN AT BAIS CHANA

A major element in a person's identity is a clear definition of her or his gender role.[13] Like the *ba'alot teshuvah* at Lincoln Square Synagogue, the women who came to Bais Chana had been unable to find within the wider society a satisfactory articulation of their role as women. Their accounts highlighted the blurring and confusion about gender in contemporary culture and emphasized that Orthodox Judaism was attractive precisely because it delineated distinct roles for women and men. One woman described her acceptance of the Lubavitch view that women and men are fundamentally distinct: "Now I see women as being very different to men mentally and spiritually, whereas before I thought there was nothing different at all." Naomi expressed the same point of view on her questionnaire:

> In feminism and in the world today womanhood is a concept that is not clear, and when explained or defined it is defined in the wrong way. Only in Judaism can a woman be a woman with all the dignity and respect she deserves.

Lisa wrote the same ideas:

> Society cries, "Women's lib! Be a modern woman! Don't get tied down and caught up in a rut of old-fashioned norms. Be fulfilled! Use birth control!" Being "just" a wife and mother, we are taught, isn't satisfying, even degrading. We must go to college, find careers, and find our own identity. I think that with all of this identity finding we have lost the true identity we had all along. . . . We *are*, first and foremost, women . . . we are meant to cleave to a man and be one together with him; we *are* meant to raise a family and, yes, even find fulfillment in it! This was God's plan from the beginning, and nothing has changed as far as He's concerned. We, as "returning" Jewish women, must acknowledge this and say "no!" to society's cries.

As these quotations illustrate, these women were aware that the gender distinctions in Orthodox Judaism contrasted sharply with contemporary feminist ideas advocating egalitarianism. Whereas most of the *ba'alot teshuvah* at Lincoln Square Synagogue denied being feminists, nearly all of the women at Bais Chana were emphatically derisive about the women's movement. Rivka asserted that although feminists said, "They want you to be freer, not as attached, I think they're slaves to what society is saying about the whole thing and they're not really themselves." Her remarks represented a fascinating play on the meaning of freedom: feminists claimed that their goal was for women to be free to do what they wanted; in fact, Rivka claimed, they were simply puppets repeating the words society put into their mouths.

Although the Bais Chana women voiced agreement with certain feminist ideas such as equal pay for equal work, they believed that feminists had lost touch with what it meant to be a woman. This led to feminists' devaluing traditional women's work and trying to be like men. Here, many of their remarks about feminism betrayed the same media stereotypes of the women's liberation movement I heard from a few of the women at Lincoln Square Synagogue. Lisa portrayed the feminist women at her college thus:

> That's why I was never in any of the women's groups because they still have this "burn the bra" kind of attitude. They were just so vehement about, you know, "We're being put down." And you know, they're still acting like the 1960s—they're going to have a sit-in; they're going to do all kinds of radical things. You know, I've seen women's groups that were very sane in their goals, they know what they're going for, they want equal pay and this kind of thing. It's not a thing where they feel they have to all of a sudden be the man and the man be the woman, which is what their attitude, well, at least at my university a lot of the groups were like that. It had to be every woman's all fired up to just go and rip everyone else apart.

Rivka also derided feminists for their ignorance:

> It seems that whenever I've had an encounter with women's lib it was always that the women were saying, "I don't feel like a woman." What do you feel like? You are a woman. You know, "We have to strive to be women." They *were* women. What they were striving to be was mostly what I saw as men. Have things that men have. And I just don't see that. I don't understand the *sechel* [brains] in it. There's so much as a woman to do. . . . I think that certain

views are imposed on people. Like, you know, people say, women say they want to be freer, not attached, yet I think they're slaves to what society is saying about the whole thing and they're not really themselves. They should be wanting to be themselves.

Rivka had been to Bais Chana the previous summer and had been involved with the Lubavitch for a couple of years. Her words reflected her integration of central ideas in the worldview of the community: she used the same language as did the rabbi in asserting that in order to be "themselves," women should reject feminism and take on the primary roles of wife and mother.

These women were examining some of the secular society's current assumptions about femininity and masculinity. They found within traditional Judaism new ammunition for rejecting contemporary norms. Whereas the ideas of the dominant culture emphasized that women should be free to choose whatever roles they wished, the Lubavitch *ba'alot teshuvah* echoed the rabbis of this community, who insisted that in fact contemporary women were not free to choose because the traditional role was devalued. These women articulated a profound critique of the ostensible feminist position that women could be truly fulfilled only in the public arena of work: Tamar, who had been married for nine years, expressed these ideas pointedly:

> Women are intrinsically there for family, to serve. But I think the world at large has been misinformed. They think the woman raising the family is being subservient. Something to be ashamed of. On the contrary, I think it's one of the most responsible, most beautiful, most creative roles there is. It's only in these last decades, since 1959, 1960, that we've made being a housewife into drudgery. Something to be ashamed of. They think a woman who's working for IBM is happy? No, it's—there's always somebody that can do that, be an executive. There's always somebody that can take over my job being a nurse. But there is only one person that can raise a child like you.

It is striking how she described her job as a function anyone could do. She felt that if she were lifted out of her work, nothing would change—not her or the workplace setting. For her, real fulfillment derived from engaging in an irreplaceable action, such as being a mother. Tamar's remarks were particularly interesting in light of the comments from the women at Lincoln Square Synagogue that they did not derive the meaning of their lives from their work.

Those were the women who worked for "IBM," and yet as Tamar astutely pointed out, they clearly were not happy with the lives they were leading as single professional women.

The women at Bais Chana were critical of what they understood to be feminism. Nevertheless, they had been brought up in a society in which at least some feminist ideas were rather widely known. In addition, they all had met at least a few potential recruits who voiced concerns about women's roles in the community. Thus, even while these women were attracted to the traditional gender distinctions delineated by Orthodox Judaism, they felt a need to respond to possible feminist critiques by asserting that women's roles in Judaism were more open than was commonly believed. According to Beth:

> If people were to actually know Judaism's approach to women (for example, "Woman of valor," a psalm of homage read by a husband to his wife at the Friday night Shabbat dinner) I don't think there would be as much conflict as there is. I think the conflicts come from ignorance. . . . I believe I think more of womanhood now.

A nineteen-year-old former college student declared:

> Women's roles aren't as restrictive as a lot of people seem to think they are. There's quite a few Lubavitch women, Hasidic women, who have careers and who are working. And their husbands are working, too. It's either for economic reasons, or some of them, well, the woman wants to work and the man wants to study and they work things out. It's not—a lot of people seem to think it's well, barefoot and pregnant; that's the way it's supposed to be. Well, if that's the way it's supposed to be, I certainly wouldn't have converted. And I can see, I think in the long run there's a lot more respect for women in Judaism than there is in anything else.

These women argued that Judaism offered a better alternative to contemporary norms because its conventional conception of gender actually showed more respect to women than did modern society, which, for all its freedoms, still treated women as sex objects and disregarded the importance of women's childrearing roles. The Lubavitch recruits redefined liberation as coming not from an independent professional career but rather from the respect a woman received in her family and community. Truer gratification, they felt, would come from doing something unique, such as rearing children, rather than from being a cog in the machinery of the business world. It was striking that their concern with the lack of respect for women in our culture coincided with the centrality of this idea in feminist analyses. The *ba'alot teshuvah*, however, proposed a solution that echoed the pronouncements of the rabbis in both communities, who asserted Judaism's superiority on the basis of its respect for women's dignity. One young woman at Bais Chana sounded exactly like the rabbis when she said:

> There is a connection between feminism and the *ba'al teshuvah* movement because those who don't find an answer to the problem of male-female relationships in the twentieth century are looking to Judaism for an alternative answer. Judaism looks on women not as sex objects but as something much higher, and so women are not treated as the playthings of men. They are taken more seriously. Therefore, some of the problems of feminism disappear and do not need solutions.

In this view, feminism denied women the protection offered through participation within the Lubavitch community. Essentially, the Lubavitch women argued that secular women who were single had little choice but to say "yes" to a premarital sexual relationship if they wanted to continue dating a man, whereas the Lubavitch women were free to say "no." If women followed the Lubavitch prescriptions, their relationships with men—a central problematic for feminism—would be "fixed," thereby obviating the need for a feminist analysis.

The women in both communities expressed the desire for a comfortable conception of femininity that would place them in the center of a nuclear family. The Bais Chana women were quite a bit younger than the women at Lincoln Square, yet they, too, were eager to marry and begin their own families. The central theme here, then, was shared by the two groups. But there were also critical differences: the women at Bais Chana were more willing to give up control over their lives than were the women at Lincoln Square Synagogue. They sought substitute parents and the chance to work out parental relations with a new set of parents as part of the process of eventually forming nuclear families of their own. The Lincoln Square women had already established their independence and were ready to marry and have children. The women at Bais Chana were younger and less established in the world. Therefore, they had less to give up and more to gain in accepting the tighter social controls of the Lubavitch community. Also, they were in much greater need of structure. The women at Lincoln Square, in contrast, would probably not have been attracted to the Lubavitch community even when they were younger: they did not describe having experienced the same degree of disorder in their lives. Each group of women, then, was likely to be receptive to a different set of teachings: the women who came to Lincoln Square were more attracted to an approach to Orthodoxy that was open to the world and therefore allowed them to maintain elements of their former lives.

6

Teachings on Jewish
Religious Observance

The women who were attracted to the modern Orthodox and Lubavitch communities were seeking an alternative to the established ways of life offered by contemporary U.S. society. Recent cultural analyses, such as Bellah and his coauthors' study of the "habits of the heart" of the white middle class in the United States, have found "a notion of the self as pure, undetermined choice, free of tradition, obligation, and commitment."[1] Orthodox Judaism was appealing to these women precisely because it offered them a clearly articulated identity constructed in the context of an inherited religious tradition and a community of memory. Yet although these religious institutions are sought—and present themselves— as an antidote to the wider society, they exist within this society and recruit members from a population of Jews who have been socialized into its secular worldview. Thus, both the modern Orthodox and Lubavitch institutions must take a stance on the prevailing attitudes and values of modern society.

Each group's distinct stance toward modernity shapes every aspect of its teachings. A core component of each worldview is a particular conception of selfhood and of the proper relationship between obligation to others and individual self-fulfillment. Traditional worldviews, such as that of the Lubavitch, emphasize duty and surrender of control to external sources of authority; modern conceptions, such as the one at Lincoln Square Synagogue, stress individual choice and self-fulfillment. These differences are reflected in the way each group presents Jewish law, beliefs, and practices to newcomers.

Judaism as a religion is more oriented toward Halacha than toward the elaboration of a systematic theology. The rabbinical texts that have been written over the millennia of Jewish history have sought to expand on the meaning of the commandments: volumes have been dedicated to elaboration of minutiae of law rather than to nuanced analyses of the nature of God. Therefore, unlike in Christianity, in which certain beliefs such as the acceptance of Jesus Christ as the Lord are critical for membership, within Judaism acceptance of beliefs about God are much less important than is behaving in the appropriate manner. Thus, the teachings about observance at Lincoln Square Synagogue and at Bais Chana provide a good clue into the worldview of each of the communities.

The words of the rabbis, and the particular approaches they used to appeal to their different audiences, naturally echo in the women's accounts. The women's words resembled the rabbis' in their emphasis on particular themes and in their views of individual choice, gender roles, and God. This similarity has two bases. First, because the women were resocialized in the context of a particular community with its own characteristic rhetorical patterns, they learned the appropriate form and content for their accounts as they learned the other details of how to live within the community. Second, the women *self-selected* into the two different groups because the distinct worldviews they presented meshed with the women's own predispositions. Thus, the women at Lincoln Square would not have been happy at Bais Chana and vice versa. A priori the women's distinct social locations shaped their quests in different directions. That relative newcomers expressed feelings similar to those of women who had been involved in the communities for a long time suggests that the women did indeed have prior existing needs.

THE BASIS FOR OBSERVANCE

LINCOLN SQUARE SYNAGOGUE

Individual Choice and Self-Fulfillment

At Lincoln Square Synagogue, the rabbis' presentation of the nature and meaning of observance blended traditional conceptions of duty, obligation, and obedience with contemporary conceptions of individual self-fulfillment. The relative openness of the institution, and the fact that members continued to live within the wider society, militated against an absolutist stance toward religious observance. The rabbis knew that the newcomers were self-consciously "trying on" Judaism[2] and could easily be making other choices, such as any of the other religious and self-help groups proliferating in modern urban centers. The rabbis confronted contemporary cultural pluralism directly by acknowledging and legitimating the novices' right to choose.

Nevertheless, the rabbis believed that Orthodoxy represented the only viable form of Jewish religious observance. Thus, in presenting the religious teachings to urbane people raised in a pluralistic society, the rabbis marketed the religious worldview by attempting to convince recruits that it represented the *best* choice for them. The rabbis presented the religion in ways that would be attractive to the secular consciousness of the Jews in the community. Unlike the Lubavitch, who shored up their religious teachings by asserting that the newcomers really didn't have a choice about becoming observant, the rabbis at Lincoln Square Synagogue promoted this way of life by enumerating its benefits. They called it the most ethical, the sanest, and the most psychologically sound way to live.

At a "koshering party," an event one evening in which Rabbi Buchwald met with a group of beginners in one of their apartments and explained in detail the laws and practices of kashrut through a guided kitchen tour, the rabbi began his discussion of kashrut with the following rationale:

> There are many different reasons to keep kosher, not the least of which is that you can then invite other Jewish people to eat in your house. . . . An additional reason is that the bottom line of Judaism is the sanctity of life. Keeping kosher is a way of beginning to limit the life you eat.

The emphasis was on rational, ethical, and social reasons for observances. At this occasion the rabbi did not offer a single theological rationale for kashrut. In a subsequent interview, speaking about his recruitment methods, this rabbi said, "You have to give them a positive message. You have to show them that they're going to get personal fulfillment out of it." In response to the question "Do you care about what people believe or only that they take on observances?" he said:

> That's a very hard question. Obviously I do care, I do care what they believe, but at this point I care more what they feel than what they believe. Do they *feel* that they're getting something positive out of the Shabbos observance, kashrut, and learning? If they feel good, that's much more important to me than the abstract philosophical concept of belief in God. And I think that the feeling does lead to belief in God. If they feel good about it, then they feel that they're being divinely ordained in following mitzvahs.

Here, in the concern that people felt there was something to "get" out of observance, we see the ways in which utilitarian and expressive individualism—which Bellah et al. see as the dominant motifs in contemporary culture—shaped the religious teachings in this community. The emphasis was on self-enhancement through observances; the more traditional conception of duty and obligation as the basis for observance was less emphasized. This approach meshed with the portrait of contemporary individualism painted by Bellah and his coauthors:

> Contemporary culture presents a normative order of life at whose center is the autonomous individual, presumed able to choose the roles he will play and the commitments he will make, not on the basis of higher truths, but according to the criterion of life effectiveness as he judges it.[3]

The rabbis implicitly shared this perspective when they emphasized how the newcomers as individuals could benefit from this way of life. Rather than insisting that traditional laws had to be obeyed because it was the duty of all Jews to do so, the rabbis stressed that Jewish religious observances should be adopted because they would enhance the individuals' lives in every possible way.

Emphasis on Contemporary Relevance

Just as the women in this community emphasized the relevance of the ancient religion to their contemporary needs, the rabbis at Lincoln Square Synagogue promoted traditional observance by stressing how meaningful the ancient way of life of the Torah was for contemporary individuals. They claimed that even though it was developed thousands of years ago, traditional Judaism offered the antidotes so urgently needed in contemporary society. One clear instance of this reassertion of the value of traditional teachings for contemporary society could be seen in the presentation of Shabbat. The laws, practices, and rationales for Shabbat were a major focus of the religious teachings within this community—an understandable emphasis given that Shabbat was the primary religious observance that brought the entire community together every week. In teaching about the Sabbath, the rabbis frequently called it one of the major "practical antidotes" Judaism offered the contemporary individual. They highlighted the various ways in which observance of Shabbat could serve as a corrective to the stresses of modern life.

One form of correction was Shabbat's capacity to limit the encroachment of work into other areas of life. The rabbis asserted that traditional observance of the Sabbath would offer the perfect remedy to long workdays, weekends lost to overtime, and diminished contact with family. As the associate rabbi of the synagogue told his class in basic Judaism one night:

> Shabbos comes to tell us that the world can get along fine without us for a day. God is who makes the world run. . . . For the man who believes himself to be at the center of the universe, Shabbos comes to contradict that. Man thinks he's the center of the universe, but God screams back, "You're not the creator. I am."

In this view, Shabbos could also correct the strained family relations characteristic of contemporary society. As Rabbi Buchwald emphasized:

> I have become convinced that the root of evil of our modern society is the breakdown of the family. Sabbath underscores the importance of family life. . . . The Sabbath is a day to restore our soul's contact with the environment and with others. The Sabbath is the most effective psychological therapy for human beings. The Divine knew that we'd be living in this frenetic world where everyone was going to a therapist or should be. He knew that there would have to be two or three meals at which the family has to sit at the table even if you can't communicate. It forces you to communicate, even if only on the most elementary level. That's why TV is forbidden; it's an artificial means of communication. That's why tennis is forbidden. They want you to enjoy you—all six feet of you, five foot

three inches of you, or one hundred pounds of you. If there's a utilitarian purpose to the next person—like in tennis—we want them for that purpose. Shabbos says it's you I want to communicate with, talk with, on an emotional level.

These remarks highlight the blending of traditional and contemporary understandings that was manifest in the religious teachings in this community. Even as the rabbis proposed traditional religious solutions to contemporary dilemmas, their means of talking about the tradition partook of contemporary assumptions. The rabbi presented the Sabbath as the antidote to the ills of modern society and invoked the wisdom of God to account for the profound beauty of the day. Yet he did this in terms that reflected the individualistic assumptions of contemporary society: he invoked the idea that individuals have an essential self that is independent of their roles and utilitarian purposes. And in emphasizing how Shabbat was "effective psychological therapy" because it encouraged open communication between people, he incorporated elements of what Bellah et al. refer to as the dominant "therapeutic attitude," which emphasizes the "monitoring and managing of inner feelings, and . . . their expression in open communication."[4] This stress on communication between family members was a contemporary, rather than a biblical, perspective. Such a creative reinterpretation of the ancient practices was one way of making the religion attractive to middle-class individuals living in this therapeutic culture.

Presentation of the Concept of God

In the rabbis' teachings about God, we can again see this blending of traditional and contemporary worldviews. In classes and in services the rabbis talked about God and legitimated many essential rituals using traditional theological language. According to the rabbis, obedience to the law was demanded by God, was laid out in the covenant, and was the basis for the survival of the Jewish people. God was described as "the source of life," "the final authority," and "the ultimate energy and power, the source of power." In these teachings, God acted on behalf of the Jews and had chosen the Jews to survive. Thus, as Jews the recruits had to acknowledge Him and strive to connect with Him. The associate rabbi instructed his basic Judaism class thus:

> What I'd like you to get from this evening's discussion on Shabbos is the idea that God is the creator and man is not. God stands at the center of the universe and man depends on God. So when you observe Shabbos you are subjugating yourself to the will of God.

The idea of subjugating the self to God clearly challenged contemporary conceptions of self, agency, and control—that is, the U.S. ideal of individuals freely carving out their own identities and lives. The rabbi suggested that there was another, more important reality than the individual self and in so doing used these teachings as an important part of the resocialization process.

Yet although the rabbis presented to newcomers traditional conceptions of God, in general the socialization process at Lincoln Square Synagogue de-emphasized the importance of faith in the "conversion" to Orthodoxy. The rabbis were aware that they were addressing individuals who might have difficulty with the "leap of faith" and subordination of self implicit in affirming a belief in God. Thus, the teachings also presented the religion in rational and practical terms. To emphasize the "rationality" of the religion, the rabbi asserted that this way of life was compelling even without a belief in God. As Rabbi Buchwald told his Bible class one Tuesday night:

> It's really a very meaningful religion irrespective of whether you believe in God or not. The mitzvahs make sense even if you could prove black and white there is no God. This is just a meaningful way of life.

Similarly, he told me in an interview, "We don't push God at Lincoln Square Synagogue. We try to make the point that it is a meaningful and rational way to live even without God." These statements represented a "disenchanted," secularized approach to traditional religion, in which "'other-worldly' motivations" were replaced by "'this-worldly' contingencies and criteria."[5] Implicit in this approach was an acquiescence to modern rationality's refusal to recognize a transcendent, empirically nonverifiable realm. Rather than emphasizing (as did the Lubavitch) that the word of God was a sufficiently compelling reason for adopting Orthodoxy, the rabbis justified obedience in "this-worldly" terms: it would provide the framework in which individuals could construct meaningful lives.

The rabbis' teachings clearly coincided with the women's agnosticism. This was not surprising given that the rabbis pitched their appeal to the type of person they wanted to attract. This subject came up in my interview with Rabbi Buchwald:

RB: At Riskin's [the founding rabbi's] shul we believe that different approaches work for different people, and anyone who comes here who is a spiritual type, we send them to Lubavitch.
LD: What do you mean "a spiritual type"?
RB: If they seem dreamy and kind of spaced out and if they've been into these other spiritual groups before. Riskin's shul is for intelligent, well-functioning people who can support themselves and stand on their own two feet. . . . We are mainstream-type Jews, living in the contemporary world.

The rabbis in this community also appealed to their audience by emphasizing that Judaism was an ethical way of life. Whereas discussions about God concerned the intangible and could be hard for secular people to grasp, ethics concerned everyday life, and the people coming into this setting agreed with the rabbis that contemporary society was in urgent need of ethical reform. By focusing on the exemplary nature of Judaism as an ethical religion, the rabbis were able to present traditional Judaism to a secular audience in terms they could readily grasp.

In classes and at Beginners' Service, the beginners' rabbi repeatedly emphasized the ethical nature of the religion by saying, "The bottom line of Judaism is the sanctity of human life." In Bible class one night he elaborated on this idea:

Every ritual of the Torah can be traced back to what I believe is the fundamental underpinning of all of the Torah—the sanctity of human life. When you wash your hands ritually before eating of bread, you're making a statement that the bread came to you and therefore it is appreciated. The Jewish way of putting on shoes: you put on the right shoe first, then the left shoe, then tie the left shoe, then the right. This way you're not favoring one foot over the other. This is teaching you sensitivity toward human beings. This is the bottom line of Judaism. The sanctity of human life. Every mitzvah has that as its fundamental underpinning. When you trace it back to that, that's a very profound message for the world.

These statements affirmed the value of the newcomers' ethnic identity by demonstrating the lofty ethical concerns within the tradition. They also served to underline the practical benefits individuals could gain from following the religion.

THE LUBAVITCH COMMUNITY

Duty, Obligation, and Commitment

At Bais Chana the resocializing agents made much less effort to reconcile their religious teachings to modern secular consciousness. They spoke a more traditional language of duty, obligation, and commitment. Rabbi Friedman repeatedly stressed that following the dictates of Halacha was not a "lifestyle" that the women could choose but was essential to their own inner natures. As he told the women one morning in class:

> Why does a Jew do a mitzvah? For no reason. Because it's natural. They don't need a reason. . . . A Jew by definition wants to do mitzvahs. . . . When God tells us what to do, He's not telling us what to do but what we are. . . . A human being breathes; a Jewish soul mitzvahs. That's a verb. . . . God is mitzvahs, we are part of God, therefore we are mitzvahs. That's why a Jew who spent forty years living a non-Jewish life and then studied *Yiddishkeit* can be perfectly comfortable as a Jew in one week. . . . If it was a new lifestyle, it would be a struggle. But he's just being himself.

These words recall the accounts of the Lubavitch women, who, as we saw, adopted the rhetoric of compulsion in describing their attraction to Orthodoxy. Rabbi Friedman spent a great deal of time emphasizing the utter necessity of their adherence to Jewish law.

> The reasons for rejecting evil, for not doing a sin, is that the sin is not true. To sin, a Jew has to deceive himself. And not about something outside himself but about himself. On the grounds that it's crazy. So he rejects sin because it's a lie. On the grounds that it's crazy, not on the grounds of unnaturalness or inelegance.

In these words we can see one of the ways in which the rabbi tried to reverse the assumptions of the dominant society. He challenged the contemporary understanding of individuals as free to construct their own identities by choosing from available options.

He sought to minimize the possibly eroding effects of pluralism by presenting adherence to traditional Judaism as inherent in the recruits' own beings. He asserted that people's essential selves were predetermined and that for these women, as for all Jews, being true to themselves—being who they really were supposed to be—meant being connected to a larger community and following the precepts of an ancient way of life. This adherence was not a matter of choice, not the result of weighing the benefits and costs—the basis on which utilitarian and expressive individualism promotes decisions. Rather, the rabbi claimed that following the dictates of these laws was essential to the women's inner natures and that if they deviated from this obedience, they would be "insane." Thus, he shored up the worldview of the community by imbuing it with the weight of necessity.[6]

To reinforce this message that the women were really not free to choose or reject this way of life, he asserted that in general people were less free to construct their identities than they thought. As he told the class one evening:

> Individuals really have so many options. We have the notion that in America you can be anything. But you can't. If we talk about specific individuals, you'll see that any given individual does not have that many options. . . . We pride ourselves into believing that we can do anything, but we can't. We can only be what we are. What confuses us, and what really sets us off the track, is the seeming endlessness of the options. We have to realize that we don't have endless options. We have a few options. It's because of the open-endedness that people don't know who they are and say, "Well, why should I do that?" Why? Because that's what you look like you could do. "Yeah, but I'm free to do whatever I want." You're not free to do whatever you want. You're free to do whatever you can, and you can only do certain things.

The remark "People don't know who they are" reflected the rabbi's belief that identity was not socially constructed but rather inhered within a person. In contrast to the teachings at Lincoln Square Synagogue, which promoted the idea of individual choice and self-fulfillment, the rhetoric at Bais Chana repeatedly challenged the assumption that "autonomy of the self places the burden of one's deepest self-definitions on one's own individual choice."[7] The rabbi reinforced obedience to received tradition by claiming that identity was predetermined.

Paradoxically, however, Rabbi Friedman was aware that it was largely because of this conception of freedom of choice that these women were able to come to Bais Chana and create an alternative to their parents' way of life. Nevertheless, he feared that recognition of choice—awareness of pluralism—would weaken the taken-for-grantedness of the Lubavitch worldview. Thus, he emphasized that this way of life was not a choice; it was necessary and essential. He replaced the value of free choice with the concept of *hashgocha protis*, an orientation that encouraged surrender of agency by asserting that everything happened for a reason outside the individual's control.

A similar means of reversing the dominant middle-class ideal of individuals carving out their own identities "free as much as possible from the demands of conformity to family, friends, or community"[8] was the rabbi's frequent assertion that, fundamentally, the women were very much like their mothers and shared a similar destiny. The subject of mother-daughter relationships was a popular theme in the rabbi's classes. Many of the women at the institute described experiencing some tension or conflict in their relationships with their mothers. Rabbi Friedman sought to minimize this conflict. He repeatedly told the women that rather than trying to separate themselves from their mothers, their true happiness in life lay in following their mother's footsteps—that is, in getting married and having a family.

> When it comes down to what gives you satisfaction in life, it's the same thing that gives your mother satisfaction in life. Young women are really just like their mothers and find fulfillment in the same things: getting married and raising children.

The rabbi was well aware that in becoming Orthodox, these women were in fact choosing to live differently from the way they had been brought up. Yet even while knowing that these women had "left home" to become what he called *themselves*, the rabbi de-emphasized this act of choice. Instead, he emphasized how similar the women were to their mothers, in role if not in ritual behavior. This idealization of their continuity with their mothers had the effect of reinforcing traditional roles as they were cast in the Orthodox mode. It also highlighted the women's ties to the past in the context of a worldview that emphasized obedience to tradition and its history.

De-emphasizing Contemporary Relevance

The Lubavitch teachers were not interested in providing contemporary rationales for the ancient laws because they did not want to communicate that they were selling a product to a consumer who was free to choose or reject it on the basis of an evaluation of its benefits.[9] Thus, unlike the rabbis at Lincoln Square Synagogue, the resocializing agents at Bais Chana did not emphasize explanations for the various observances or the benefits that individual women stood to gain from following Jewish law. In a guest lecture entitled "Love and Marriage" given at Bais Chana by a Lubavitch woman who worked as a matchmaker within the community, the speaker described the laws of family purity, which, she explained, would govern sexual relations between the women and their husbands when they got married. The following excerpt from my field notes presents a segment of her talk and the discussion that followed. She said:

> "Girls, our rabbis have told us that we're allowed to look for rationales in mitzvahs, but we shouldn't do it because it makes sense to us, but because Hashem wants us to. Like *brit milah* [circumcision]. We always did it even though we didn't know the reason. Recently we are finding it can be beneficial."
>
> A woman in the audience asked her, "I heard a woman can't have sexual relations with her husband during menstruation because it's unhealthy for the woman."
>
> She responded, "I wouldn't even want to talk about it. We do it because Hashem says. I'm sure there must be medical benefits, but that's not what we're concerned about."

It is striking how the matchmaker's argument coincides with that of Mary Douglas, the noted contemporary anthropologist, who argues that medical explanations do not suffice to account for kosher laws, which must instead be seen as manifestations of the overall sense of order the ancient Hebrews imposed on the world.[10] The matchmaker was really making the same point: the medical (or other) benefits of the laws of family purity, if extant, were serendipitous; these laws were simply another piece of the organic way of life that the group followed.

Presentation of the Concept of God

The Lubavitch teachings on God contrasted with the de-emphasis on God within the modern Orthodox community. The worldview presented by the Lubavitch encouraged the newcomers to submit their wills to God. Rather than upholding the contemporary assumption that individuals should actively construct their own lives to suit their own needs, the rabbi taught the Bais Chana women that their own wills did not count. All of the above-mentioned teachings implicitly conveyed this message, as well as the instruction that the *ba'alot teshuvah* minimize their own needs and preferences and heed the word of God. On the first day of classes during the summer session I attended, Rabbi Friedman laid out the framework for his teachings thus:

> It is important to know that the whole pursuit of *Yiddishkeit*, when it is done properly, is done on a mission. It's not our own. This is the only way we can be sure that it remains holy, uncorrupted. Sometimes we find people who are not very Jewish in their behaviors and attitudes, and they justify it in terms of what they're studying or reading and calling it Judaism, but it's not. How does that happen? Only one way: if they came for their own purposes, on their own motivation, and forgot who sent us. So we must know who sent us and not make it our personal project. If you consider your Judaism a mission from God, you need to ask yourself, What does God want? To put it in other words, you've got no business being here except for the mission. . . . So the project is to find out what the mission is, who is sending us, exactly how we're supposed to fulfill this mission, and then go out and do it.

In this quotation we can see an example of the rabbi's characteristic attempts to negate and reverse the individualistic view of people that predominated in the wider society. Joseph Veroff, Elizabeth Douvan, and Richard I. Kulka's study, *The Inner American*, found that people in the United States utilized a "personal or individuated paradigm for structuring well-being."[11] Rabbi Friedman challenged this paradigm. Rather than assuming people should act "on their own motivation," to fulfill their own needs and desires, he explicitly told the women that their wills did not count and should be submitted to God's. This message suited the women who came into this community: they felt that they had already made so many bad decisions that they were happy to surrender the sense of responsibility for making their own choices. God, and his human representatives on earth, such as the Rebbe, would guide the women in the correct path.

The Rebbe

The Rebbe, as he is called by his followers, is the leader of the Lubavitch Hasidim. The current Lubavitcher Rebbe, Menachem Mendel Schneerson, is seventh in the line of revered teachers and leaders of this sect. He is believed to have profound spiritual knowledge and insight: his followers claim that "the Rebbe knows all things about all Jews."

The teachings concerning the Rebbe, which were a major emphasis throughout the summer, provided a clear example of the attempt to teach surrender of the self. According to this worldview, all members of the community are in a particular relationship with the man called the Rebbe, who is believed to be "God's representative on earth in this generation." Rabbi Friedman used stories to teach the women the nature of this relationship with the Rebbe. Stories about the Rebbes (past and present) were frequently told in this setting by the *madrichot* as well as by the rabbis. Some of the stories were about the Rebbe's extraordinary insights, miraculous cures, and so forth. Other stories were about people who had failed to follow the Rebbe's advice and ended up in trouble. One such story Rabbi Friedman told in class provides an example:

A Lubavitcher rabbi from Israel wrote this "true confession" in an Israeli magazine [the language here is Rabbi Friedman's summary of the story]. He came to New York to raise money for his yeshiva. He made a big dinner, raised money. Then he had to collect it, and by then it was late August, so he decided to stay for Rosh Hashanah. But then he thought he had to get back to get school organized for the school year, so he wrote and asked the Rebbe what to do. The Rebbe said the guy should pack, go back to Israel, and get ready for the school year.

But as he was packing, some of his friends had arrived from Israel. They said he was crazy to pack. He said the Rebbe had said it was a priority to go. His friends said, "That doesn't mean you can't stay." So he got confused. He wrote to the Rebbe again. He didn't get an answer. By that time it was a week before Rosh Hashanah, so he stayed.

Between Rosh Hashanah and Yom Kippur [Day of Atonement], he went to California to raise money. He went with a friend. . . . He arrived in Los Angeles past midnight, took a little motel room on the ocean, so he decided to go for a swim. The beach was deserted. (Now the guy I'm talking about is a young guy, either a year younger or older than me [mid-thirties].) Suddenly the guy got dizzy, got completely disoriented. His friend didn't see him, it was so dark. He started thinking, this is it, he's dead. So he thought, Who will run the school? So he thought, he's not indispensable. Someone else will run the school. So he thought, What will I do when I'm dead? Seek out the previous Rebbes and ask directions.

As he was going through these thoughts, his friend pulled him out. He had swallowed quite a bit of water. It took him a few days to recuperate. He was shaken and made his friend swear not to tell his family.

Back in Crown Heights he was driving a rented car—Hertz. One corner a policeman stopped the car for a spot check. He asked for a license. The rabbi said he's from Israel. The policeman checks the license, says, "Get out of the car," and frisks him. He puts on handcuffs—the supposed rental car is really a stolen car. He's a very delicate guy, and he's arrested. . . . A couple of hours later a court-appointed lawyer came to see him in his cell. . . . Within fifteen minutes the whole thing was straightened out. . . .

So the guy wrote to the Rebbe to ask why he had suffered so. If it's to make up for his sins, that he accepts, but there's something weird about this. Within an hour he had an answer: the Rebbe had told him to go back to Israel for the school year. These two events happened outside Israel, after the beginning of the school year. Now that it's over you should correct the disobedience and turn it into a virtue to serve God with joy and confidence.

He thought to himself that he could undo the events by publishing his story so others could learn from it.

Through such stories, Rabbi Friedman communicated the group's beliefs concerning the Rebbe—that he knew better than they did what was best for them; therefore, they should submit their wills to his. They were to seek his advice in all major decisions in their lives and follow it. These stories, then, were a didactic means of teaching surrender of the mind and will.

The message in the rabbi's stories about the Rebbe was reinforced by the *madrichot*, who encouraged the women to write letters to the Rebbe for advice concerning important life issues. Thus, the women were taught in practical terms how to relate to a Rebbe. Naomi had been troubled since the first day of the program about how to figure out what her "mission" was—did it involve going to Israel the following year and following her plan to attend a non-religious high school there? Or should she move into the Lubavitch community in Crown Heights? The *madrichot* encouraged Naomi to write to the Rebbe about the decision: it was too important to make alone. They sat with her and helped her compose the letter.

The world presented to these women was well ordered and had a beneficent, omniscient father at the head. And not only could this man shape their own lives for the better; he had the power to change the course of Jewish history. These attributes were taken as evidence that the Rebbe was the Moshiach. In class one day the rabbi presented this understanding of the Rebbe:

> The Rebbe feels that for a Jew coming back to Judaism is not a miracle. It's not unusual and it's not strange. It's just natural. But the fact that the Rebbe created a *ba'al teshuvah* phenomenon does indicate that he's Moshiach because as far as we can tell, one of the requirements of Moshiach is that he has to bring all Jews back to *Yiddishkeit*. . . . We see someone accomplishing what Moshiach is supposed to accomplish, so we say, "This is Moshiach." And he's going to say, "I'm not Moshiach. I'm just doing what needs to be done." But we'll pester him long enough until he'll accept. He'll agree to be Moshiach. And he will be. So just like Hasidim make the Rebbe a Rebbe, Jews will make Moshiach a Moshiach.

In an interview, Rabbi Friedman articulated the same belief concerning the Rebbe's messianic role:

RF: As far as I'm concerned, who created the sixties was the Lubavitcher Rebbe. Who created *ba'al teshuvah* is the Lubavitcher Rebbe. Who created the rejection of materialism is the Lubavitcher Rebbe. Who created idealism among youth is the Lubavitcher Rebbe.

LD: How did he create it?

RF: He generated it. That's what he is, and he just gives off that kind of energy. And that kind of attitude is very contagious.

LD: Is the Rebbe the Moshiach?

RF: He's got my vote.

LD: What does that mean?

RF: That if the Rebbe keeps doing what he's doing, he will change the world, which is what Moshiach is supposed to do. So if we look around and we say, we believe that the world can become

> good, that there's some future for mankind, where is it going
> to come from? As far as I'm concerned, from Brooklyn. I can't
> see it coming from anyplace else. Right now it's happening to
> Jews in increasing numbers and eventually it will spread to the
> non-Jew and that's it. The world is fixed.

The millenarian cast of these teachings was a powerful way of
creating order: the bad old world in which the women "messed
up" and "got into trouble" was ending, and the new era was about
to begin. And the rabbi assured them that this had to be so.

> It's not possible that a bunch of Jews are giving an individual credit
> that he didn't deserve. People will not give credit to someone unless
> he deserves it. The Jews, more than most people, are very selective
> and very stingy with approval, with respect. We don't respect easily.
> We're great cynics. So what I'm telling you is you should listen
> exactly to what his Hasidim are saying, and then you'll know exactly
> what he is. For they will not give him credit for things he's not.

The message that we are on the threshold of a new age is common in sectarian religious groups. In her book on Catholic Char-
ismatics, Meredith McGuire describes how "the millenarian dream
that the perfect New Order is imminent" operated within the community as a powerful order-creating mechanism.[12] The millenari-
anism in the Lubavitch worldview similarly served to create a well-
ordered universe for the *ba'alot teshuvah*. It reassured them that
although the world did indeed seem to be in a critical state, that in
itself was a sign that change was imminent. And because by joining this community they were allying themselves with "the ultimate source of order"—the Rebbe—they would "have a privileged
position in the unknown glorious future."[13]

Within the Lubavitch community the Rebbe was the focus of
millenarian beliefs; he would usher in the new era, in which peace
and harmony would reign. And each woman would have a role to
play in hastening the process:

> God wouldn't give people a mission that they couldn't do. The
> success in this mission produces a greater devotion and deeper com-
> mitment to bring more Godliness into the world. This hastens the
> coming of Moshiach, at which time the world will be perfected. . . .
> No war, no animosity . . . true peace and lasting peace. And this
> will come about sooner by each person fulfilling their individual
> responsibility. When we experience the coming of Moshiach in our
> days, then we will see the world established on its proper basis.

Through this vision, the *ba'alot teshuvah*, who previously had felt at odds with the world, were given a special place in ushering in the new age. Through their actions in following the teachings of the community, they could create order in their lives as well as help restore order in the world.

In an ironic borrowing from contemporary culture, one of the *madrichot*, an earnest young *ba'alat teshuvah*, asserted that the existence of technology capable of broadcasting simultaneously all over the world proved that the millennium was near.

> It's supposed to be that when Moshiach comes everyone all over the world will know at the same time. How could that be? But now that we can see the Rebbe on cable TV all over the world, that means that we have the technology to broadcast the coming of the Moshiach. So the time must be near.

An understanding of their place in the community and in relation to God and the cosmos was a significant aspect of the new identity taught to these two groups of women. This new self-understanding was a major aspect of what the women were seeking when they first entered the synagogue. But these *ba'alot teshuvah* wanted to be rooted not only in a community of memory but also in the immediate context of a family, a nuclear family. Their desires coincided with the Orthodox Jewish promotion of nuclear families.

TEACHINGS CONCERNING WOMEN'S ROLES, MALE-FEMALE RELATIONS, MARRIAGE, AND THE FAMILY

In both communities the teachings concerning marriage, the family, and women's roles were an essential component of the resocialization process. The women were taught not only the laws and practices that guided all aspects of their daily activities as observant Jews; they were also encouraged to accept the community's conception of their appropriate role as women. The difficulty of forming a family and the confusion about gender within the secular society were frequently highlighted by the women as contributing to the sense of disorder that brought them into the religious community. Thus, the order the community projected and attempted to impose in this area was a major attraction of the Orthodox Jewish way of life. In this fundamental aspect of their teachings we can see further evidence of the characteristic differences between the modern Orthodox and Lubavitch approaches to modernity.

LINCOLN SQUARE SYNAGOGUE

Promoting Nuclear Families

Coincident with the desires of the women who came in, and shaping those desires through the resocialization process, the rabbis in this community devoted a great deal of energy to promoting nuclear families. The importance of family life was repeatedly emphasized. Even in teachings about other aspects of ritual observance, such as Shabbat or holidays, the discussion inevitably included references to the traditional family setting within which many of these rituals were performed.

In a class in basic Judaism one evening, a woman asked the associate rabbi to explain the significance of the two candles lit on Friday nights to usher in the Shabbat. He responded:

> It represents the ideal household. Judaism has this very strong bias. It wants you to get married. People in the world are seen as being almost incomplete when they're not married. . . . Why doesn't God create woman like he created man? Instead he takes him and makes a similar creation. So why didn't He create woman separate? Because the essence of woman is a creation from man so that they can be combined into union again. In the sexual act, in living a life together on a spiritual level. So the bias of the Torah is to get married.

The message here was very similar to what was taught in the Lubavitch community: people were incomplete unless married. Yet, as we will see, the Lubavitch had clearly established norms for ensuring that its members got married—they arranged marriages and did not allow people to date casually. They thus set up an alternative to prevailing patterns of dating and mating. The modern Orthodox community, in contrast, had a much looser social structure; the rabbis and other members of the community generally did not exercise strict control over members' lives. Because the people in this community remained rooted in the secular world, there was no attempt to completely restructure their dating and mating practices. They were not limited to dating only other members of the community. Essentially, then, they were able to carry on, even as members of the synagogue community, the same patterns of male-female relationships that prevailed in the wider society. How, then, did the rabbis foster the formation of nuclear families?

One of the ways they encouraged the formation of heterosexual attachments was through informal matchmaking. This practice was common. On my first day in the setting, people who had just met me briefly, and did not know that I was married at the time, were already interested in introducing me to men in the community. Many of the women I interviewed mentioned that members of the community had tried to introduce them to men. Sometimes the rabbis introduced women and men to each other. There was also an official "matchmaker" in the community who had been appointed by the former rabbi of the synagogue. Most of the women I interviewed, however, had not met or even heard of her.

The rabbis used other subtle (and not so subtle) means to promote marriages. It was widely known in the Jewish community that this synagogue was a place where singles came to meet each other, and the rabbis did not hesitate to use this as a selling point. One woman remarked to me that when she told the rabbi about her engagement, his response was, "Great! That's good for our statistics." One Saturday, during the section at the end of Beginners' Service in which the rabbi regularly encouraged new people to introduce themselves, a woman introduced herself and announced her engagement. The rabbi seemed very pleased and warmly wished her *mazel tov* (congratulations). He then said, "See, if you want to get married, you only have to come to beginners' minyan." Whenever the engagement of a person in the Beginners' Service was announced, at the kiddush following the service the rabbi would lead people in energetic singing and dancing in honor of the *simcha* (joyous occasion). (The dancing was traditional circle dancing, with men and women in separate circles.) On one such Saturday, in the midst of much merriment over a member's forthcoming marriage, the rabbi said, "If anyone has any resistance to getting married, let them come over to me right now; I'll break it down."[14]

Conceptions of Gender

The presentation of women's role in Judaism within this modern Orthodox community resembled its teachings on other aspects of Jewish religious observance: it represented an attempt to challenge and reverse contemporary values and assumptions, even while upholding many modern attitudes and behavioral patterns. The modern Orthodox conception of women's roles blended traditional, essentialist understandings of women's nature—the idea that women have a unique and distinct nature that is rooted in their biology—with contemporary voluntaristic ideas.[15] Although a majority of women within this community worked outside of the home—particularly the new *ba'alot teshuvah*, who were predominantly single and had no other means of support—Rabbi Buchwald taught that Judaism assigned women primary responsibility for the care of the home and family.

> Men and women have roles and basic areas of responsibility. That's incontrovertible. Nothing can be used to rationalize that away. . . . The woman basically is ascribed the responsibility for the raising and nuturing of children. The men are assigned the responsibility for the cognitive education of the children.

On another occasion he told the newcomers, "I think that women have a very particular role in Judaism, and that's to create the religious atmosphere in the home."

No one missed his criticism of those who pressed for women's equality in the public realm. Woman's place was in the home, as he told the group at Beginners' Service one Saturday morning:

> I would argue that the emphasis on synagogue life today is destructive to Judaism rather than constructive. I would say that the emphasis should be on home life; I think men should be arguing in favor of more rights in the home rather than women arguing for more rights in the synagogue. And you mark my words . . . within ten years you'll see a marked swing of emphasis on the home. If our society is going to survive, it's only going to be on the basis of a heightened concentration on efforts within the home, and people will be arguing and fighting for rights within the home. . . . Our

contemporary society has *facocked* [confused] values, as if to say the job, the career, is the most important thing. But I'm telling you that if I came to my senses, if the rest of the people came to their senses, we would be arguing about having the opportunities to raise our children. . . . That should be our prized possession.

This conception of women and the importance of the home was reminiscent of the nineteenth-century "cult of true womanhood," in which, at a time of great social upheaval, women's ability to create a warm, loving haven away from the heartless world was lauded by preachers and social philosophers alike.[16] The religious community offered its own solution to the dilemmas about women's roles in the late twentieth-century United States. The rabbi frequently made clear his perception that we were in a time of great crisis; women's capacity to create peaceful, comforting homes that could serve as a refuge was urgently needed.

Nevertheless, the rabbis in this community also (implicitly and explicitly) upheld modern ideas in their teachings about women's roles. The adult education program included a course entitled "Feminism and Halacha." Offering such a course implied that the two—feminism and traditional Jewish law—could and should be reconciled. In basic Judaism class one night the associate rabbi made clear his belief that Judaism had to change to accommodate the changes in gender roles in modern society. He was describing the rituals associated with Shabbat and was talking about candle-lighting. Here is the excerpt from my field notes of this event:

> The rabbi asked the class, "Who lights the candles?" Someone answered, "The woman." He asked, "Why?" and then continued to say, "I'll say it. Down here [points to heart] I believe what I'm saying. Up here I don't. So I'll say it. In the traditional household, hundreds of years ago—thousands of years ago, so we won't get too nervous—man's basic purpose was to represent values outside the home. Woman was responsible for home and children. In modern society, these roles have changed, so Halacha, which deals with these issues, must be changed."

Rabbi Buchwald, too, asserted that even though Orthodox Judaism believed in certain forms of sex roles, it was not opposed to modern egalitarian ideals. One Saturday he told the group at Beginners' Service:

There's nothing in Judaism that says men and women can't share household responsibilities, that a man can't change a baby. Judaism—Jewish people—adopted the norms of the culture, and now that is changing, and there is no reason that it can't change in Judaism. But the primary responsibility for children is assigned to the mother.

During my stay in the community I observed many instances in which the tradition was creatively reinterpreted to show how attuned it was with feminist thinking. For example, the *niddah* laws (laws of family purity that govern the sexual relations of married couples by forbidding physical contact during menstruation and for seven days thereafter) have been highlighted by feminists as reflecting negative attitudes toward women's sexuality. The rabbis reinterpreted these laws in a way that incorporated feminist ideas.[17] In services one Saturday, Rabbi Buchwald emphasized how these laws actually benefited women by encouraging men to see women as individuals, not as sex objects:

> I would say that the relationship of impurity has to do with sexual attitudes. I would say that it has to do with the sanctity of life, which is a broad concept. But it also has to do with not being seen as a sexual object, which I think is a totally prowoman attitude. You have to love me for what I am, and not for what you can get off me, and that's the laws of *tum'ah* [ritual impurity] and *taharah* [ritual purity] in Judaism. . . . Take a look at what's going on out there, how women have been objectified. Do you see women in Judaism objectified as sexual objects? On the one hand you can say it's keeping women down on the farm by keeping their heads covered. On the other hand, you could say, hey, it's by maintaining a certain attitude towards women which is not to objectify them as a sexual object.

In this reinterpretation of *niddah*, the rabbi used one aspect of contemporary culture to criticize another: he incorporated a modern feminist analysis of the sexual objectification of women to reinforce a traditional religious critique of current sexual norms. Even though the rabbi's intention was to oppose modern trends, he actually presented a contemporary analysis according to which people were to be valued for their own individuality: "Love me for what I am." Implicit was the notion that people had an essence apart from their roles or functions.

The rabbi's affirmation of individualism was incorporated into his explanation of other Jewish laws concerning women. In services one Saturday morning, he offered an explanation of the law that a bride had to wear a veil at the wedding ceremony—that it affirmed women's individuality:

> Judaism doesn't have the notion that the two merge into one, but that they maintain separate identities, so the veil is a way of saying symbolically, "*Ad can* [until here], you can have me, but only till here. We cannot melt into each other." The veil represents the individual identity of the woman. And this is related to why we have separate seating in the synagogue. That Jews pray as a community, but also as individuals. The husband and wife are not supposed to merge into one.

Here the rabbi engaged in the practice Samuel Heilman, a contemporary sociologist of Jews, calls contemporizing—"the effort to make Torah a part of and relevant to the modern world"—by reinterpreting a traditional practice in present-day terms.[18]

The teachings in this setting about women's roles, then, highlighted some of the dilemmas of presenting traditional religious norms to modern individuals. On the one hand, the rabbis maintained traditional conceptions—women, because of their biological capacities, were assigned responsibility for childrearing. On the other hand, the rabbis also affirmed contemporary sentiments about the need to change women's and men's roles. How did they reconcile these seemingly contradictory viewpoints?

One way they did so was by making a distinction between the public and private spheres and relegating religion to the private sphere. In discussing gender roles in the religion, the beginners' rabbi asserted that although women were clearly assigned responsibility for the raising and nurturing of children, they could also work outside of the home:

> In terms of breadwinner, there is no limitation and no recommendation made. . . . In terms of their commitment to the study of the Torah, yes, there is a recommendation—that a woman should sacrifice her study of Torah for the raising of children.

Through such remarks the rabbi suggested that religion pertained to the private sphere—the home and private study—but did not pertain to the public sphere of work. This represented a secularized, U.S. understanding of religion.

Such a separation between the public and private realms coincided with the desires of the women who came into this community. As we saw, these women were not looking to change their work roles; although they were not heavily invested in their careers, they did not articulate a desire to seek change in this realm. Rather, they were seeking family and community to fulfill their private lives. The religious community's advocacy of traditional roles at home together with equality in the workplace corresponded with their concerns.

Sexuality

Because there were few direct means of enforcing social control beyond the boundaries of the synagogue, the rabbis were essentially unable to control the sexual activities of the members. On this issue the rabbis sent out mixed messages.

On the one hand, they explicitly taught the traditional Jewish laws concerning sexuality—that premarital and extramarital sexual activities were forbidden. On the other hand, even while cautioning members against sexual activity, the rabbis were aware that the newcomers to this community were not likely to change their sexual behavior. Because these adults remained involved in the secular world and sexuality was such a basic drive, the community was not in a position to enforce a drastic change in sexual mores. This was implicitly acknowledged, sometimes in humorous ways. One evening in Bible class the rabbi was going over the relevant laws and explained that one of the reasons premarital sexual relations were forbidden was that only married women were required to immerse themselves in a *mikveh* (ritual bath) seven days after their menstrual periods. It was only after this immersion that men were permitted to have sexual relations with them.

> A woman in class asked, "You're saying that the only thing prohibiting sexual relations between single men and women is *mikveh*?"
> The rabbi answered, "Only *mikveh*. If a woman doesn't go to *mikveh*, she's considered a menstruant. If you have sexual relations with a menstruant, the punishment is excision. If you eat bread on Passover, the punishment is excision."
> A man asked, "But if she goes in the ocean?" The rabbi responded, "Look, if you're making plans, she could also put on a ring and cover her hair and go to a *mikveh*."
> A woman then asked, "Is it better to go to the *mikveh* and lie or

not acknowledge that a person is a sexual being?" The rabbi said, "I'll answer these questions on an individual basis."

The humorous tone in which this interchange was carried out was one means of dispelling the tension that might have arisen over the discrepancy between the community's norms and the recruits' behavior. Samuel Heilman, in his study of a modern Orthodox community, suggests a similar explanation of joking behavior: "It blocks out—literally as well as symbolically—the possibility of the speakers' having to come to terms with the deeper antinomies inherent in their modernity and Orthodoxy."[19] Because the rabbis knew how difficult it would have been to change the newcomers' sexual attitudes and behaviors, they either ignored the discrepancy or engaged in light joking about it.

Thus, we can see that in their teachings concerning women, marriage, and male-female relations, the representatives of this community were unable to reverse the prevailing norms of the wider society. Instead, they maintained a precarious balance between upholding the implicit assumptions of the wider culture and advocating a retreat to a more traditional way of life. They engaged in a creative reinterpretation of the tradition that blended elements of contemporary feminism and individualism with a traditional religious conception of gender roles. This represented a significant contrast with the Lubavitch community, whose teachings more directly challenged and attempted to replace modern U.S. ways of life.

THE LUBAVITCH COMMUNITY

Both communities clearly communicated their conceptions of the appropriate gender roles and ideals of family life, but within the Lubavitch community these teachings were emphasized a great deal more, and given much more explicit attention, than at Lincoln Square Synagogue. The Lubavitch community's goal in this area was complete resocialization: teaching the women entirely new patterns of behavior in their interactions with men. The modern Orthodox community did not presume to regulate its members' behaviors so closely; even though in some respects Orthodoxy's beliefs and ideology challenged contemporary trends, the community did not really attempt to completely override contemporary cultural patterns of male-female relations. Because the transformations demanded by the Lubavitch were much more strenuous and thorough, it makes sense that they would focus more attention on teaching the new norms.

Promoting Nuclear Families

Given that within this community the most significant means for women to fulfill God's will was through marriage and childbearing, teachings on marriage and the family were a major emphasis in all of the classes. This explicit part of the agenda was announced on the first day of the session: "Anything that we learn that's got any value has to be useful to you in your *Yiddishkeit* and in your marriage. If it's useful in only one of them, you're in trouble." That teachings about marriage predominated at Bais Chana was well known within the community—one young *ba'alat teshuvah* who was engaged to be married told me she came there to "learn to be a *kallah* [bride]."

The rabbi's concentration on the subject of marriage stemmed from his conviction that it was the essence of Judaism: "Marriage is synonymous with all of Judaism. The whole point of *Yiddishkeit* is to bring a man and a woman together." Marriage was also seen as an essential component of a woman's identity: a single woman was not complete, as Rabbi Friedman told me in an interview:

> My pet subject is that women should get married when they're fourteen. . . . Past the age of fourteen they're already frustrated by being single . . . because biologically, psychologically, they're ready to be married, and it's the preferred state. Together is better than alone. . . . That's why I really think that a woman who's into her twenties and is not married already has a problem. Before anything else is said, it's already a problem because she's just not complete. She's at odds with the world. I think every need then becomes desperate because life doesn't have a stable comforting base. . . . I don't know why it is, but marriage is much more of an issue with a woman than it is with a man. He can easily lose himself in other things and delay marriage and children, but she can't.

To promote the women's socialization into wives, Rabbi Friedman devoted a great deal of time replacing the contemporary U.S. ideal of romantic love with a sense of relationships based on duty, obligation, and commitment. As Robert Bellah and his coauthors point out, there is a tension in our culture between the belief that "love and marriage are supposed to be spontaneous, and a rich source of psychical satisfactions," and the reality that marriage also entails commitment and obligation.[20] Rabbi Friedman resolved this tension by spurning an individualistic emphasis on feelings and self-fulfillment and replacing it with a more traditional conception of people as bound together by ties of duty. He belittled the ideal of romantic love by emphasizing its individualistic nature.

> Between two people, love isn't the ultimate experience. Love in our society is based on our own selfish needs and desires. There's very little doubt that when a man says to a woman or vice versa I love you, what it means is I enjoy loving you. In our society we're so needy and so selfish that basically you have 200 million people running around wanting to enjoy their own emotions, most of all love. But love involves another person. They're not ready for that. So they bump into another person who'll permit them to love them without getting involved.

People in the United States, Bellah et al. write, "believe in love as the basis for enduring relationships."[21] They "tend to assume that feelings define love and that permanent commitment can come only from having the proper clarity, honesty and openness about one's feelings."[22] Rabbi Friedman reversed this order. Rather than relying on feelings as the basis for forming permanent relationships, he advocated the primacy of commitment over feeling. Love should be seen not as the reason for marriage but as the result of it.

> What is love? The desire for closeness. . . . In order for love to exist—to desire closeness—you need to already have a relationship, and that relationship permits or cultivates the emotion of love. Until the guy proposes it's not love. Only when the guy proposes, when he's made the ultimate sacrifice for you, is that love. . . . Love comes only *after* marriage. In most relationships outside of marriage the love isn't love at all but the comfort we feel with *ourselves*. . . . Through *conviction* you create a relationship that in the end will reward you with love.

The rabbi recognized that emotions alone could not provide a stable base on which to build a permanent relationship. Thus, he stressed the obligations first—establish a commitment to the relationship, and then the feelings would follow. Feelings could and should be subordinated to duty through the exercise of the will: "Through conviction you create a relationship."

Traditionalists fear that the expressive individualism that underlies our culture's preoccupation with feelings will threaten family life. Like the Lubavitch Hasidim, Evangelical Christians attempt to reverse the current primacy of emotion over obligation in relationships. An Evangelical minister cited by Bellah sounds exactly like Rabbi Friedman:

> Most people are selfish . . . looking at relationships for themselves only. . . . Scriptures teach there is a love we can have for other people that is selfless. We have to learn it. It's actually a matter of the will. [23]

The attempt by fundamentalist religions to reestablish the supremacy of nuclear families necessitates a reformulation of the relationship between feeling and will. The rabbi and the Evangelical minister were posing a model of family in which duty, obligation, and commitment took precedence over the spontaneous flow of feelings. Even when it might be inconvenient for oneself, or go against one's immediate preferences, marriage required putting the commitment to one's partner first, as Rabbi Friedman told his class:

> Let's say they get married and they find out he has some rare allergy, and he can't live in the United States, and so they have to move to Honduras. Even though she doesn't want to move, they *will* because *he* has an allergy. And she won't consider it an infringement on her life—he's not *ruining* her life—because that's what a marriage is. She has made his reality hers. . . . That's the ultimate demand—that you have to, to some degree, forget yourself and be tuned in to the other person. [24]

This view of marriage encourages permanence and commitment by emphasizing the primacy of roles over individual selves. An opposite view to this, and one which Bellah and his coauthors claim is widespread in our society, is what they call the "therapeutic attitude." "The therapeutic attitude begins with the self, rather than with a set of external obligations." [25] This worldview rests on the assumption that people have an essential self, independent of their roles, and encourages people to "get in touch with" this self. Rabbi Friedman belittled this ethos, arguing that the only way to relate to people was through their roles.

> The Gemara [the codified oral law, together with its rabbinic analysis and commentary] says, "Women—stay away from them, they're ugly, they're not nice. What do you need them for?" . . . But right alongside all these statements about how women are distasteful and unlovable you have the exact opposite statements of esteem and devotion on the part of the rabbis towards their wives and mothers. . . . This tells us something very interesting. If we remove the role— not mother, not wife, not daughter—then what's left is not acceptable, according to the Gemara. Same with a man. If he's not functioning as a son, a father, or husband, then he's not acceptable. And what we're trying to do in our society is take away the roles and see what's left. . . . But if you eliminate all the roles, then you're not dealing with the person. You're dealing with an abstraction.

His assertion that individuals did not have an essential self apart from their roles was an attempt to reverse the contemporary individualistic preoccupation with the self and its fulfillment. Such statements served the function of turning the women's attention away from intrasubjective musings and reinforcing proper fulfillment of their roles in the community. This process was an example of the commitment mechanism that Rosabeth Moss Kanter, in her studies of religious communities and their commitment mechanisms, labels "mortification":

> Mortification processes provide a new set of criteria for evaluating the self; they reduce all people to a common denominator and transmit the message that the self is adequate, whole, and fulfilled only when it lives up to the model offered by the community.[26]

The "self," in the Lubavitch worldview, does not exist apart from the roles filled by the individual. Because the central role women play within the Lubavitch community is as mothers and wives in nuclear families, the explication of how to fulfill these roles is an essential process in the reconstruction of the *ba'alot teshuvah* into Lubavitch women.

Conceptions of Gender

During the first class on the first day of the summer session I attended, Rabbi Friedman announced to the assembled group of women that "when a woman comes into *Yiddishkeit* she has to rethink her whole being as a woman." Thus, he communicated that within this community, the process of resocialization to Orthodoxy demanded a radical reconceptualization of femininity. A great deal of his time in class was spent breaking down contemporary understandings of women's role, male-female relations, and marriage and presenting the Hasidic alternative.

The Hasidic interpretation of women's proper role rests on an essentialist view of women, the idea that women's nature is rooted in their biology and expressed in all aspects of their beings. Woman's greater involvement in childbearing is taken as a metaphor for her essential nature, as Rabbi Friedman told the *ba'lot teshuvah:*

> That's why, for many women, to relearn devotion, to replace narcissism with devotion, is really a very natural thing because it's more feminine to be devotional than to be narcissistic. . . . Biologically, a man does not give of himself in any real sense to have children. A woman does. So right there before we even get into any profound mystical stuff, just the way our bodies are built, a woman is, by nature, going to give of herself. . . . For the woman it's almost inevitable, natural.

"Femininity," as a rabbi's wife told the women in a special class (offered once during my stay) on women's role in Judaism, "is attained to a great extent through marriage, through bearing children and nurturing children."

As with other aspects of obedience to Jewish law, the women were taught that any deviation from this conception of women's roles was a violation of their own inner natures. During one of the many classes devoted to this topic, Rabbi Friedman told the women:

> For a woman to wait to have children is wrong because she's violating herself. It seems to be that that's part of the definition of being a woman and when you tamper with the definition you're tampering with yourself. I think the proof of it is that the women who decided not to have children, in the last moment panicked and dropped their jobs and go out and have children at an age when the doctors are saying it's not so safe anymore. . . . So the only logical assumption is to say that it's within the woman to want children. . . . Women should not castrate themselves in order to have a career. I think birth control is a violent violation of a woman's being.

In contrast to the feminist ideal that women are free to choose their roles and that they may reasonably elect to fulfill several different primary roles either simultaneously or in succession, the message here was that women's inherent nature is consistent with the demands of a domestically based feminine role.

Sexuality

One of the practical effects of these teachings is the restructuring of the women's behavior in terms of male-female relationships. The Lubavitch Hasidim maintain a different pattern of courtship from that prevailing in the wider society. Adolescent boys and girls are not permitted any casual interactions or dating. At the age of eighteen or nineteen, when the woman is deemed ready for marriage (early twenties for a man), a third party arranges a *shidduch.* Lifers' parents make these arrangements for them, whereas BTs' matches are typically arranged by their *mashpiim.* The woman and man are encouraged to go out only a few times before deciding on the suitability of the person as a marriage partner. The couple is allowed no physical contact prior to marriage.

When new recruits adopt the way of life of this community, they come under the community's auspices in this realm. The "sacrifice" of their control over their dating and sexual relationships is a commitment mechanism, one frequently employed in utopian communities.[27] During the resocialization process at the institute, while the women are taught the new norms they are completely isolated from men. The community's regulation of behavior in this realm is complete and thorough—the women are told they are not even allowed to shake hands with men. Once the women join the community, there is generally a waiting period of at least a year to ensure that their commitment to Hasidism is solidified before they are deemed "ready" to go out. Then they follow the prescribed pattern of dating only men who have been selected for them as possible marriage partners.

These obviously are enormous changes to make for women who have been brought up in an era of sexual freedom and who have already experienced sexual relationships with men. The rabbi fostered the women's acceptance of these restrictions by emphasizing that the prevailing patterns of dating and mating did not guarantee, and indeed might hamper, strong marriages, which were the desired goal. Given that many of these women had had negative experiences with sexual relationships prior to joining, they were receptive to his arguments. One morning he told an attentive class:

> Why would you want to get to know anybody if you're not interested in getting married? It was only forty to fifty years ago that all people behaved like Hasidim today. Very recently, and predominantly in America after World War II, this thing with dating became very prominent. . . . People thought that young people should get to know each other before getting married. . . . Now there's no chaperons, no polite sipping of sodas; you can do everything but get pregnant.

A woman in class objected, "But the idea of getting to know each other doesn't seem bad to me. You just should talk." He responded:

> But now we think you need to get an apartment, move in together, and practice being married. But did marriages get better? No, they're often worse. So the whole argument in favor of teenagers dating has got to be thrown out. The argument is it'd make marriages better. It doesn't. I'd argue it makes it worse. . . . Every psychologist and sociologist would tell you people don't marry the kind of person they date or date the kind of person they'd want to marry. The excitement in dating is primarily in meeting a man who's very unlike your father. It's exotic, challenging. Marriage means meeting a man who's like your father. In dating, you develop a certain mannerism or approach that works, and you convince yourself that that's the way to get along properly with a man. When you get married it has to switch, and it's very difficult to switch to a new way of getting along. Dating is a distraction from marriage. The better you are at dating, the worse you are at marriage.

Because many of the women in this community felt that they had been "unsuccessful" at dating, they were relieved to hear the rabbi's critique of the practice. His words essentially told them that they should not worry, that their failure at dating actually boded well for their marriages.

The underlying message of the rabbi's teachings concerning male-female relationships and sexuality was self-control. He told the women, "The Rebbe says you can say no to the desires of the heart. That's a radical statement in light of contemporary psychology. Use your mind to bring your emotions into line." In contrast to contemporary culture, which intoned, "If it feels good, do it," the community's norms required restraint. The rabbi proffered advice on how to achieve this restraint:

> A person has to consider sex as not so nice so that the animal soul will be turned off . . . has to consider how aesthetically unpleasing, aesthetically inelegant, sex is . . . in order to control the desires or the passions. Is that why you shouldn't do it? Certainly that is not why. But it is how. Why you shouldn't do it is because God said not to. How will you get yourself not to do it? Turn yourself off. Think about the inelegant side of it.

The teachings in this setting promoted an interesting balance of self-control and surrender of control. On the one hand, the rabbi taught the women submission and surrender of their wills—to God, the Rebbe, and the norms of the community. On the other hand, following the religious laws required enormous self-control. So even as the rabbi taught them the concept of divine providence, he was also teaching them a way of life that demanded rigorous control over their basic drives. Both of these messages, however, fit into his overall framework—the attempt to reverse the prevailing assumptions of the larger society.

The rabbi's primary goal was resocialization. To do that, he needed to erode their commitment to their former ways of life. His teachings suggested that they could begin life anew—they could return to their native "innocence" and start again. Even though this clean slate applied to their observance of all aspects of Jewish law, the rabbi's repeated emphasis on sexual renunciation was not accidental. He knew this was a particularly sensitive area for these women. One morning he told them:

> I think that innocence is a native condition and that there's an intrinsic need to be innocent. The innocence that the Torah demands is the same innocence that your own gut level condition demands, and that's why a Jew will take to *Yiddishkeit* like a fish to water. . . . Innocence means that you're created a certain way and that you've never corrupted that condition. You never tampered, a virginal territory. Untouched. That's innocence. And if God says, "I created you kosher," then to have eaten nonkosher means you've been tampered with. You introduced an ingredient that didn't belong. Discoloration. So you're no longer virginal, and that hurts—in spite of what everybody else says.

Although here the rabbi explicitly pointed to the violation of kosher laws as his example of lost innocence, his use of the words *virginal, tampered,* and *untouched* suggests that he was also talking about sexuality. He promoted the goal of resocialization by reinforcing the women's discomfort about their past sexual activities. Many of them did indeed feel "tampered with" and were concerned about whether they could erase that taint now that they were embracing a new way of life. Two of the women had expressed to me their anxiety about ever signing the traditional Jewish marriage contract, which explicitly states that the woman is a virgin. (The community handles the matter of virginity by employing the legal device claiming that once someone "returns" in repentance, all her or his prior sins are erased.) By tapping into the women's discomfort and guilt, the rabbi encouraged their acceptance of the community's strict regulation of their sexuality.

But what happened to the sexual energy of the sixty women who were living together in this institute? Was it manifest in other forms? One channel for this energy might have been the excesses of food offered at Bais Chana. Food was served five times a day— three very large meals (lunch and dinner consisted of several courses) and many sweet snacks in the afternoon and at night. All of the women claimed to be eating much more than normal, and most gained five to ten pounds in the month I was there. My hunch about some of the latent functions of food at the institute were implicitly confirmed by the rabbi in our interview. We had been talking about sex and how people in our society felt the need for sex therapists, an indication that people were out of touch with their basic drives. When I suggested that the prevalence of eating disorders confirmed the same point, he responded immediately:

> RF: Sex and food are also intimately related. . . . It's the same urge. We have an appreciation for music, we get pleasure from a beautiful scene, but we have an appetite for food, and we have an appetite for sex. So those two share the same kind of urging. Of all the sensations, of all the drives and pleasures that we have, eating and sex are indistinguishable in terms of their urge. Others are more distinguishable. . . . We need love, but we don't have an appetite for love. But sex and food are exactly the same. And sometimes, they're confused.
>
> LD: What about around here?

RF: I told you anything over fourteen [the age at which he felt girls should be married] and you're in trouble. The urges are there in full force, subliminally and all that stuff. Sublimation.

LD: And how's that dealt with?

RF: Best left alone. Yeah, if you're going to eat that extra sandwich, ok, so?

Some of the repressed sexual energy was projected onto the rabbi. Many of the women's conversations revolved around him—how special, brilliant, insightful, sensitive, and attractive he was. One woman who was in charge of tape recording his classes would come into his class at noon wearing her house dress and stare at him dreamily while turning over the tape. The rabbi was aware that he was the recipient of these projections; I imagine that he enjoyed it. In an interview with me, he legitimated this transference by saying that the women's fantasies helped them develop "an ability to look at a man, cry on his shoulder, and not have sex enter into the picture." From his perspective he was trying to teach them that they did not always have to act on their sexual desires. Because sexuality was so tightly controlled in this community, even after marriage, the women were being taught a new way to relate to men. As Rabbi Friedman said, "You have to develop a sense of holiness, to where the attraction is genuinely lessened, decreased, so that you're not constantly biting at the bit."

One particularly interesting display was provided in a mock wedding staged one Saturday evening. It was after *tish'a ba'av* and the "nine days," a period of mourning and added renunciation (no meat, no hot showers, no music) commemorating the destruction of the ancient temple in Jerusalem. On the Saturday night following this period, some of the pent-up energy of the past weeks was released in a lavish "wedding" celebration. Here is an excerpt from my field notes of that event:

Half of the women dressed as men, painting beards on their faces and even borrowing the rabbi's pants. Some of these women presented themselves as very tough men: particularly striking was a young "*frum* from birth" Lubavitch woman, who had a cigarette dangling from her mouth and a pack of Marlboros in her chest pocket (she was not a cigarette smoker). One woman was chosen to be the bride (a twenty-eight-year-old woman who was very concerned about getting married) and dressed in a wedding gown made of sheets. The other women were assigned roles as relatives of the bride or groom or as guests. The evening involved a great deal of very lively dancing between the women and the "men." At one point the "men" performed a particularly vibrant dance involving sparklers, which they twirled feverishly while they stomped their feet forcefully. The energy and power in the room were quite impressive.

Through the staging of this event, the women were enacting their understanding of the centrality of marriage within this community and expressing their desire to get married. They were also making use of a permitted release for some of their pent-up energies. Thus, even within this environment, in which severe restrictions were placed on sexual expression, the women invented creative means of channeling their sexual energy.

CONTRASTING CONCEPTIONS
OF SELFHOOD

The modern Orthodox and Lubavitch communities each offered the women a clearly defined sense of self that was rooted in a community. Yet each community's stance toward modern society carried with it a particular understanding of the individual's relation to the larger community. Thus, the rabbis at Lincoln Square taught the women to construct an individualized self that would be fulfilled through participation in a community of similar selves. God was de-emphasized; the women were instead encouraged to follow religious law not because God said so but because they would individually benefit from it. The Lubavitch rabbis, in contrast, taught their newcomers to submerge themselves in the community and emphasized duty and obligation over individual fulfillment and self-expression. These teachings appealed to God as the ultimate religious authority, and the rabbis promoted religious practice by encouraging the women to submit their will to God's.

The *ba'alot teshuvah* in both communities were seeking clarity about gender, models of nuclear family life, and assistance in finding partners. Both communities emphasized the centrality of the nuclear family within Orthodox Judaism. Overall, the two groups of women spoke of common needs. Yet the different life experiences and positions of the two groups of women led them to seek out different religious conceptions of femininity, marriage, and the family. Because the women who came to Bais Chana were less established in the secular world, they were more in need of comprehensive guidelines. They were therefore more prepared to adopt religious definitions and roles that contrasted sharply with those offered in secular society. With respect to gender and family norms, the two communities differed in the comprehensiveness of their guidelines, their accommodation to secular ideology, and degree of social enforcement. These differences were central in the communities' appeal to the two different groups of women.

7

The Dynamics of Conversion

Conversion is a dynamic process shaped by the interactions and mutual influence between conversionist institutions and their recruits. Most of the literature on conversion looks at the issue either from the perspective of the convert (the more common approach) or from the perspective of the organization. My approach is to develop an interactive model that analyzes individual experiences and institutional contexts simultaneously. When applied, this model reveals that the conversion experience in each setting was shaped by certain characteristics of the settings, such as the strength of their boundaries with the wider society, and of the women, such as their availability for dramatic change in their lives.

Lincoln Square Synagogue and Bais Chana, which are examples of what sociologists call "identity transforming organizations," were set up specifically to produce changes in the recruits. These communities' ability to get newcomers to adapt their way of life and the speed with which this was accomplished were affected by the community's ability to "encapsulate" the recruits during the period of resocialization. The need for encapsulation—the mechanisms by which institutions shield potential recruits from the claims of competing commitment demands—increases with the size of the difference between a group's worldview and that of the wider society.[1]

Nevertheless, all identity transforming organizations are limited in their ability to set up strong boundaries with the wider society because they are also forced to interact with this society to obtain necessary resources. The conflicting needs for isolation and contact are particularly complicated when the "necessary resources" are members, as in the two communities discussed here. Because both Lincoln Square and Bais Chana are actively engaged in "outreach" programs for the unaffiliated, their members and representatives must come into contact with the wider society. Thus, the groups are constantly faced with the dilemma of how to be in this world but not of it—how to interact with the wider society and nevertheless maintain a distinct worldview and way of life.

The divergent stances toward modern society in each group result in their creating different types of boundaries between themselves and the wider society: those at Lincoln Square Synagogue are obviously more permeable than those at Bais Chana. The boundaries each community establishes can be analyzed by comparing them on the three characteristic dimensions of encapsulation: physical, social, and ideological. The women's responses to the settings, and the stages in their conversion processes, can be analyzed along three parallel dimensions of commitment: behavioral, social, and ideological. The differential strength of the institutions' encapsulating mechanisms interacts with the types of recruits in each to produce different conversion experiences.

MAINTAINING GROUP BOUNDARIES

LINCOLN SQUARE SYNAGOGUE

Physical Encapsulation

Lincoln Square Synagogue had rather weak physical boundaries with the wider society. The synagogue as the primary resocializing institution was unable to physically encapsulate the potential converts during the resocialization process. The new recruits continued to live within the larger community of the Upper West Side (and East Side) of Manhattan. They attended events at the synagogue one to several times a week, but the rest of the time they participated fully in the activities of the secular society. The women I met in this community continued to go to their workplace settings daily; live in large, heterogeneous apartment buildings; and spend most of their time in secular contexts. Thus, their exposure to competing worldviews could not be effectively shut off by physical absence.

Social Encapsulation

At Lincoln Square synagogue the options for social encapsulation were also minimal. The synagogue community's ability to control the social interaction of its members was quite limited because their occupations and residential arrangements kept them in constant contact with people in the secular world. Thus, the *ba'alot teshuvah* continued to maintain relationships with individuals who did not share the worldview of the religious community.

Nevertheless, even in this setting obedience to religious law entailed some degree of social encapsulation. Many of the women I met told me that it was difficult to maintain relationships with people outside of the community, particularly once they began to keep kosher and thus to limit what and where they ate. Nevertheless, in many spheres of their lives, the members of this community continued to participate in the wider culture (as was permitted by the ideology of modern Orthodoxy): they watched television; went to movies, theater, and the opera; read popular literature; and socialized with "outsiders."

Ideological Encapsulation

Because Lincoln Square Synagogue could not rely on physical and social encapsulation to reinforce its religious ideology, the community had to work harder to maintain its ideological boundaries with the secular society than the Hasidic group did.[2] One way the rabbis projected insulating boundaries, and thus reinforced the group's distinctiveness, was by engaging in scathing critiques of the wider society. Rabbi Buchwald spent a great deal of time excoriating the evils of contemporary Western society and demonstrating Judaism's value as the urgently needed antidote. In Beginners' Service, in classes, and in interviews and conversations, this rabbi repeatedly pointed to the confusion over values in contemporary society. In impassioned terms and with great animation he derided the "decadence" of contemporary culture:

> Our society is eating us up alive because of the decadence. In the last days I learned of the violent deaths of two young men who were associated with the synagogue. Our minds, bodies, psyches are not capable of absorbing as much trauma as we do in the twentieth century. The media bombards us with so much of it we don't have the capacity to cope with it all. When we hear that 225 soldiers were killed in Beirut, we should get down on the floor and rend our clothes and wear ashes, but we can't absorb it all. The only way to

survive is to build this shell. We are slaves. We have become immoral because of our society. The guy on the eleven o'clock news, he
has blond hair and blue eyes and he's always smiling as he reports,
"Twenty-five people were killed in a crash, three people burned in
a fire." There was a survey in *Time* magazine, 87 percent of the
people had had premarital sex. I read it and I felt I'm not part of this
society. But if you read it and have no moral strictures, then you feel
you might as well.

Such steady and insistent critiques of the wider society served as
a boundary-creating device. Through them, the rabbis reminded
the recruits that although they were unable—and not even required—to give up all their contacts with the outside world, they
had to recognize the world's corruptness and maintain their emotional distance from it. The rabbis at Lincoln Square Synagogue
thus asserted and established the group's distinctiveness by criticizing the "outside" society and demonstrating how the religious
community presented a morally and cognitively superior alternative. As Rabbi Buchwald told the group at Bible class one Tuesday
evening:

> We're in a crisis situation . . . of where our world is going to be.
> We need a redirection of our world order and our societal structure.
> I think it's virtually impossible for us to separate ourselves from our
> environment. But that's precisely what we need to do, and I think
> this is what Torah does for me—it enables me to separate myself from
> the environment. To look at what's going on with a more clear
> perspective. In our country they think they can legislate what your
> morality is. But that's just relative morality and changes from year to
> year. One hundred years ago it was the law in New York that a
> woman couldn't walk around without a corset. . . . Anything can be
> legislated, just as the Nazis called the Jews subhuman. However, if
> you have absolute morality, it gives you freedom. It gives you a
> jaundiced eye to look at the newspapers and the trends. Recognize
> God and you'll be free.

But as the rabbis in this synagogue recognized, it was difficult
for newcomers to continue interacting with the wider society on a
daily basis and still maintain a sense of distance from it. This tension between living in the secular world and not being swallowed
up by it was a frequent subject of discussion at the Beginners'
Service. Even though the philosophy of modern Orthodoxy asserted precisely that observant Jews could follow the laws of traditional Judaism and still participate in the wider society, some-

times the beginners' rabbi expressed doubts about the successful merger of the two. He said that the "extreme decadence" and "intrusiveness" of our society made him question whether the traditional religion actually could coexist with secular norms and values.

One day during my sojourn in this community, a representative from the Satmar, one of the most insular groups of Hasidim, came to the synagogue to speak as part of the lecture series, "The Future of Orthodoxy in America." This rabbi had agreed to lecture at the synagogue only on condition that an opaque *mehitzah* be set up in the room, completely screening the women from his view. At the Beginners' Service for several Saturdays before and after this event, this opaque *mehitzah* was the subject of much heated discussion. Deborah, who frequently brought up questions having to do with women's roles in the religion, was outraged about the women having to be invisible to this rabbi. Rabbi Buchwald justified the visiting rabbi's requirement:

> They have taken an additional restriction upon themselves as a way of surviving in this hostile environment. This culture intrudes upon us so much in every way that we have to take additional restrictions upon ourselves to ensure that it doesn't engulf us. The Hasidic position is preferable to what goes on in our society, which is that you go to a cocktail party and end up in bed with someone else's wife. So by setting up *mehitzah*s for public gatherings, they are not subject to that temptation. This is the basis for an incredible statement Rabbi Riskin [the founding rabbi of the synagogue] made before he moved to Israel—he said that in order for Orthodoxy to survive in this country, they would have to build ghettos, that it wouldn't survive otherwise [because] the culture is too overwhelming.

A woman asked, "But Rabbi, don't we have self-control?" He responded:

> We have no self-control. Billions of dollars are spent on weight reduction each year in our society because people can't control themselves. In our society people have no control. Their palate controls them. Their sexual urges.

The rabbis of this community were highly conscious of the dangers weak boundaries could pose to the group's survival. They could appreciate why other groups of traditional Jews employed more extreme boundary-creating mechanisms—participating in the larger culture might threaten the integrity of the traditional way of life. Rabbi Buchwald was aware of that danger and therefore was occasionally ambivalent about the wisdom of modern Orthodoxy's openness to the secular society. In an interview quoted in a *New York Times Magazine* article on the revival of Orthodoxy in the United States, he challenged the premise of modern Orthodoxy: the idea that it was possible to participate in the wider society and still maintain a demanding religious commitment.

> Some well-intentioned [very liberal] Orthodox Jews . . . make it in the business place, move to the Five Towns or Scarsdale [wealthy suburbs of New York City] with every idea of remaining committed. But they find themselves integrating into the secular world at a dizzying pace. Off goes the *yarmulke* [skullcap], up come the island vacations where they compromise on *kashrut* and don't go to *shul*. Their two worlds have merged, but at the expense of Orthodoxy. And what will happen to their children? How Jewish will they be? How will they be Jewish? Confrontation with modernity theoretically strengthens Judaism, but now is not the time for it. We are in a state of siege. The outside environment is pernicious. We need higher walls, stronger shelters, and more committed Jews in order to reduce the threat of Jewish extinction in America.[3]

But even while this rabbi made such dramatic statements about the need for observant Jews to drastically reduce their contact with the outside environment, the teachings in this community (in his classes and services as well) actually supported various contemporary attitudes and values alongside the traditional religious worldview. This ambivalence toward the wider society—the push and pull, attraction and resistance—provided a clue to some of the complexity, difficulty, and ambiguity of maintaining a "modern Orthodox" approach to Judaism. The individuals in this community, including the rabbis, were caught between two worlds. Thus, the rabbis' teachings on religious observance and their attitudes toward contemporary culture revealed their simultaneous attempts to uphold and challenge the norms of the wider society. They engaged in scathing critiques of modern society even while admiring some of its most deeply held values, such as the importance of the individual, freedom of choice, and material and professional success.

BAIS CHANA

Physical Encapsulation

Many of the beliefs the women were taught during their socialization at Bais Chana radically challenged the assumptions of the dominant society. The insularity of the group allowed it to establish a tightly knit community that served as the social base within which its particular vision of reality was made plausible. Because the Lubavitch way of life required even greater "deviation" from secular culture than did that of the modern Orthodox community, the socialization process demanded much more effective insulation of newcomers from the wider society.[4]

At Bais Chana the recruits were physically removed from the mainstream society to a much greater extent than were the *ba'alot teshuvah* at Lincoln Square Synagogue. To attend the session at Bais Chana, the women had flown from their hometowns. The geographic isolation acted as a strong mechanism of renunciation. Additionally, attending Bais Chana already required a great deal more commitment on the part of the recruits than did walking into a neighborhood synagogue for a class or service. Once the women were at Bais Chana, the daily routines were so full that to participate completely the *ba'alot teshuvah* had to stay within the confines of the setting. Thus, they were physically removed from competing versions of reality.

This process of physical encapsulation, begun at Bais Chana, continued in Crown Heights for women who moved there. Some of the women I met, about 15 percent, had already relocated to Crown Heights prior to attending Bais Chana that summer. About 30 percent of the other women moved there immediately after the summer session ended. In Crown Heights, they were provided by the Lubavitch community with apartments, usually in the homes of members of the community; employment, often within the community; and eventually the introduction of a *ba'al teshuvah* as a potential marriage partner. All of the newcomers' and members' needs were provided within the community: there were local Lubavitch-run and -supervised kosher butchers, grocery stores selling only certified extrakosher dairy products (the Lubavitch require that their milk be boiled during processing at higher temperatures than usual), beauty parlors, clothing stores, and so on. Bais Chana resembled the primary Lubavitch community in also meeting its members' needs within the confines of the household: the "girls" were fed all their meals, taken by bus to do their laundry, brought to the local Y for an all-female swim, and taken out for a day of recreation. Thus, the Lubavitch community was able to minimize the recruits' exposure to alternative belief systems.

Social Encapsulation

The high level of physical encapsulation at Bais Chana supported an intense degree of social encapsulation. Individuals in the Lubavitch community—the novices at Bais Chana as well as the established members in Crown Heights—socialized very little with "outsiders." Their lives were structured in such a way that interaction with outsiders was made extremely difficult. At Bais Chana, the women's contacts with friends and family members who might have opposed the Lubavitch way of life were minimal. The women spent all their time in the Lubavitch setting interacting with the rabbis, other recruits, and the *madrichot*. The novices' intense interactions with the *madrichot* were critical for resocialization into the new worldview.

Rosabeth Kanter's studies of utopian and sectarian communities found that one way "alternative" communities establish insulating boundaries with the wider society is by maintaining a distinctive language and style of dress.[5] In the Lubavitch community, all of the men wore black hats and suits, and the women always wore three-quarter-length-sleeve blouses, long skirts (or dresses), and stockings, even in the extreme heat of summer. The recruits at Bais Chana were encouraged to gradually adopt this style of dress.

Ideological Encapsulation

The Lubavitch's physical and social encapsulating mechanisms were supported and reinforced by ideological commitment mechanisms. According to Rosabeth Moss Kanter, successful utopian communities establish clear boundaries with the outside, developing a language that conceives of the group's way of life positively and that of the wider society negatively. Such groups shut out the wider society as much as possible by eliminating many avenues through which it can intrude. Newspapers are generally not read, nor are national holidays celebrated.

The women at Bais Chana were cut off from the wider society in just these ways. National holidays such as July Fourth were not noted or celebrated, there were no newspapers or radios in the house, and there was strong cross-boundary control—novices did not leave the setting very much to interact with the wider society. The community functioned as an enclave that minimized its recruits' and members' exposure to the wider society.

The physical and social commitment mechanisms at Bais Chana were reinforced by the rabbis' declarations that contemporary society was in a state of chaos, turmoil, and confusion and that Lubavitch Hasidism provided the remedy. As Rabbi Friedman told his class early in the summer session:

> This is not a holy world. If you live in this world you're bound to mess up, to get unholy. . . . This is a time of extraordinary darkness, in which we don't even know right from wrong. So we need the extraordinary light of the Tanya to show us the way.

Overall, however, Rabbi Friedman devoted a surprisingly small amount of time to highlighting and excoriating the evils of the outside society. Whereas at Lincoln Square Synagogue the beginners' rabbi used nearly every class and every Beginners' Service as an occasion to lash out at the secular culture, at Bais Chana this topic was not a major focus of the rabbi's teachings. The only aspect of contemporary life whose disorganization Rabbi Friedman repeatedly referred to was the area of personal relationships (which, as we saw in the previous chapter, was a central focus of his teachings). One morning he drove this point home to the class:

> People's lives are being devastated because of the confusion in their personal relationships. With all the good intentions in the world we're ruining ourselves, we're hurting ourselves, we're scarring ourselves. The emphasis on materialism and things outside the family was so overdone, so exaggerated, that the inner family, the inner workings, was completely neglected.

On another day he stressed similar ideas about the devastation of personal relationships between women and men. He was discussing the alienation from their own true natures experienced by people caught up in the normlessness of contemporary society. He referred to contemporary society as "decadent" and said that the real index of this decadence was that contemporary men and women did not seem to understand what sex was and were uncomfortable with their sexuality. He mockingly mimicked an imagined conversation: "Do you know what the truth is?" "No, I don't know. Leave me alone. I'm not interested." "Well," Rabbi Friedman said,

> that's a little decadence. But when you no longer know what man, woman, is, that's real decadence. . . . That's when Rome ended. When they forgot what a man and woman are. A society that needs sex therapists is finished. It's the end of the line.

Yet, as we have seen, it was the Lubavitch community that was much more concerned with attempting to reverse contemporary norms. Why, then, would their leaders spend less time criticizing the wider society than did the rabbis in the modern Orthodox community? One possible explanation is that the institution already had so many effective boundary-creating devices that this particular one was less important. At Lincoln Square Synagogue, the newcomers might have come to services and classes, but otherwise they remained immersed on a daily basis in the secular society. At Bais Chana, recruits were effectively segregated from the wider society. Thus, the women who attended could be presumed to agree with the rabbi about the "corruptness" of contemporary culture, so he did not need to emphasize this theme to such a great extent.

Rabbi Friedman did, however, devote a great deal of time to challenging contemporary norms in male-female relationships. A possible reason for this emphasis was that within this setting, the resocialization of the women into the community's conception of Jewish mother and wife was a major focus of the teachings. Thus, the rabbi's attempts to convert the women required denouncing contemporary norms and patterns and presenting the Hasidic alternative.

Just as the rabbis at Lincoln Square Synagogue found that their particular stance toward modernity confronted them with a characteristic dilemma—they would sometimes find themselves simultaneously upholding and resisting the norms of contemporary society—the resocializing agents at Bais Chana, too, faced some distinctive tensions. Their worldview and way of life more consistently and effectively shielded members from the claims of competing commitment demands than did the socialization attempts at Lincoln Square Synagogue. But Bais Chana's strong boundary-creating devices effectively limited the community's appeal exclusively to women who were more available for a radical transformation of their lives. Thus, the stronger the group's boundaries were, the greater was the chance at complete transformation, but only for a more limited group of people.

STAGES IN THE CONVERSION PROCESS

The varying degrees and mechanisms of encapsulation in the two communities made them each attractive to women with different degrees of readiness to radically alter their lives. Because the women who came to Lincoln Square Synagogue were much more invested in mainstream society—they had their own professions, apartments, and established friendships with secular Jews and non-Jews—they were less available for intensive resocialization. The women who came to Bais Chana, in contrast, were less invested and less firmly rooted in the mainstream society, and therefore they were more available for a dramatic transformation.

Given the nature of Judaism as a religion—it is more oriented to observance of law than to theology—changes in the women's *behavior*, rather than beliefs, were the most significant aspects of their religious conversion. These behavioral changes included strictly observing the Sabbath, following the laws of kashrut, and even changing sexual behavior to conform to the community's norm of no physical contact with men before marriage. "Conversion" to Orthodoxy involved no professions of faith or testimonials; rather, it comprised an accretion of observances. Within the Lubavitch community, there was the additional ideological commitment of accepting the Rebbe, which meant adopting the community's belief that the Rebbe was the leader of the Jewish people of this generation and the major religious counselor. The newcomers had to learn to ask him all of their religious as well as personal and business questions.

The socialization processes at both institutions in this study followed a model that has been articulated by Arthur Greil and David

Rudy in their study of commitment processes in Alcoholics Anonymous.[6] For both groups of women, behavioral changes occurred first, often simultaneously with the social changes, and then ideological commitment followed.

Not surprisingly, all three types of change involved in commitment occurred much more slowly among the women at Lincoln Square Synagogue. The interaction of this setting, with its relatively loose boundaries and weak mechanisms of social control, and the women who came there seeking to supplement rather than transform their lives, was conducive to a slow process of change. At Lincoln Square Synagogue the *ba'alot teshuvah* adopted an "experimental" attitude, slowly testing out the group and deciding over time whether to stay. John Lofland and Norman Skovond, in their analysis of the variety of conversion "motifs," describe experimental conversion as occurring when religious identity, behavior, and worldview are transformed quite tentatively and slowly.

> Experimental conversions involve relatively low degrees of social pressure to participate since the recruit takes on a "try-it-out" posture. The actual transformation of identity, behavior, and world view called conversion takes place over a relatively prolonged period.[7]

Although several of the Bais Chana women also revealed an experimental attitude in their initial approach to the community, the large majority were relatively quick to adapt their behavior to suit the community's norms. The accounts of the Lincoln Square women indicated much more hesitation and resistance.

One reason that the women at Lincoln Square were slower to change their lives was that they were already rooted, at least somewhat comfortably, in the secular world. They expressed fear that if they were to change their behavior very quickly, they might lose their friendships and relationships with family members. The decision to adopt the kosher laws was highlighted in particular as an extremely difficult commitment to undertake. Many of the women I met had been involved in the synagogue for several months, a year, and even longer and had not yet taken the basic step of koshering their kitchens. Stephanie, for example, attended the synagogue for more than a year and a half before she made the commitment to have a kosher home. She described her hesitations as follows:

> The part that I find the hardest is the idea of the food and beyond that what it symbolizes in terms of the separation from the rest of my life because my life to this date has been involved with many Gentile people. So the greatest problem that I have is the idea of separation. Intellectually I understand that the whole thing is structured to keep you together, to keep us from being assimilated. I understand that it's the only way that the thing will survive, and yet, philosophically, I object. Because what it seems to me, and to other people as well, to be saying is, well, "If I don't want to be with you, then I think I'm better than you." I object to the idea that if I were really true to this thing I would become more isolated from those people. I don't want to be separated. And yet, even in saying "these people," I have admitted to you that I have begun to see a separation.

Stephanie's remarks illuminate the ways in which behavioral and social changes were necessarily related in this conversion process. By adopting the laws of Judaism, such as becoming kosher and not traveling on Shabbat, the *ba'alat teshuvah* gradually but inevitably had to change the people with whom she shared her time. These transformations could be particularly difficult for family members to accept. Stephanie's commitment to attend Saturday services, for example, led to some difficulties with the members of her family. Because they lived several hours away, her weekend visits now began Saturday evenings rather than midday on Saturday. Her parents were not pleased with the new arrangement:

> They have seen that just in terms of the way time is structured, that I want to be in the synagogue a lot, it takes me away from them, and they don't like it. They see it as a threat.

Despite this resistance, however, Stephanie slowly began to take on the various observances:

> We [a group of young adults from the Beginners' Service] had Shabbos lunch at the rabbi's house. He lives on the third floor and we walked up his stairs and when I left I walked down his stairs. And when I got into my own building, I walked up the stairs. It was a conscious decision to walk up the stairs to continue the experience.

When I got into the apartment, I turned on the light and it felt funny. Now, I continue to walk up the stairs, but I also continue to turn on lights. I use my hair dryer Saturday mornings. They can't ask you not to wash your hair and use a hair dryer. Anyway, the more education I got on the subject, and the more I shared the experience with people, the more entrenched I became, so that I don't have a feeling of "Oh damn, I can't do so and so on Shabbos."

This quotation illustrates how behavioral changes often take place first in the context of participating with other people; changes in feelings follow.

The women at Lincoln Square did not radically change their lives in a short amount of time, nor did they have an intense "conversion experience," a moment of decisive and sudden realization that this was the true path. As Ellen said:

I went for over a year and I finally decided to kosher my house after talking about it for quite a while. I wanted to do this so then I could invite people over. But I never quite made a decision to abide by all the laws and do everything that is expected.

Stephanie, too, reported on the absence of a clear-cut moment of transformation:

I don't remember a moment when I just said, "This is for me." But once I got involved with David [a man in Beginners' Service], it helped us both to accelerate since we were doing Shabbat together.

THE WOMEN AT BAIS CHANA

Although a few of the Lubavitch women's accounts revealed a process of "experimental conversion" similar to that described by the women at Lincoln Square Synagogue, the majority recounted experiences of rapid and sudden transformations. Behaviorally, some of the changes were already made simply by the women's presence at the institute: they were fed kosher food, and Sabbath was observed, as were the other Jewish holidays. Socially, they were isolated from the wider society, so that the behavioral and social changes took place simultaneously and in a more organic fashion. For example, Beth noted that after she had been at Bais Chana for three days she had already decided to change her mode of dress to conform with the Lubavitch norms: "I wrote to my

mother and asked her to send me stamps and postcards and a
laundry bag and money and blouses, size 38–40, midarm length
sleeves, very modest neckline."

These changes in the details of how the women lived their daily
lives were actually some of the most profound aspects of their
transformation to Orthodoxy. Rivka described how, much to her
own surprise, after spending just a few Shabbosim in a religious
community, she was no longer comfortable violating the Sabbath.
She described her great discomfort when, after these few weeks of
Sabbath observance, she spent the day with secular friends engaging in ordinary activities.

> I went there and I knew it was Shabbos. We went to the pool.
> And it freaked me out how weird it felt to be in a bathing suit. And
> then, I went into the bathroom, [and] there was no toilet paper
> ripped. [Orthodox Jews do not tear or cut anything, including toilet
> paper, on the Sabbath.] That I should feel crazy for ripping a piece
> of toilet paper on Shabbos? So what! Who cares! Twenty years I
> ripped a piece of toilet paper on Shabbos! And then I was in B'nai
> Brak [a religious town outside of Tel Aviv] for three Shabbosim, and
> it makes me feel strange that I'm ripping a piece of toilet paper! How
> bizarre that is. And then we took the bus before Shabbos ended and
> I knew it was before Shabbos ended and that was the end. By then
> I was miserable: why did I come here for the weekend? I should
> have just gone where I was content, where I knew I would be happy
> in celebrating Shabbos. That particular Shabbos obviously said a lot
> to me. It told me that the feelings that I wanted to make those
> commitments now was totally right. I just knew it was right; it was
> time, obviously.

Most of the women at Bais Chana described a similar decisive
moment when they realized that this was the path they had to
follow. Tamar described her initial encounter with the Lubavitch as
follows:

> I remember when I went to Chabad house in [my hometown]. . . .
> I met people similar to myself and a whole world opened up. And in
> a span of about a week I knew that this is where I had to be. That this
> was it. Anything else would again have been a procrastination. And
> I was tired. I was emotionally and physically drained from the
> searching. And I said this is it. This is where you should be. This is
> where you should learn, study. . . . I was burnt out, you know.
> What was I going to turn back to? To what? Music? Art? The uni-
> versity? It was dead.

The Lubavitch women did not display the same resistance expressed by the women at Lincoln Square partly, I imagine, because they felt they had less to lose and more to gain in radically changing their lives. To reinforce to themselves and others the value of changing their behavior and social circles so rapidly, these women described the dramatic improvements in all aspects of their lives that followed their contact with the Lubavitch. Several women told me of going through very hard times and struggling with difficult issues—such as fear of an unwanted pregnancy or excessive use of drugs—which suddenly cleared up as soon as they got involved with Orthodox Judaism. Naomi related these experiences:

> When I got into this my friends would try to get me to smoke dope with them, and it was very strange how much I've changed. And my grades went up. . . . Everything just zoomed. And I was getting really better with the drugs. Before I was taking coke and I was going to all different kinds of parties and like it was really sick and everything was going wrong. Everything you could, like with guys and everything. Things that I didn't want to happen happened. And things like that. Something happened with this guy and I was scared that I wasn't going to get something that you get on the month, you know, but then when I went to this Lubavitch girl's house for Shabbos; as soon as I got to her house everything went positive. When I got there good news came [laugh].

Rachel Stein also described the improvements in her life that followed her "conversion" to Orthodoxy:

> Since I've been religious everything that was wrong has been starting to go my way a little bit. My mother is getting better, my grandmother is getting better, I'm not so confused, I know where I'm going. I don't do drugs anymore. . . . I made good friends who care. When I pray to God my prayers are answered.

Although Lincoln Square Synagogue and Bais Chana had similar goals—the resocialization of secular Jewish women to Orthodoxy—their distinct ways of being "Orthodox" had significant consequences for the processes of change the women experienced. The Lubavitch worldview was more "deviant" from the dominant culture than was that of the modern Orthodox community. Thus, the Lubavitch socialization process involved the construction of stronger boundaries—physical, social, and ideological—with the secular world than were required at Lincoln Square Synagogue.

The Lubavitch appealed to women like Beth who had a greater need for structure and were more readily available to change their lives. Lincoln Square Synagogue, in contrast, appealed to women who, like Stephanie, were fairly well established in the secular world. Thus, the Lubavitch women's experience of conversion was more sudden, dramatic, and far-reaching than was the more "experimental" approach to conversion adopted by the women at Lincoln Square Synagogue.

8

On Women and Religious Traditions
in Modern U.S. Society

The two central themes in this book—women's nature and role in the social order and the place of religion in secular society—have been in the forefront of social discourse in industrial societies for the past one hundred fifty years. Recent structural changes in women's roles and signs of religious resurgence have resulted in a revitalization of these concerns in the late-twentieth-century United States and elsewhere around the globe. A close examination of a particular case in which these issues converge—that of *ba'alot teshuvah*—allows us to see more general stresses and strains in the culture. Although few women in our society choose to search for fulfillment in Orthodox Jewish communities, the concerns of the *ba'alot teshuvah* are common nonetheless. Many women in our society face similar difficulties in finding husbands and desirable models for nuclear families, puzzle about the place of family and work in a woman's life, and express more generalized needs for certainty and fulfillment. Similarly, although these Orthodox Jewish institutions are marginal, they are confronted by those same features of modernity that challenge all contemporary religious communities. Therefore, they, too, must find strategies for responding to these challenges and constructing new forms of religious worlds in the context of modern secular society.

This book has explored two diverse instances of "return" to Orthodox Judaism by contemporary U.S. women: a modern Orthodox and a Lubavitch Hasidic. I have traced the two groups of women's parallel but quite distinctive journeys as they entered Lincoln Square Synagogue or Bais Chana, interacted with the rabbis and other resocializing agents, learned the distinctive way of life of that variety of Orthodoxy, and gradually began to adopt its practices.

The comparisons between the two groups of women and the religious institutions they entered have been a central focus of this book. Modernity is not uniform in its impact on individuals or institutions. Even within the seemingly small worlds of newly Orthodox Jewish women, we are able to see quite a range of women's and religion's responses to the conditions of modernity. The *ba'alot teshuvah* and the rabbis at Lincoln Square Synagogue and Bais Chana were self-consciously constructing religious worlds in the context of modern secular society. Therefore, the rabbis were forced to articulate in clear terms their central concerns, their worldviews, and the alternative way of life they were offering. The women, who were engaged in a process of evaluating their needs against what they saw the institutions offering, likewise were in a position of having to make explicit for themselves and others the issues that loomed largest. A close examination of the details of women's religious resocialization in these two unusual groups provides the opportunity to reflect on more general social issues such as the questions about women's roles and about how religious communities respond to the secularizing forces of modernity.

WOMEN AND RELIGION IN THE CONTEMPORARY UNITED STATES

The decision to explore Orthodox Jewish ways of life represents one possible solution to widespread questions about women's proper roles. The structural changes in U.S. society in the past twenty-five years, in particular the changing demographics of women's educational, occupational, marital, and childbearing patterns, have occasioned a debate in our culture about women's nature and social roles similar to the late-nineteenth-century "woman question" that followed the Industrial Revolution. Within our society there are a wide variety of competing definitions and prescriptions for women's roles, far more than there are for men's roles. Traditionalists clash with women's liberationists, and even within the various feminist communities there are numerous alternative visions. Women may now choose among the numerous

variants of the "radical" solution (which creates alternative structures of meaning outside the framework of mainstream society),
the liberal feminist approach (which seeks equality in the public
sphere), and the "traditional" model (which emphasizes the centrality of woman's place in the home).

A popular contemporary image of womanhood is that of the
"superwoman" who excels at her career and manages both a home
and a family, all with aplomb and grace. The ideal of the modern
woman who can "have it all," however, has begun to fade with
women's growing realization that fulfilling the competing demands
of these multiple roles is no simple task. In the past two decades we
have read reports of professional women who opt to pursue their
careers and forego marriage and childbearing. We have also heard
of career women who decide in their mid-thirties to give up the
juggling act and devote themselves primarily to their children.
Recently, the media have also publicized cases of highly successful
women in their forties who have suddenly shifted their focus and
tried to become pregnant. In the 1980s it became clearer that even
though women had indeed made significant advances in the educational, occupational, and political spheres, women earned only 70
percent of what men earned, and their career paths were still often
stymied by overt and subtle forms of discrimination.[1]

The women featured in this book never intended to become
career women. Although the respondents at Lincoln Square Synagogue were professionals, almost none thought of her job as a
career. Their work did not provide them with a central defining
core to their identities. These women, who grew up in the 1950s
and 1960s, had been brought up with the expectation that they
would get married and raise families. Although they pursued college educations and professional work, two-thirds of them did not
have graduate degrees. Their intent had been to subordinate work
to family demands once they had children. When these plans did
not work out, they drifted into the lives of single professional
women. Yet this group of women, who to some extent had "made
it" in the world of work, found their lives too empty. Instead, they
sought to create a new sense of self within communities of memory
that might also help them establish themselves in nuclear families.

The women who came to Bais Chana also did not define themselves in terms of their work. Most of them lacked either the re-

sources to pursue careers or the interest to do so. Even though they felt that many people in contemporary society looked down on women's roles of wife and mother, this was the life they were seeking.

Both groups of women were attracted to a religious community that seemed to suit their needs and the choices they had already made. For the women at Lincoln Square these choices included investing in education, establishing themselves in apartments, and maintaining independent lives. At Lincoln Square this degree of independence was normative; joining the religious community did not require that the women give up the autonomy they had so successfully established. In contrast, the women at Bais Chana commonly arrived there in search of the basic structures of a stable life. Most of these women felt that exercising their choices in modern society—such as the free expression of their sexuality—had resulted in great problems for them. Therefore, they were searching for one all-encompassing way of life within a community that would completely take charge of their lives.

Although both groups of women found Orthodox Judaism appealing precisely because it offered a conception of femininity in which women's roles as wives and mothers were honored and seen as central, each of these women was attracted to the Orthodox vision of Jewish womanhood that best suited her life circumstances. The modern Orthodox rabbis articulated a definition of femininity that prioritized women's roles in the home but also allowed for women's seeking secondary fulfillment in other spheres. This conception meshed with the situations of the *ba'alot teshuvah* at Lincoln Square Synagogue, who described themselves as being "settled" at work but wishing to develop a role and identity at home. The Lubavitch rabbis, in contrast, offered a definition of femininity that focused exclusively on women's roles as wives and mothers. This vision was attractive to the Lubavitch women, who sought one all-embracing role. In the context of a differentiated society, these two diverse groups of women were able to seek out those religious communities that validated their life choices and gave them meaning.

The concerns highlighted by these two groups of women are in fact widespread. Newspaper articles, numerous books, and radio and TV talk shows all feature stories on some of the central issues discussed by the *ba'alot teshuvah*: the difficulties for single women in finding male partners in the appropriate age range who are willing to make commitments, the question of how to figure out the proper place of work and family within a woman's identity, and how contemporary women struggle to balance the various demands of work and family. The women in this book described their attempts to find a fulfilling way of life. They also articulated their struggles with such questions as, What is the true nature of femininity? What should be women's primary roles? What are the appropriate gender identities for men and women? How, as women, can they construct a sense of self and place in the world that would achieve the proper balance between work and family?

The need to make choices about priorities for work and family is a problem more common to women than to men in our culture. Although many men in our society spend time and take pleasure in caring for their children, they rarely express concern about whether they can have both satisfying work and family lives. That this concern remains central to the women in this book, as well as to many other women, reflects the persistence in our society of social structural and ideological features that define women primarily by their childrearing functions. Joining a religious community in which women are placed squarely in the home is thus one way of avoiding the tensions and difficulties that face the women who challenge the system by attempting to have both successful careers and families.

RELIGIOUS INSTITUTIONS' STRATEGIES FOR SURVIVAL IN MODERNITY

For Lincoln Square Synagogue and Bais Chana to attract newcomers to their Orthodox worlds, their representatives had to find ways of reaching out into the wider society and recruiting among the contemporary generation of secular Jews. The most important strategy for accomplishing this goal was to present what these representatives claimed to be a traditional religious way of life in terms that clearly reflected engagement with modern culture. The Orthodox religious groups reinforced their credibility to new recruits by emphasizing the longevity of the tradition. In contrast to so many of the recently constructed available means for finding oneself—the various self-help groups popular in large cities and imported Eastern religions such as the Hare Krishnas and the Moonies—the rabbis claimed that Orthodox Judaism was true because it had survived the test of time. Its validity and strength rested on the fact that it was ancient and unchanging.

But the leaders at Lincoln Square and Bais Chana actually introduced modern features into their interpretation of the religious tradition. They reached out into the modern society and incorporated elements of it in order to reconstruct the tradition and make it appealing to modern secular Jews. The rabbis and representatives of these communities engaged a great deal with the secular world. They knew about feminism, evolutionary theory, and contemporary psychology, and they used this knowledge to enhance their communities' appeal. Nevertheless, they staked their legitimacy on their claims to traditional religious authority. In the context of a constantly changing society, a religion presented as ancient and unchanging could indeed be appealing. The religious worlds they constructed represented two distinct types of new religious forms whose validity was reinforced by reference to the weight and authority of tradition.

Although both institutions legitimated their authority by emphasizing their traditionalism, the meaning of tradition was interpreted and reconstructed differently in each religious community. The representatives of Lincoln Square Synagogue and Bais Chana each devised their own strategies for creating a religious world in the face of the challenges of modern society. They developed unique approaches to contemporary secular society that ranged along a continuum from accommodation to resistance. Their different degrees of engagement with the larger society affected all aspects of the religious worlds they constructed, such as their teachings, forms of social organization, and types of religious authority.

In this book I have analyzed each group's responses to modernity through a close examination of the ways they dealt with several challenging features of contemporary life: differentiation, pluralism, individualism, rationalization, and the changing of women's roles. What we have seen is that instead of being eroded by these difficult features of modernity, each institution found a way to directly deal with them and utilized them to its own advantage in attracting new recruits.

The religious leaders at Lincoln Square Synagogue created a mode of existence in the modern secular society by constructing a religious world that accommodated many features of contemporary life. The representatives of this community did not resist differentiation, pluralism, rationalization, or the changing of women's roles. Instead, the rabbis openly acknowledged all these features of modern life and incorporated them into their presentation of Orthodoxy. For example, they offered newcomers an Orthodox religious way of life in which differentiation was still possible. The synagogue made available numerous opportunities for newcomers and members to adopt the religion as the central focus of their lives. But the rabbis also acknowledged and accepted the recruits' commitment to a continued differentiation of their lives into occupational, residential, social, and religious spheres.

Similarly, the rabbis minimized the threat of pluralism by acknowledging that Orthodox Judaism was indeed one choice among many available options. The women who came to this community had exercised their choices and constructed reasonably stable lives within the freedoms of modern society. Thus, instead of negating the idea of choice and challenging the dominant individualism and functional rationality of our culture, the rabbis appealed to their urbane, secular audience by actually emphasizing mainstream middle-class U.S. values: freedom, choice, and the power of reason.

The leaders and members of the Lubavitch community, in contrast, interacted to produce a contemporary Orthodox world that attempted in many ways to resist the encroachment of modernity. They created an alternative to the differentiation of life in secular society by establishing structures in which all recruits' and members' needs were met within the confines of the community. The rabbi challenged pluralism and individualism and appealed to women who had gotten "in trouble" making the wrong choices by asserting that individuals were not really free to make their own life-shaping decisions. Instead, their essential selves were predetermined. He negated the element of choice in the women's attraction to Orthodoxy and instead asserted that this transformation was inherent in, and demanded by, the women's own inner beings. Thus, the representatives of this community vigorously opposed rationalization: they did not present the women with rationales for the various observances but instead claimed that they were to be followed simply because God so commanded.

The particular approaches to tradition and modernity in the two communities were especially visible in the rabbis' teachings about gender. At Lincoln Square Synagogue they accommodated contemporary feminist ideals by presenting a religious definition of women's roles that supported women's activity in the workplace, if the woman desired it, even while emphasizing the importance of women's roles in the home.

In contrast, the Lubavitch teachers' positions on sexuality, women's roles, marriage, and the family resisted many contemporary liberalizing trends. The teachers downplayed the importance of romantic love as the basis for successful marital relationships and instead promoted the women's commitment to the proper fulfillment of their roles. The rabbis taught that women, by nature, were meant to be exclusively mothers and wives and derogated the feminist emphasis on women's career advancement. Nevertheless, their arguments against feminism revealed some knowledge of and engagement with it, a necessary consequence of their existing and attracting newcomers within the modern secular society.

The attention devoted in these Orthodox communities to questions about women's roles, gender definitions and norms, and the nuclear family was a reflection of the centrality of these concerns in the general culture. The rabbis were well aware of contemporary trends and capitalized on them by offering solutions to these most difficult dilemmas.

The religious communities in this study each claimed to offer one type of solution—a "traditional" one—to the issues that were problematic for the *ba'alot teshuvah:* the need for clarity about gender, guidelines for nuclear family life, and, for the women at Bais Chana, an end to sexual exploitation. Many recent studies of religious communities have also found that the provision of "traditional" solutions to these modern dilemmas was a significant dimension of their appeal.[2] These groups offered models of gender, sexuality, and family that competed with those prescribed by most feminists. Instead of the feminist program of broader gender definitions and options, sexual liberation, an emphasis on careers, and the acceptance of a variety of family patterns, Orthodox Judaism proposed clearly circumscribed gender norms, the control of sexuality, assistance in finding partners, and explicit guidelines for nuclear family life.

Both religious communities offered their own version of a distinct alternative to the liberal feminist goal of equality: that of equity, the idea of separate but equal roles. The religious groups were attractive to some contemporary women precisely because they legitimated the women's desires for the "traditional" identity of wives and mothers in nuclear families. The rabbis told the recruits that woman's role was highly valued in Orthodoxy and that woman's primary place in the home, where a majority of the rituals took place, gave her special status within the Jewish religious world. In addition, Orthodox Judaism's emphasis on the nuclear family and women's place in it actually provided the women with an additional benefit: they gained support for a conception of men's roles that placed great stress on men's involvement in the home and with their families.

Although the conception of women's roles in these two Orthodox communities was conventional, their vision of masculinity and prescriptions for male roles were actually modern. Achieving men's increased involvement in the family has been a goal of many feminists. The Lubavitch and modern Orthodox attempts to construct "traditional" religious responses to contemporary gender ambiguity reveal the significant influence of modern social norms.

Religion acts as a mediator between the public and the private spheres. In modern society we are often taught to seek a great deal of our satisfaction within the private sphere because the public realm has become too institutionalized and bureaucratic. But we are simultaneously surrounded by signs of trouble in the private sphere, such as family violence, the rising rates of divorce, drug addiction, and the difficulty of maintaining stable relationships. Even though modern individuals seek solace within private life, many of them find that the private realm has become fraught with ambiguity and emptiness. The women profiled in this book found it hard to create the kinds of family lives they wanted. They sought an institutional context that would legitimate their desires and help to achieve them. The Orthodox Jewish communities represented here, and other religious groups like them, thus offer solutions, difficult to find elsewhere, to the dilemmas of modern life.

CONVERSION

In this book I have analyzed the process of resocialization to Orthodox Judaism from the perspectives of both the women and the religious institutions, in contrast to most recent studies of conversion that typically focus more on the institutional resocialization mechanisms. The women's conversion experiences in each setting were shaped by their own life experiences and by several important features of the religious institutions, such as the nature of their boundaries with the wider society.

The women attracted to Lincoln Square Synagogue differed initially in significant ways from those attracted to Bais Chana: they had attended universities and obtained professional positions, they lived in comfortable apartments, and they had found reasonably successful ways of fitting into the secular society. Most of the women at Bais Chana, in contrast, were not as securely established in the world. They had not attended college, did not hold professional positions, and for the most part did not live on their own. Many of them lived with parents from whom they were still struggling to differentiate themselves. These differences shaped the nature of the women's search and their availability for radical transformations. The Lincoln Square women sought to supplement lives that were basically stable and in order; the Bais Chana women, in contrast, were embarked on a quest for an all-encompassing way of life.

The women's divergent situations within modern society shaped the kind of Orthodox Jewish community to which they were attracted. The modern Orthodox and Lubavitch institutions each had a distinct form of social organization that reflected varying levels of engagement with the larger society. At Lincoln Square Synagogue, the community's greater openness to modernity was reflected in the more permeable boundaries it established with the secular world. Newcomers were free to carry on most aspects of their lives outside the confines of the synagogue community. In contrast, at Bais Chana, the Lubavitchers' resistance to secular society resulted in their encapsulating the recruits during and after the resocialization process. In order to resocialize the women into this all-pervading way of life, the resocialization process demanded the establishment of more stringent boundaries with the secular society. In addition, at Bais Chana the authority and knowledge of the Rebbe and even of Rabbi Friedman, the teacher of the *ba'alot teshuvah*, were seen as absolute, thereby setting up a more authoritarian structure in which conformity was established and maintained.

The interactions between the women, who entered these communities with divergent sets of experiences and needs for structure in their lives, and the religious worlds as presented to them by the representatives of Lincoln Square Synagogue and Bais Chana produced a distinct process of change at each institution. The women at Lincoln Square adopted an "experimental" attitude toward their conversion, slowly testing out the group and deciding over time whether to stay. Consequently, many women at Lincoln Square remained involved in this community for months, sometimes even years, without fully adapting the basic norms of the community, such as kashrut and Sabbath observance. The women at Bais Chana, in contrast, rapidly began to change their behavior, and their accounts included more descriptions of rapid and sudden transformations that led to improvements in all areas of their lives.

The clear differences between the conversion experiences of the women at each setting highlights the need for a new model of conversion, one that directs researchers to study both individual experiences and institutional characteristics simultaneously. Conversion must be reconceptualized as a dynamic, interactive process shaped as much by institutional resocialization strategies as by the attributes of the converts.

THE IMPACT ON
CONTEMPORARY JUDAISM

Most of the *ba'alot teshuvah* who came to Lincoln Square Synagogue and Bais Chana thought that these communities might offer attractive solutions to some of the common dilemmas of contemporary life. Nevertheless, despite the prevalence of the concerns that shaped these women's quests, I do not expect that Orthodoxy will appeal to enough other secular Jews to form a significant *"ba'al teshuvah* movement." Although membership in the Orthodox communities offered a great deal to these particular groups of women, this solution will not be attractive to all Jews or even to all Jewish women in the same situation as the women portrayed here. The price of joining is too high for most people because of (1) the ritualism of Orthodox Judaism, (2) the marginality and separation involved in adopting this way of life, and (3) the limits set on a person's choice for a partner. In addition, the conventional definitions of gender within Orthodoxy reduces its appeal for women who are devoted to careers and to women and men with feminist perspectives.

In terms of its ritualism, the religious law involves numerous restrictions in the habits of daily life, such as what and where a person eats. Observance of the Sabbath requires radical changes in the rhythm of life because of the ban on work on Friday evenings and Saturdays and the many restrictions on routine daily activities, such as use of the telephone, electricity, and transportation. Ritual observance is time intensive, particularly the requirement of stopping all productive activity for one full day each week. It also can be labor intensive, especially for women, because of the need to prepare in advance special meals for Friday nights and Sabbath lunches.

The Orthodox world is parochial and requires at least some measure (although the degree varies between Orthodox communities) of separation from the recruits' past lives and their friends and families. This separation can be difficult and painful. Many women reported how unhappy their parents were that their daughters were rejecting their upbringing and were seeking a different way of life. Similarly, keeping kosher can result in difficult interactions with family members and friends, such as when the *ba'alei* and *ba'alot teshuva* decline food in others' homes and severely limit options for eating out.

Joining the community also seriously restricts a woman's choice of a marital partner. Given that the demographic data indicate that there are already too few men available for single women in their thirties, many women will not want to further restrict their pool of

potential partners to ritually observant Jewish men. Although joining the religious community increases the likelihood that the men
a woman meets within it will be interested in getting married and
forming families, the absolute numbers of available men will certainly decline.

The influx of *ba'alot* and *ba'alei teshuvah* into Orthodox communities is thus not likely to result in any significant swelling of the
ranks of the Orthodox. Because many individuals who grow up
Orthodox leave the fold (there are no reliable estimates of these
numbers), the net result is at best a zero gain. Nevertheless, the
appeal of traditional rituals, liturgy, and practices has recently occurred in other Jewish denominations as well. Over the past de-
cade there have been numerous newspaper and magazine articles
reporting the increased use of Hebrew in Reform liturgies, some
rise in ritual observance at college Hillels (Jewish student organizations), and other examples of a seeming rise of the appeal of the
traditional, precisely because it is traditional. So the movement of
these women to Orthodoxy, while unique in many ways, is also
part of a more general trend of resurgence of interest in "traditional" religiosity in other Jewish denominations, in numerous
Christian groups, and in Muslim cultures around the globe.

Secularization theorists see the multiplicity of options for religious observance as a sign of the decline of the importance of
religion in the social order. Bryan Wilson and Peter Berger argue
that the modern option of choosing a religious community weak-
ens the seriousness of that commitment because recruits and members can so easily switch allegiances from one day to the next.[3]
Students of contemporary Jewish life and Jewish community leaders similarly worry about the impact on Judaism of the broadening
of options available to Jews. They express concern that in the absence of the overarching dominance of the Judaism of the
shtetlach, the religion will become diluted.[4]

In contrast, those sociologists of religion who do not see religous
decline as inevitable in modern society assert that pluralism can
actually enhance religious vitality. As Mary Jo Neitz concludes in
her book on Charismatic Catholics, their newly adopted way of life
is not threatened by the presence of other options because they
have already taken the competing beliefs into account and have
consciously chosen the Charismatic reality.[5] Similarly, Stephen

Warner suggests that contemporary pluralism and the emphasis on choice do not necessarily weaken religious commitments: people in the United States have always had religious freedom, and they have nevertheless been highly religious.[6] Many scholars of contemporary Judaism argue in parallel fashion that although traditional forms of religious cohesion have declined, other forms have emerged to take their place.[7]

I conclude that although modernity does pose serious challenges to religious ways of life and that religious leaders must develop suitable responses, the pluralization and multiplicity of choices available in the contemporary United States can actually strengthen religious communities. I believe that the specialization of institutions and available options for "being Jewish" brings vitality to modern Jewish life. Contemporary Jews may choose to join a mainstream congregation, one of its smaller subgroups called a *havurah* (literally, group of friends), an independent *havurah*, or a Jewish social action, Zionist, or feminist group; they may emigrate to Israel; or they may even enter specialized settings for learning to be Orthodox. The availability of these options actually increases the range of secular people who might become involved with the religion and opens opportunities for involvement to people who might well remain unaffiliated if the only option was, for example, a sectarian Hasidic community.

INSIGHTS EMERGING FROM
A STUDY OF WOMEN

The large majority of sociological studies of U.S. Jews have been conducted by men. Their research samples have generally consisted of other Jewish men, or if the samples included women and men, the reports rarely distinguish between the women's and men's responses.[8] Although there have been some exceptions to this rule, such as Calvin Goldscheider's *Jewish Continuity and Change* and portions of Herbert Danzger's *Return to Tradition*,[9] there has not yet been any full-length sociological study of Jewish women. Similarly, the sociological literature on religious conversion rarely looks at gender as a central category in the analysis of religious experience.[10] The growth of feminist knowledge in the past two decades, however, has highlighted the gendered nature of all forms of social experience, including the religious. Thus, I conclude by reflecting on the new insights into U.S. Jewish life and the sociological study of religion that can be derived from an exclusive focus on women. Even though some of these ideas involve men and may well apply to them, they have not been visible in studies in which men comprised all, or the majority, of respondents. Here I suggest some modifications in basic concepts and understandings that can arise from a women-centered analysis.

This book has revealed that there are likely to be gender differences in belief in God among Orthodox Jewish women and men. Existing analyses of contemporary Jewish life do not compare women and men on key dimensions of religious belief and practice. Therefore, we have no data on whether and in what ways Jewish women and men relate to God differently.

Nevertheless, we know that religious behavior, like all behavior, is gendered. This is especially the case in an Orthodox Jewish community in which roles and privileges are so sharply distinguished by sex. The extremely high level of agnosticism I found among the women I interviewed at Lincoln Square Synagogue—more than 50 percent of the women were uncertain about their belief in God—is unprecedented in the literature. Samuel Heilman and Steven Cohen's recent book, *Cosmopolitans and Parochials*, was based on a sample of one thousand members of Lincoln Square Synagogue. The authors report a level of 85 percent belief in God among the "centrist" (that is, modern) Orthodox.[11] As we do not know how many of their respondents were male and how many were female, the differences in my findings and theirs about the levels of belief in God in this community might reflect gender differences.

These possibly important distinctions in the religious beliefs of Orthodox Jewish women and men may reflect, and in turn shape, the broad assignations of female and male roles within the world of traditional Judaism. These gender distinctions have not appeared in other studies of contemporary Jewish life in which most or all of the respondents were men. Thus, by beginning with women and comparing their responses to previous findings, I have located a heretofore unexamined dimension of Orthodox Jewish life. We now need a great deal more research exploring gender differences in religious beliefs and experiences among Jews, connecting these distinctions to the related aspects of the Jewish religion and culture, and comparing these findings with those on other religious traditions.

This book has also highlighted the emphasis on the nuclear family as the primary type of interpersonal bond sought by the new recruits. This characteristic might be relevant to other contemporary religious groups as well. As I discussed in chapter 4, the literature on conversion to new religious movements reports that the formation of interpersonal bonds between members and recruits is a central factor in the recruitment of new members. The types of bonds generally described are those of friendship between peers. Some of the literature also describes the search for a substitute family and for a benevolent patriarchal authority. This is reflected in the way members often refer to each other as "brother" or "sister" and to the leader as "father."[12] But almost none of these analyses highlights the formation of a nuclear family as the primary type of interpersonal bond sought by recruits entering contemporary religious movements. The *ba'alot teshuvah* at Bais Chana and Lincoln Square Synagogue came to these institutions with that end clearly in mind. Focusing on their experiences reveals a concern that may be important in many experiences of conversion.

Research that begins with women's experiences—even those of a small minority group—exposes us to more widespread concerns in the culture. By focusing exclusively on women and the issues that were central in their religious resocialization, I was afforded glimpses into several more general social phenomena, such as the concerns that trouble many contemporary women and the variety of ways in which "traditional" religious communities recreate themselves in the modern world. The *ba'alot teshuvah*'s accounts echoed other current reports about the difficulty of satisfying key personal desires, such as those for a partner, a comfortable sense of oneself as a gendered being, and a satisfying family life. The stories of the women at Lincoln Square and Bais Chana make vivid for us how religious groups maintain themselves in the face of the challenges of modernity by reaching out into the world, learning about the important and troubling issues in modern individuals' private lives, and proffering newly reformulated "traditional" religious solutions.

Appendix A:
Interview Guide for
Ba'alot Teshuvah

THE RETURN

How did you come to be interested in Orthodox Judaism?
    context in which it occurred
    what was going on in her life
    source of exposure
    where learned new norms, etc.
    how learned them

Parental response, reaction of "significant others"—family and friends

Background—religious upbringing, education, practices, etc.
    parents' practices
    grandparents
    siblings
    parents' place of birth; work experience

What aspects of this change did/do you experience as the hardest to make?
    The easiest?
    Was it a struggle or easy? Sudden or gradual?

Do you call yourself a *ba'alat teshuvah?*

Did you ever have an experience that you would call a religious experience?
    What form did it take?
    What did you take with you from that experience?
    Did you experience any voices or visions in the course of the change?

What is your sense of God?

Did this feel, to some extent, like a coming home?

Are there, or were there, important role models for you in this transformation?

Are there any books, ideas, or events that influenced you in this path?

DAILY LIVING, LIFE AS AN ORTHODOX JEW

To what extent is your life today a break from the past?

Are there aspects of your life that are unchanged?

What was the most important thing you learned about being Jewish?

What does being Jewish mean to you now? What did it mean before?

What do you like most about the Orthodox way of life? Least?

Are there some things you don't observe now that you want to observe at some point? What prevents you from observing them now?

Are there things about which you have questions?

Have your friendships changed since your involvement with Orthodox Judaism? Your relationships with men?

Who are your three closest friends?

On a daily basis, are you mostly in contact with Orthodox Jews?

Is there a particular community with which you identify?

Do you want to live in an Orthodox neighborhood in the future?

Have your career and/or family plans changed since your involvement? Describe these plans.

Feelings about secular world activities
    movies
    novels
    television
    newspapers
    secular education

Are you interested in helping others to become more religious? In what ways?

Do you think there is a *ba'al teshuvah* movement?

What would you say you "get" out of participating in traditional Jewish life? Are there any ways in which you are dissatisfied with what you get?

What kind of work do you do for a living? Does it mesh easily with your new observance?

(Make sure to get age, marital status, level of education.)

WOMEN'S ROLES AND ISSUES IN JUDAISM

What do you think are the most important issues for women in Judaism?

Has the women's movement of the past twenty years had any impact on Orthodox Judaism? Elaborate.

Do you think there are any differences between women who were brought up Orthodox and those who become Orthodox?
    In terms of their Jewishness?
    In terms of their feelings about women in Judaism?

Feelings about family purity laws?
    From whom and in what context did they learn them?
    Do you (or do you plan to) observe them?
    What are your feelings about, use of birth control?

Sexual practices

Feelings about the distinctions in Orthodoxy between male and female roles, about *mehitzah*.

Feelings about women covering their head.
    If applicable—do you cover your head?
    What meaning does this have for you?

Appendix B:
Interview Guide for Rabbis

What do you think are the major factors that lead a woman to *teshuvah?*

What do you call these women?

What is your goal?

Are you happy if the women end up more observant but not totally *frum,* or is the goal for the women to end up completely observant?

Ask for examples: tell me a story about a situation in which you were successful . . . and one in which you weren't.

How do you know if someone is ready to hear your message?

Do you have a way of telling when the woman has been socialized? Are there a set of indicators you look for?

Can you tell the difference between just learning a new set of behaviors and the internalization of a new identity and set of beliefs? How?

Do you ever wonder about what the women believe? Does it matter?

Do you have any sense of changes in this phenomenon over time—for example, any difference in the women who are doing this now versus the women who did this a few years ago?

Do you see any differenes in the women of different ages who go through this experience?

What do you think are the most important things for a *ba'alat teshuvah* to learn?

What do you teach them first?

What is your sense of the relationship between *ba'alei/ba'alot teshuvah* and the rest of the Orthodox community?

Do you think it's best for the women to adopt Orthodox Jewish practices all at once or one step at a time?

What do you think are the easiest things for the women to change? The hardest?

What do you think is the impact of the women's movement on Orthodox Judaism?

What are the differences between women's and men's roles in the religion?

Are there differences you can see between women and men who become Orthodox?

What do you do with someone who comes to you?

How did you get involved with this work?

Can you give me names of women to interview—both those who've stayed within the fold and those who've moved away from Orthodox Judaism?

Appendix C:
Questionnaire for
Bais Chana Women

July 1983

Guarantee of anonymity: Everything that is written here will be read only only by me. In addition, everyone's identity will be disguised in my report.

1. Name:

2. Address:

3. Phone number:

4. Age:

5. Marital status:

6. Children:

7. National origin:
   Place of birth:
   Place lived most recently:
   If American, please specify first, second, or third generation, etc.

8. Religious upbringing (check the appropriate responses):
   Jewish _____   Other (please specify) _____
   Please specify: Hasidic _____   Orthodox _____
   Conservative _____   Reform _____
   Other (please specify) _____

9. Which of the following religious practices were observed in your home as you were growing up? Indicate your parents' observances with a P under the correct heading.

	Yes	No
a. Mother lit Shabbos candles regularly.	___	___
b. Mother lit Shabbos candles on occasion.	___	___
c. Father made kiddush every Friday night.	___	___
d. Father made kiddush on occasion.	___	___
e. Money was handled on Shabbos.	___	___
f. Traveling was forbidden on Shabbos.	___	___
g. Yom Kippur and Rosh Hashanah were observed (for example, synagogue attendance).	___	___
h. Fasting done on Yom Kippur.	___	___
i. Passover seder was celebrated.	___	___
j. Leavened foods were not eaten on Passover.	___	___
k. Kashrut was strictly observed (separate dishes, pots and pans, a wait of six hours between meat and milk).	___	___
l. Kashrut was moderately observed.	___	___
m. *Cholov Yisroel* was consumed.	___	___

Now please go back through the questions and answer them according to your grandparents' observance, marking an MP for your mother's parents and an FP for your father's parents.

10. Education: What grade of school did you complete?
    Less than 12th
    12th grade
    Some college
    Completed college
    Graduate school
    Degrees?

11. Work experience (describe briefly):

12. What was the extent of your religious education?
    a. Attended yeshiva   No. years _____
    b. Attended Hebrew Day School   No. years _____
    c. Attended Hebrew School   No. years _____
    Number of times per week

13. Have you been involved in any other religious groups before coming to Lubavitch? Please specify which group. What was the extent of your involvement (for example, for how long, nature of commitment)?

14. Were you active in any political, secular, or religious organizations (such as political groups, Jewish youth groups, women's groups, service organizations)? Please specify.

15. How did you hear about Bais Chana?

16. What did you hear about Bais Chana prior to coming?

17. What were your reasons for deciding to come to Bais Chana?

18. How long have you been at Bais Chana? _____ weeks
    Were you ever here before? Please specify.

19. Have you ever been involved with Lubavitch Hasidism before? How did you come into contact with it?

20. If you have been involved with Lubavitch before, what factors were important in your continuing involvement with Lubavitch? Describe the extent of your participation in Lubavitch activities prior to coming to Bais Chana.

21. Have any of your religious observances changed within the past few years? For each observance, indicate the month and year of the change under the heading that applies.

	Do Not Observe at All	Observe to Some Extent	Observe Strictly	Plan to Observe
Shabbos observance	_____	_____	_____	_____
Holiday observance	_____	_____	_____	_____
Davening (daily praying)	_____	_____	_____	_____
Blessings before eating	_____	_____	_____	_____
Nagel vasser (washing hands in morning)	_____	_____	_____	_____
Tzniyus	_____	_____	_____	_____
Kashrut	_____	_____	_____	_____
Family purity (if applicable)	_____	_____	_____	_____

22. What is (or do you anticipate would be) your parents' reaction to your deepening involvement with *Yiddishkeit?*

23. Are there any religious women whom you know and admire? Any religious men?

24. What is your definition of a *ba'al teshuvah?* Do you consider yourself one?

25. Do you believe there is a *ba'al teshuvah* movement?

26. Do you see any connections and/or conflicts between feminism and the *ba'al teshuvah* movement? Between feminism and a traditional Jewish lifestyle?

27. What are your plans and goals for the future? (Please be specific in terms of education, work, marriage, family.) Have your goals and plans changed, or stayed the same, since your involvement with *frum* Judaism?

28. What do you believe is the ideal role for a Jewish woman in today's world?

29. Has your image of womanhood stayed the same or changed as a result of your learning at Bais Chana? Please describe.

30. Do you think Jewish married women should work outside of the home? If so, in what capacity?

31. Have your personal moral standards and/or your involvement in male/female relationships changed since you became involved with *Yiddishkeit?*

32. What is your relationship to the Lubavitcher Rebbe?
    a. Do you write letters to the Rebbe for *beruchos* (blessings)?
    b. Do you sell Sefer Torah letters?
    c. Other:

33. What is the mission of the Lubavitcher Rebbe to the Jewish people?

34. Are you interested in helping others to become more observant? In what ways?

35. Do you think your involvement with (commitment to) *Yiddishkeit* will increase _____ , stay the same _____ , or decrease _____ in the next six months? What about in the distant future?

36. In the past, what sort of people were your close friends? In the present?

37. Do you plan to live in a religious community in the future?

38. Are you willing to participate in a follow-up questionnaire? Yes _____ No _____

Notes

CHAPTER ONE

1. "Stephanie" is a pseudonym for a real woman I met during my research. To protect the anonymity of my respondents, I have changed their names and some of their identifying characteristics. I made a decision, however, to reveal the names of the institutions and their rabbis because each institution is distinct and will be immediately recognizable to people familiar with Orthodox Judaism.

2. Throughout the book, foreign words are defined only at their first appearance in the text. For easy reference, a glossary near the back of the book gives a definition of every foreign word used in the text.

3. Within this community the Sephardi (Spanish and Portuguese) and the Ashkenazi (Eastern European) pronunciations of the Hebrew word for the Sabbath were used interchangeably. In this book I follow this practice in order to give a flavor for the language.

4. The use of the English language plural *s* in Hebrew and Yiddish words is grammatically awkward but commonly practiced in the communities I studied.

CHAPTER TWO

1. Geertz, 1983, p. 58.

2. Precise statistics on the percentages of Jews in each denomination are difficult to obtain because there has not been a national survey since the National Jewish Population Study of 1970–71. The percentages of Jews in each denomination that are reported in this book are the 1987 figures reported by Barry Kusmin, director of the North American Jewish Data Bank, as cited by Wertheimer, 1989, pp. 80–81.

3. I am using the term *conversion* not in the conventional sense, given that nearly all of the women discussed here were Jewish from birth, but to connote a "transformation of self concurrent with a transformation of one's central meaning system" (McGuire, 1982, p. 49).

4. Durkheim, 1965.

5. Bell, 1980; Wilson, 1985.

6. Berger, 1969.

7. Ibid.

8. Douglas, 1982.

9. Ibid., p. 35.

10. Ibid., p. 33.

11. Neitz, 1987, p. 258.

12. Ibid.; Snow & Machalek, 1982.

13. Stark & Bainbridge, 1985, p. 1.

14. Ibid., p. 6.

15. Shupe & Bromley, 1985, p. 58.

16. J. Richardson, 1985; Stark & Bainbridge, 1985.

17. Shupe & Bromley, 1985, p. 58.

18. Ibid.

19. Ammerman, 1987; Barker, 1984; McGuire, 1982; Neitz, 1987; Rochford, 1985; Warner, 1988.

20. Hunter, 1982.

21. Neitz, 1987, p. 253.

22. Ammerman, 1987, p. 3.

23. Ibid.; Lechner, 1985.

24. Ammerman, 1987, p. 8.

25. R. Stephen Warner, personal communication, 1987.

26. Clifford, 1988, p. 14.

27. For more detail on the historical origins of these groups see the section "Judaism and Modernity."

28. Aviad, 1983; Bulka, 1983; Cohen, 1983; Goldscheider & Zuckerman, 1984; Herberg, 1960; Himmelfarb, 1973; Leventman, 1969; Sklare, [1955] 1972; Waxman, 1983.

29. Some notable exceptions are works by Heilman, 1976; Mayer, 1979; Poll, 1962; Shaffir, 1974; Sklare & Greenblum, 1979.

30. Goldscheider & Zuckerman, 1984.

31. Berger, 1969.

32. Goldscheider & Zuckerman, 1984, p.68.

33. Raphael, 1984, p. 5.

34. Ibid., p. 7.

35. Whereas the milder forms of accommodation maintain the centrality of the tradition, Reform Judaism in many ways actually subordinates the uniqueness of the religion to modern styles of thought and practice. To traditionalist Jews, such radical changes are to be avoided because they presage the complete incorporation of Jews into the mainstream society.

36. Raphael, 1984, p. 8; Sklare, [1955] 1972.

37. Rudavsky, 1967, p. 321.

38. Raphael, 1984, pp. 180–182.

39. The remaining 26 percent of Jews not accounted for in any of these denominations identify themselves as "other" or "just Jewish" (Wertheimer, 1989, p. 81).

40. The Reform rabbinical academy is the Hebrew Union College; its rabbinical assembly is the Union of American Hebrew Congregations. Conservative rabbis are nearly all trained at the Jewish Theological Seminary, and their governing body is the United Synagogue of America. Similarly, the Reconstructionist Rabbinical College ordains all Reconstruc-

tionist rabbis; their congregations belong to the Reconstructionist Federation of Congregations. See also Raphael, 1984, p. 155.

41. Goldscheider & Zuckerman, 1984; Raphael, 1984; Rudavsky, 1967.
42. Heilman, 1976, p. 97.
43. Geertz, 1973b, pp. 93–94.
44. Ryan, 1975, p. 79.
45. Ehrenreich & English, 1978.
46. Ryan, 1975, p. 76.
47. Ehrenreich & English, 1978; Ginsburg, 1989; Lasch, 1977; Ryan, 1975; Welter, 1966.
48. Braude, 1989.
49. Aidala, 1985; Kanter, 1972a.
50. Rix, 1988.
51. Aidala, 1985.
52. Ammerman, 1987; Neitz, 1987; McGuire, 1982; Rochford, 1985; Rose, 1987.
53. McGuire, 1982, p. 57.
54. Ibid., p. 197.
55. Ibid.; Neitz, 1987; Rochford, 1985; Rose, 1987.
56. Danzger, 1989; Kaufman, 1985, 1987.
57. Aviad, 1983; Danzger, 1989; Kaufman, 1985, 1987.
58. Kaufman, 1985, p. 547.
59. Danzger, 1989.
60. Clifford, 1988, p. 34.
61. Matthews, 1984.

CHAPTER THREE

1. Kovacs, 1977.
2. Schreiber, n.d.
3. Marcus & Fisher, 1986, p. 18.
4. Clifford, 1988, p. 34.
5. In mainstream anthropology and qualitative sociology the interpretive framework for analysis of the cultures studied has typically been that of the researcher. In the 1980s, and now in the 1990s, some anthropologists began advocating an approach to ethnography rooted in a critique of the amount of control—and distortion—involved in ethnographers' translations. These researchers are attempting to develop new experimental ethnographic forms that aim to represent more fully the multiple voices that the researcher actually hears in the field. See Clifford, 1988; Clifford & Marcus, 1986; Marcus & Fisher, 1986; Stacey, 1988.
6. Geertz, 1983, p. 56.
7. Clifford, 1988, p. 47.
8. Nash, 1963.
9. Ammerman, 1987; Neitz, 1987; Richardson, Stewart, & Simmonds, 1979; Warner, 1988.

10. Warner, 1988; McGuire, 1982.

11. Gouldner, 1970, p. 497.

12. The idea of selecting categories of interviewees and saturating the categories derives from the grounded theory method first developed by Barney Glaser and Anselm Strauss (1967).

13. Stacey, 1988, p. 23.

14. Clifford, 1988, p. 25.

15. Ibid., p. 39.

16. Clifford & Marcus, 1986, p. 7.

17. Clifford, 1988, p. 50.

18. Clifford & Marcus, 1986, p. 6. Within contemporary anthropological literature, scholars have been attempting experimental approaches that try to avoid imposition of the sole authoritative voice of the ethnographer in presenting the results of field studies.

CHAPTER FOUR

1. Aviad, 1983; Danzger, 1989.

2. Lofland, 1977, 1978; Stark & Bainbridge, 1980. Rochford, 1985, found that these personal connections were particularly important in women's religious recruitment to the Hare Krishna.

3. See, for example, Lofland, 1978; Neitz, 1987; Snow & Machalek, 1982.

4. Gilligan, 1982, p. 2.

5. Burke, 1953; McGuire, 1982.

6. Neitz, 1987.

7. Ibid., pp. 257–258.

8. Aviad, 1983; Danzger, 1989.

9. Richardson, White, & Simmonds, 1979.

10. Bellah, Madsen, Sullivan, Swidler, & Tipton, 1985.

11. Ibid., p. 82.

12. Berger & Luckmann, 1967; Berger, 1969.

13. Goldscheider & Zuckerman, 1984; Goren, 1970.

14. Glanz & Harrison, 1978; Gordon, 1974; Shaffir, 1978; Travisano, 1970.

15. Berger & Luckmann, 1967, pp. 144–147; McGuire, 1982, p. 50.

16. Herberg, 1960.

17. Aidala, 1985; Ammerman, 1987; Rochford, 1985; Rose, 1987.

18. This finding is similar to that of Rosanna Hertz (1986), who in her study of high-earning "dual-career" couples also found that the women did not feel that they had "chosen" to become career women.

19. Bellah et al., 1985, p. 153.

20. Although this choice does "make sense" for these women, it is by no means attractive to all Jews. The roots, stability, and order offered in Orthodoxy also come with a price: newcomers must make changes in their behavior that affect all aspects of their daily and social lives. There are

many individuals who value the relative absence of restrictions in their lives enough to find Orthodoxy unattractive. This book, however, does not intend to establish what makes some individuals willing to take on the discipline of a strenuous religious life while others are not.

21. Geertz, 1973b, p. 112.

22. McGuire, 1982; Mol, 1977.

23. Durkheim, 1965.

24. Aviad, 1983, p. 81.

25. These findings are developed and analyzed in Davidman, 1988.

26. Danzger, 1989.

27. Argyle & Beit-Hallahmi, 1975; De Vaus, 1984; Nelson, Cheek, & Au, 1985.

28. Weber, 1958.

CHAPTER FIVE

1. Robbins, 1988, p. 48.

2. Aidala, 1985, p. 289.

3. Ibid., p. 311.

4. Aviad, 1983; Aidala, 1985; Ammerman, 1987; Danzger, 1989; Kaufman, 1985, 1987; Neitz, 1987; Rochford, 1985.

5. L. Richardson, 1985, p. 2.

6. Kerr, 1985, p. 82.

7. This theme of how some Orthodox communities become very involved in arranging marriages for their new recruits is featured in Roiphe, 1987.

8. See, for example, Susan Rose (1987) and R. Stephen Warner's (1988) studies of Evangelical Christians, Mary Jo Neitz's ethnography of Charismatic Catholics (1987), Nancy Ammerman's book on Fundamentalist Christians (1987), and E. Burke Rochford's study of the Hare Krishna (1985).

9. E. Becker, 1975, p. 13.

10. For example, at the Lincoln Square Synagogue, the fliers announcing the annual "Turn Friday Night into Shabbos" dinners were prepared by a professional advertising company. Some Jewish organizations sponsor seminars to teach Jewish professionals how to be more effective "outreach" workers; marketing professionals are brought in to do some of the presentations.

11. This quotation highlights an interesting distinction between private and public spheres. Secularization locates religion in the purely private sphere. By affirming the distinction between how she felt about work and how she felt about religion, this woman was articulating a peculiarly U.S. and secular expression of freedom, even while she was talking about the appeal of a traditional religion. Her words resemble those of the beginners' rabbi, who, as we shall see in chapter 6, asserted that the religion did

not object to women's equality in the workplace but nevertheless pre-scribed traditional gender roles for the home and synagogue.

12. This finding resembles that of Rosanna Hertz's study on high-earning dual-career couples in their mid-thirties, which found that even in a group that was highly successful professionally, many of the women had never really planned or thought about careers (1986, pp. 42–54).

13. Aidala, 1985; H. Eisenstein, 1983; Gilligan, 1982; Miller, 1976.

CHAPTER SIX

1. Bellah et al., 1985, pp. 152–153.

2. This strategy of "trying out" religious ways of life prior to joining is referred to in the sociological literature as "experimental" conversion and is reported to be one of the most common forms in contemporary society. See Balch & Taylor, 1978; Downton, 1980; Lofland, 1977; Neitz, 1987; J. Richardson, 1985.

3. Bellah et al., 1985, p. 47.

4. Ibid., p. 138.

5. Hill, 1973, p. 237.

6. Berger, 1969, chapters 6 and 7.

7. Bellah et al., 1985, p. 65.

8. Ibid., pp. 23–24.

9. Berger, 1969.

10. Douglas, 1966, pp. 29–32.

11. Veroff, Douvan, & Kulka, 1981, pp. 529–530.

12. McGuire, 1982, p. 39.

13. Ibid., p. 41.

14. How successful was the rabbi in accomplishing his goal of helping the singles to marry? It was impossible to say because the institutions did not keep good records. And when asked, the rabbis, I believe, made up numbers. Rabbi Buchwald told me that at the Beginners' Service they had more marriages than in the main congregation, fifty a year. What this number meant, however, was that anyone who had ever been associated with the Beginners' Service—including people who had since moved away or dropped out—who let the rabbi know they were getting married be-came part of his statistics. What happened to the singles who did not get married within the community? Some found partners elsewhere and ei-ther dropped out or brought their partners in. Others remained in the community because they derived enough other benefits. Others dropped out after a period of time, ranging anywhere from a few months to several years. What were the percentages of women who chose each of these options? It was extremely difficult to say given the paucity of data. I myself met several women who fit into each category.

15. H. Eisenstein, 1983.

16. Degler, 1980, pp. 26–51; Lasch, 1977; Welter, 1966, pp. 151–174.

17. Other studies of contemporary Orthodox communities have found

similar processes of reinterpretation of *niddah*. See Heilman, 1978, p. 34; Kaufman, 1985, 1987.

18. Heilman, 1978, p. 33.

19. Heilman, 1976, p. 209.

20. Bellah et al., 1985, p. 85.

21. Ibid., p. 90.

22. Ibid., p. 90.

23. Ibid., p. 98.

24. I wish I could find out what is said to men about these issues in the parallel men's institution in Morristown, New Jersey. Unfortunately, I have been unable to find any literature dealing with the gender role socialization of men in a Lubavitch institution.

25. Bellah et al., 1985, p. 98.

26. Kanter, 1972a, p. 103.

27. Ibid., pp. 77–78.

CHAPTER SEVEN

1. Greil & Rudy, 1984, p. 261.

2. Goffman, 1961.

3. Gittleson, 1984, p. 71.

4. Greil & Rudy, 1984.

5. Kanter, 1972a, p. 84.

6. Rudy & Greil, 1987, p. 48.

7. Lofland & Skovond, 1981, pp. 378–379.

CHAPTER EIGHT

1. U.S. Department of Labor, 1989.

2. Ammerman, 1987; Kaufman, 1985, 1987; Neitz, 1987; Rochford, 1985; Rose, 1987.

3. Berger, 1969; Wilson, 1982, 1985.

4. Helmreich, 1982; Hertzberg, 1983; Mayer, 1979; Shaffir, 1974.

5. Neitz, 1987, p. 258.

6. Personal communication, May 1988.

7. Cohen, 1988; Goldscheider, 1986; Goldscheider & Zuckerman, 1984.

8. For a fuller discussion of these issues, see Davidman & Tenenbaum, 1990.

9. Goldscheider, 1986; Danzger, 1989. Samuel C. Heilman and Steven M. Cohen's *Cosmopolitans and Parochials* (1989) contains some tables comparing women and men but does not indicate how many of their respondents were female and how many were male.

10. Two notable exceptions to this are Jacobs, 1984; Rochford, 1985. See also Davidman, 1988.

11. Heilman & Cohen, 1989, p. 89.

12. Parsons, 1986.

Glossary

ad can	"until here"
Adon Olam	"Lord of the Universe"; the prayer sung at the closing of Shabbat and holiday services
ahavas Yisroel	love for fellow Jews
Aleinu	"It is our duty"; the prayer sung or chanted toward the end of daily, Sabbath, and holiday services
alter Rebbe	the first Lubavitcher Rebbe
Amidah	the central prayer in the services, which is read in silence
aron hakodesh	ark where Torah scrolls are kept
Ashkenazi	Eastern European Jewish
ba'alat teshuvah	(pl. *ba'alot teshuvah*) a woman who adopts Orthodox Judaism as an adult
ba'al koreh	person who chants the Torah portion of the service aloud
ba'al teshuvah	(pl. *ba'alei teshuvah*) a man who adopts Orthodox Judaism as an adult
bar mitzvah	"son of commandments"; an adult with religious responsibilities; a ceremony in which a thirteen-year-old boy is initiated into religious adulthood
baruch Hashem	"thank God"
bashert	ordained by God, i.e., not a coincidence
bat mitzvah	"daughter of commandments"; an adult with religious responsibilities; a

	ceremony in which a thirteen-year-old girl is initiated into religious adulthood
beinoni	the man, neither saint nor sinner, who is the major subject of the Tanya
bentching	the prayer recited after meals
Berchot Hashachar	morning blessings
Bereshith	"in the beginning"; the beginners' newsletter
berucho, brachah	Ashkenezic and Sephardic forms of the word for "blessing"
binah	"'understanding'; the second of the *sefiros*, or divine emanations; . . . reason *in potentia*" (Schneerson, 1990, p. 288)
bobbe	"grandmother"
brachot	"blessings"
B'reishit	"in the beginning"; Genesis (the first book of the Bible)
brit milah	circumcision
bubbe meisa	"old wives' tale"
Chabad	acronym for *chochma, binah,* and *da'as,* the Lubavitch approach to Hasidism
challah	special bread for Shabbat
Chanukah	festival of lights; holiday in December commemorating the victory of the Maccabees over the Greeks
chassan	"husband"
chavrusa	a one-on-one study session. At Bais Chana it referred to sessions in which the *madrichot* taught the women whatever they were interested in.
chochma	"'wisdom'; the first of the *sefiros*, or divine emanations; . . . developing the original concept" (Schneerson, 1990, p. 290)
cholov Yisroel	milk that is watched and closely supervised from the moment of milking the

	cow—which is done by a Jewish person—through processing and packaging
chulent	a stew, usually containing beans, beef, and potatoes, that is a traditional Sabbath food because it may be placed in a warm oven prior to Shabbat and will stay hot through all of the Sabbath
Chumash	Pentateuch
da'as	" 'knowledge'; the third of the *sefiros*, or divine emanations; . . . *da'as* is not knowledge in the ordinary sense, but in the sense of concentration and attachment—the mental faculty where concepts mature into their corresponding dispositions or attributes of character" (Schneerson, 1990, p. 290)
davening	prayers, praying
dvar torah	a brief talk on a Jewish theme
Echod	newsletter of the main congregation
facocked	confused
friedeker Rebbe	the previous Lubavitcher Rebbe
frum	traditionally observant
Gemara	the codified oral law together with its rabbinic analysis and commentary
Haggadah	the prayer book read at the seder
Halacha	the body of religious law that governs both the religious and secular behavior of observant Jews
Hamotzieh	blessing over bread or *challah*
Hashem	God
hashgocha protis	divine providence—the idea that God knows and controls everything that happens to people
Hasidim	(pl.) a sectarian group of ultra-Orthodox Jews
Hasidus	the Hasidic way of life

havurah	"a group of friends"; alternative types of Jewish communities, formed in the late 1960s and early 1970s, dedicated to creating innovative services, often with an emphasis on integrating radical politics with Jewish observance
Hillel	Jewish student organization
kaddish	prayer for the dead
kallah	"bride"
kashrut	the kosher laws that regulate the dietary behavior of Orthodox Jews
kehilla	Jewish community; also refers to the internal governing bodies of the Jewish communities in premodern Europe
kiddush	ritual blessing over the wine, part of the Shabbat meal
kiruv	bringing assimilated Jews to traditional religious practice
klal Yisroel	all of Israel
k'neina hara	without an evil eye
lashon hara	gossip
madricha	(pl. *madrichot*) counselor and teacher
mashpiah	(pl. *mashpiim*) "one who influences"; a term used within the Lubavitch community to refer to the person who brings a *ba'al* or *ba'alat teshuvah* into *Yiddishkeit*
mazel tov	congratulations
mehitzah	the partition in an Orthodox synagogue that separates the women's section from the men's
merkos	center
mezuzah	(pl. mezuzot) sacred scroll in a casing that is hung on the doorposts of Jewish homes and rooms
mikveh	(pl. *mikvaot*) ritual bath in which Orthodox women immerse themselves one

	week after completing their menstrual cycles
minyan	the quorum of ten men needed for Orthodox communal prayer; prayer service
Mishnah	a text codified in C.E. 200 that is the compilation of Jewish oral law
mitzvah	(pl. mitzvot) commandment
mivtza	project, campaign
Modeh ani l'fanecha	"I give my thanks to you."
Moshiach	Messiah
Mussaf	additional *Amidah*
nagel vasser	water poured from a cup over the hands on arising
niddah	menstruant or state of ritual impurity resulting from menstruation
parsha	chapter; Torah section that is read in Shabbat services
Pesach	Passover
Pesukei Dezimrah	Psalms of Praise
pintele yid	Jewish soul or spark
premie	a follower of Maharaj ji
Purim	festive, playful holiday in early spring commemorating the victory of Jews over the wicked Haman, who plotted to eradicate them
Rebbe	the title for a rabbi who is head of a community or movement, as in Bostoner Rebbe or Lubavitcher Rebbe
rebbetzin	rabbi's wife
Rosh Hashanah	the Jewish New Year
schmooze	chat, discussion (can be used as a noun or a verb)
sechel	"brains," wisdom
seder	Passover ritual dinner

Sefer Torah	scrolls of the Torah
sefiros	divine emanations
Sephardi	Spanish or Portuguese Jewish
Shabbat, Shabbes, Shabbos	(pl. Shabbosim) the Sabbath
Shabbaton	a special weekend Shabbat program with meals, singing, lectures, and discussions
shadchan	matchmaker
shalach manos	treats distributed to friends and relatives to celebrate the holiday of Purim
shaliach	(pl. *shlichim*) outreach worker, representative
shalom	hello or goodbye
shalosh seudos	meal eaten Saturday in the late afternoon toward the end of Shabbos
Shema	Hear, O Israel; a central prayer affirming the unity of God
shidduch	(pl. *shidduchim*) date arranged by a third party for the explicit purpose of marriage
shivah	seven-day ritual mourning period for the dead
shtetl	(pl. shtetlach) the small, tightly knit, bounded community in which Jews in premodern Europe lived
shtick	in this instance, hang-up; more generally, one's "thing" or one's "bag"
shtiebl	small synagogue
shul	synagogue
sicha	(pl. *sichot*) discussion, discourse
siddur	prayer book
simcha	joyous occasion
taharah	ritual purity
taharat hamishpacha	laws of family purity governing sexual relations between wives and husbands
Talmud	a series of texts, dating from C.E. 200 to

	600, that are a commentary on the Mishna
Tanya	main Lubavitch text
tashlich	ritual for the Jewish New Year in which one goes to a body of water and casts away one's sins
tefillin	phylacteries; leather straps connected to a box containing sacred scrolls that Orthodox Jewish men wrap around their arms and head for their weekday morning prayers
Tehillim	Psalms
teshuva	return
tish'a ba'av	a fast day commemorating the destruction of the ancient temple of Jerusalem
Torah	the Jewish Bible; "the corpus of Jewish law, lore, and rabbinic commentary which is the central organizing element of Jewish religion and tradition and which is considered by believers to be divinely inspired" (Heilman, 1976, p. 289); the traditional Jewish philosophy, learning, and way of life, as in "the Torah things that I learned"
Torah im derech eretz	"Torah together with the ways of life of the surrounding people"
tum'ah	ritual impurity
tzniyus	modesty
ulpan	course for the intensive study of Hebrew
yarmulke	skullcap
Yasher coach	"You did well."
yeshiva	(pl. *yeshivot*, yeshivas) institution of Jewish education
yeshivishe velt	"yeshiva world"
yetzer hara	instinct to do bad
yetzer hatov	instinct to do good
Yiddishkeit	Judaism, Jewish way of life

Yom Kippur	Day of Atonement
zaddik	holy man
zaide	"grandfather"

References

Adler, Rachel. 1973. "The Jew Who Wasn't There." *Response* 18 (Summer), pp. 77–82.

Agar, Michael. 1980. *The Professional Stranger: An Informal Introduction to Ethnography.* New York: Academic Press.

Agudath Israel of America. 1980. *The Ba'al Teshuvah Movement.* Special Issue of the *Jewish Observer* 14, 9 (June 1980).

Aidala, Angela. 1985. "Social Change, Gender Roles, and New Religious Movements." *Sociological Analysis* 46, 3, pp. 287–314.

Ammerman, Nancy Tatom. 1987. *Bible Believers: Fundamentalists in the Modern World.* New Brunswick, N.J.: Rutgers University Press.

Anthony, Dick, and Thomas Robbins. 1974. "The Meher Baba Movement: Its Effect on Post-Adolescent Social Alienation," pp. 479–501. In I. I. Zaretsky and M. P. Leone, eds., *Religious Movements in Contemporary America.* Princeton, N.J.: Princeton University Press.

Argyle, Michael, and Benjamin Beit-Hallahmi. 1975. *The Social Psychology of Religion.* London: Routledge & Kegan Paul.

Aviad, Janet. 1980. "From Protest to Return: Contemporary Teshuvah." *Jerusalem Quarterly* 16 (Summer), pp. 1171–1182.

———. 1983. *Return to Judaism: Religious Renewal in Israel.* Chicago: University of Chicago Press.

Balch, Robert W. 1980. "Looking Behind the Scenes in a Religious Cult: Implications for the Study of Conversion." *Sociological Analysis* 41, 2, pp. 137–143.

Balch, Robert W., and David Taylor, 1978. "Seekers and Saucers: The Role of the Cultic Milieu in Joining a UFO Cult." In James T. Richardson, ed., *Conversion Careers: In and Out of the New Religions,* pp. 43–64. Beverly Hills, Calif.: Sage.

Barker, Eileen, 1984. *The Making of a Moonie: Choice or Brainwashing.* Oxford: Blackwell.

Baruch, Grace, Rosalind Barnett, and Caryl Rivers. 1983. *Lifeprints: New Patterns of Love and Work for Today's Women.* New York: Plume/New American Library.

Baum, Charlotte, Paula Hyman, and Sonya Michel. 1975. *The Jewish Woman in America.* New York: New American Library.

Becker, Ernest. 1975. *Escape from Evil.* New York: Free Press.

Becker, Howard S. 1963. "Becoming a Marijuana User" and "Marijuana

Use and Social Control." In *Outsiders: Studies in the Sociology of Deviance*, by Howard S. Becker, pp. 41–58, 59–78. New York: Free Press.

Beckford, James A. 1978. "Accounting for Conversion." *British Journal of Sociology* 29, pp. 249–262.

Bell, Daniel. 1980. *The Winding Passage: Essays and Sociological Journeys, 1960–1980*. Cambridge, Mass.: Abt Books.

Bellah, Robert N. 1967. "Civil Religion in America." *Daedalus* 96, pp. 1–21.

———. 1970. *Beyond Belief: Essays on Religion in a Post-Traditional World*. New York: Harper & Row.

Bellah, Robert N., and Charles Glock, eds. 1976. *The New Religious Consciousness*. Berkeley and Los Angeles: University of California Press.

Bellah, Robert N., Richard Madsen, William M. Sullivan, Ann Swidler, and Steven M. Tipton. 1985. *Habits of the Heart: Individualism and Commitment in American Life*. Berkeley and Los Angeles: University of California Press.

Berger, Peter. 1969. *The Sacred Canopy: Elements of a Sociological Theory of Religion*. Garden City, N.Y.: Anchor Books/Doubleday.

———. 1980. *The Heretical Imperative*. Garden City, N.Y.: Anchor Books.

Berger, Peter, Brigitte Berger, and Hansfried Kellner. 1974. *The Homeless Mind: Modernization and Consciousness*. New York: Vintage Books/Random House.

Berger, Peter, and Thomas Luckmann. 1967. *The Social Construction of Reality*. Garden City, N.Y.: Anchor Books.

Bibby, Reginald. 1978. "Why Conservative Churches *Really* Are Growing: Kelley Revisited." *Journal for the Scientific Study of Religion* 17 (June), pp. 129–137.

Bibby, Reginald W., and Merlin B. Brinkerhoff. 1973. "The Circulation of the Saints: A Study of People Who Join Conservative Churches." *Journal for the Scientific Study of Religion* 12 (Fall), pp. 273–284.

Bird, Frederick, and B. Reimer. 1982. "Participation Rates in New Religious and Para-Religious Movements." *Journal for the Scientific Study of Religion* 21 (March), pp. 1–14.

Bowles, Gloria, and Renate Duelli Klein, eds. 1983. *Theories of Women's Studies*. London: Routledge & Kegan Paul.

Braude, Ann. 1989. *Radical Spirits: Spiritualism and Women's Rights in Nineteenth-Century America*. Boston: Beacon Press.

Buchwald, Ephraim. 1976. "Reaching Out to the Uncommitted." Address delivered to the Rabbinical Council of America convention, Ellenville, New York, May.

Bulka, Reuven P., ed. 1983. *Dimensions of Orthodox Judaism*. New York: Ktav Publishing.

Burke, Kenneth. 1953. *A Rhetoric of Motives*. Englewood Cliffs, N.J.: Prentice-Hall.

Bush, Diane Mitsch, and Roberta G. Simmons. 1981. "Socialization Processes over the Life Course." In Morris Rosenberg and Ralph H.

Turner, eds., *Social Psychology: Sociological Perspectives*, pp. 133–164. New York: Basic Books.

Chodorow, Nancy. 1978. *The Reproduction of Mothering: Psychoanalysis and the Sociology of Gender*. Berkeley and Los Angeles: University of California Press.

Christ, Carol. 1977. "The New Feminist Theology: A Review of the Literature." *Religious Studies Review* 3 (October), pp. 203–212.

Christ, Carol P., and Judith Plaskow. 1979. *Womanspirit Rising: A Feminist Reader in Religion*. San Francisco: Harper & Row.

Clifford, James. 1988. *The Predicament of Culture: Twentieth Century Ethnography, Literature, and Art*. Cambridge, Mass.: Harvard University Press.

Clifford, James, and George E. Marcus, eds. 1986. *Writing Culture: The Poetics and Politics of Ethnography*. Berkeley and Los Angeles: University of California Press.

Cohen, Steven M. 1980. "American Jewish Feminism: A Study of Conflicts and Compromises." *American Behavioral Scientist* 23 (March–April), pp. 519–558.

———. 1983. *American Modernity and Jewish Identity*. New York: Tavistock.

———. 1988. *American Assimilation or Jewish Revival?* Bloomington: Indiana University Press.

Comte, Auguste. 1970. *Introduction to Positive Philosophy*. Edited with a revised translation by Frederick Ferre. Indianapolis: Bobbs-Merrill.

Cox, Harvey. 1977. *Turning East: Why Americans Look to the Orient for Spirituality—and What That Search Can Mean to the West*. New York: Simon & Schuster.

Cushman, Thomas O. 1983. "The Fallen Family as Fallwell's Symbol of Social Decadence: A Content Analysis of 'Listen America!'" Paper presented at the meeting of the Society for the Scientific Study of Religion, Knoxville, Tennessee, November.

Damrell, Joseph. 1977. *Seeking Spiritual Meaning: The World of Vedanta*. Beverly Hills, Calif.: Sage.

Danzger, M. Herbert. 1989. *Returning to Tradition: The Contemporary Revival of Orthodox Judaism*. New Haven, Conn.: Yale University Press.

Davidman, Lynn. 1988. "Gender and Religious Experience." Paper presented at the meetings of the American Sociological Association, Atlanta, Georgia, August.

———. 1990a. "Accommodation and Resistance: A Comparison of Two Contemporary Orthodox Jewish Groups." *Sociological Analysis* 51, 1 (Spring), pp. 35–51.

———. 1990b. "Women's Search for Family and Roots: A Jewish Religious Solution to a Modern Dilemma." In Tom Robbins and Dick Anthony, eds., *In Gods We Trust II*, pp. 385–407. New Brunswick, N.J.: Transaction Books.

Davidman, Lynn, and Shelly Tenenbaum. 1990. "Towards a Feminist Sociology of American Jews." Paper presented at the meetings of the Association for the Sociology of Religion, Washington, D.C., August.

Davis, Murray. 1971. "That's Interesting! Towards a Phenomenology of Sociology and a Sociology of Phenomenology." *Philosophy of Social Science* 1, pp. 309–344.

Degler, Carl. 1980. *At Odds: Women and the Family from the Revolution to the Present*. New York: Oxford University Press.

Demerath, N. Jay III, and Wade Clark Roof. 1976. "Religion—Recent Strands in Research." *Annual Review of Sociology*, vol. 2, pp. 19–33. Palo Alto, Calif.: Annual Reviews.

De Vaus, David A. 1984. "Workforce Participation and Sex Differences in Church Attendance." *Review of Religious Research* 25, pp. 247–256.

Douglas, Mary. 1966. *Purity and Danger*. London: Routledge & Kegan Paul.

———. 1982. "The Effects of Modernization on Religious Change." In Mary Douglas and Steven M. Tipton, eds., *Religion and America: Spirituality in a Secular Age*, pp. 25–43. Boston: Beacon Press.

Douglas, Mary, and Steven M. Tipton, eds. 1982. *Religion and America: Spirituality in a Secular Age*. Boston: Beacon Press.

Downton, James V., Jr. 1979. *Sacred Journeys: The Conversion of Young Americans to Divine Light Mission*. New York: Columbia University Press.

———. 1980. "An Evolutionary Theory of Spiritual Conversion and Commitment: The Case of the Divine Light Mission." *Journal for the Scientific Study of Religion* 19 (September), pp. 381–396.

Dunn, Thomas P. 1983. "Religious Mindopoly: The Co-optation of the Family as a Conversion Tool." Paper presented at the annual meeting of the Society for the Scientific Study of Religion, Knoxville, Tennessee, November.

Durkheim, Emile. 1951. *Suicide: A Study in Sociology*. Translated by John A. Spaulding and George Simpson. New York: Free Press of Glencoe.

———. 1965. *The Elementary Forms of the Religious Life*. New York: Free Press.

Ehrenreich, Barbara. 1984. *The Hearts of Men: American Dreams and the Flight from Commitment*. Garden City, N.Y.: Anchor Books.

Ehrenreich, Barbara, and Deirdre English. 1978. *For Her Own Good: 150 Years of the Experts' Advice to Women*. Garden City, N.Y.: Anchor Press/Doubleday.

Eisenstein, Hester. 1983. *Contemporary Feminist Thought*. Boston: G. K. Hall.

Eisenstein, Zillah. 1981. "Antifeminism in the Politics and Election of 1980." *Feminist Studies* 7, 2 (Summer), pp. 187–205.

Eister, Alan. 1972. "An Outline of a Structural Theory of Cults." *Journal for the Scientific Study of Religion* 11 (December), pp. 319–334.

Freeland, Edward P. 1983. "Religion and Family Politics: A Historical Perspective." Paper presented at the meeting of the Society for the Scientific Study of Religion, Knoxville, Tennessee, November.

Gans, Herbert J. 1956. "American Jewry: Present and Future." *Commentary* 21 (June), pp. 422–430.

Geertz, Clifford. 1973a. "Deep Play: Notes on the Balinese Cockfight." In

Clifford Geertz, *The Interpretation of Cultures*, pp. 412–453. New York: Basic Books.

———. 1973b. "Religion as a Cultural System." In Clifford Geertz, *The Interpretation of Cultures*, pp. 87–125. New York: Basic Books.

———. 1973c. "Thick Description: Toward an Interpretive Theory of Cultures." In Clifford Geertz, *The Interpretation of Cultures*, pp. 3–30. New York: Basic Books.

———. 1983. "From the Native's Point of View: On the Nature of Anthropological Understanding." In Clifford Geertz, *Local Knowledge: Further Essays in Interpretive Anthropology*, pp. 55–70. New York: Basic Books.

Gerlath, Luther, and Virginia Hine. 1970. *People, Power and Change: Movements of Social Transformation*. Indianapolis: Bobbs-Merrill.

Gilligan, Carol. 1982. *In a Different Voice: Psychological Theory and Women's Development*. Cambridge, Mass.: Harvard University Press.

Ginsburg, Faye. 1989. *Contested Lives: The Abortion Debate in an American Community*. Berkeley and Los Angeles: University of California Press.

Gittleson, Natalie. 1984. "American Jews Rediscover Orthodoxy." *New York Times Magazine*, September 30, pp. 40–41, 60–61, 63–65, 71.

Glanz, David, and Michael J. Harrison. 1978. "Varieties of Identity Transformation: The Case of Newly Orthodox Jews." *Jewish Journal of Sociology* 20, 2, pp. 129–141.

Glaser, Barney, and Anselm L. Strauss. 1967. *The Discovery of Grounded Theory: Strategies for Qualitative Research*. Chicago: Aldine.

Glasner, Peter. 1977. *The Sociology of Secularization: A Critique of a Concept*. London: Routledge & Kegan Paul.

Glock, Charles. 1964. "The Role of Deprivation in the Evolution of Religious Groups." In Robert Lee and Martin Marty, eds., *Religion and Social Conflict*, pp. 24–36. New York: Oxford University Press.

Glock, Charles, and Rodney Stark. 1965. *Religion and Society in Tension*. Chicago: Rand McNally.

Goffman, Erving. 1959. *The Presentation of Self in Everyday Life*. Garden City, N.Y.: Doubleday.

———. 1961. *Asylums*. Garden City, N.Y.: Doubleday.

Goldenberg, Naomi R. 1979. *Changing of the Gods: Feminism and the End of Traditional Religions*. Boston: Beacon Press.

Goldscheider, Calvin. 1986. *Jewish Continuity and Change: Emerging Patterns in America*. Bloomington: Indiana University Press.

Goldscheider, Calvin, and Alan S. Zuckerman. 1984. *The Transformation of the Jews*. Chicago: University of Chicago Press.

Gordon, David F. 1974. "The Jesus People: Identity Synthesis." *Urban Life and Culture* 3, 2, pp. 159–178.

Goren, Arthur A. 1970. *New York Jews and the Quest for Community: The Kehilla Experiment, 1908–1922*. New York: Columbia University Press.

Gouldner, Alvin. 1970. *The Coming Crisis of Western Sociology*. New York: Avon.

Greenberg, Blu. 1981. *On Women and Judaism: The View from Tradition.* Philadelphia: Jewish Publication Society of America.

Greil, Arthur L., and David R. Rudy. 1983. "Conversion to the World View of Alcoholics Anonymous: A Refinement of Conversion Theory." *Qualitative Sociology* 6, 1 (Spring), pp. 5–28.

Greil, Arthur L., and David R. Rudy. 1984a. "Social Cocoons: Encapsulation and Identity Transformation Organizations." *Sociological Inquiry* 54 (Summer), pp. 260–278.

———. 1984b. "What Have We Learned from Process Models of Conversion? An Examination of Ten Case Studies." *Sociological Focus* 17, 4 (October), pp. 305–323.

Hacker, Andrew. 1982. "Farewell to the Family?" *New York Review of Books*, March 18, pp. 37–45.

Hammond, Phillip E., ed. 1985. *The Sacred in a Secular Age.* Berkeley and Los Angeles: University of California Press.

Hansen, Marcus L. 1952. "The Problem of the Third Generation Immigrant." *Commentary* 14 (November), pp. 492–500.

Hargrove, Barbara. 1979. *The Sociology of Religion.* Arlington Heights, Mass.: AHM Publishing.

———. 1985. "Gender, the Family, and the Sacred." In Phillip E. Hammond, ed., *The Sacred in a Secular Age*, pp. 204–214. Berkeley and Los Angeles: University of California Press.

Heilman, Samuel C. 1976. *Synagogue Life: A Study in Symbolic Interaction.* Chicago: University of Chicago Press.

———. 1977. "Inner and Outer Identities: Sociological Ambivalence Among Orthodox Jews." *Jewish Social Studies* 39 (Summer), pp. 227–240.

———. 1978. "Constructing Orthodoxy." *Society* 15 (May–June), pp. 32–40.

Heilman, Samuel C., and Steven M. Cohen. 1989. *Cosmopolitans and Parochials: Modern Orthodox Jews in America.* Chicago: University of Chicago Press.

Helmreich, William. 1982. *The World of the Yeshiva: An Intimate Portrait of Orthodox Jewry.* New York: Free Press.

Herberg, Will. 1960. *Protestant, Catholic, Jew*, rev. ed. Garden City, N.Y.: Anchor Books.

Hertz, Rosanna. 1986. *More Equal Than Others: Women and Men in Dual-Career Marriages.* Berkeley and Los Angeles: University of California Press.

Hertzberg, Arthur. 1983. "Assimilation: Can Jews Survive Their Encounter with America?" *Haddassah Magazine* 65, 1 (August–September), p. 16.

Heschel, Susannah, ed. 1983. *On Being a Jewish Feminist: A Reader.* New York: Schocken Books.

Hewitt, John P., and Randall Stokes. 1978. "Disclaimers." In Jerome G.

Manis and Bernard M. Meltzer, eds., *Symbolic Interaction: A Reader in Social Psychology*, pp. 308–319. Boston: Allyn & Bacon.

Hierich, Max. 1977. "Change of Heart: A Test of Some Widely Held Theories About Religious Conversion." *American Journal of Sociology* 83, 3 (November), pp. 653–680.

Hill, Michael. 1973. *A Sociology of Religion*. New York: Basic Books.

Himmelfarb, Milton. 1973. *The Jews of Modernity*. New York: Basic Books.

Hoffer, Eric. 1951. *The True Believer*. New York: Harper & Row.

Hoge, Dean R. 1981. *Converts, Dropouts, Returnees: A Study of Religious Change Among Catholics*. New York: Pilgrim Press.

Hoge, Dean R., and David A. Roozen, eds. 1979. *Understanding Church Growth and Decline: 1950–1978*. New York: Pilgrim Press.

Hood, Ralph, Jr., and James R. Hall. 1980. "Gender Differences in the Description of Erotic and Mystical Experiences." *Review of Religious Research* 21, pp. 95–107.

Hunter, James Davison. 1982. "Subjectivization and the New Evangelical Theodicy." *Journal for the Scientific Study of Religion* 20 (March), pp. 39–47.

———. 1983. *American Evangelicalism: Conservative Religion and the Quandry of Modernity*. New Brunswick, N.J.: Rutgers University Press.

Jacobs, Janet. 1984. "The Economy of Love in Religious Commitment: The Deconversion of Women from Nontraditional Religious Movements." *Journal for the Scientific Study of Religion* 23 (June), pp. 155–171.

Jaggar, Allison, and Paula Rothenberg Struhl, eds. 1978. *Feminist Frameworks: Alternative Theoretical Accounts of the Relations Between Women and Men*. New York: McGraw-Hill.

Jernigan, Jack D., and Steven L. Nock. 1983. "Religiosity and Family Stability: Do Families That Pray Together Stay Together?" Paper presented at the meeting of the Society for the Scientific Study of Religion, Knoxville, Tennessee, November.

Jewish Publication Society of America. *American Jewish Yearbook*, vols. 31, 43, 68, 79. Philadelphia: Author. 1930, 1942, 1967, 1978.

Kanter, Rosabeth Moss. 1968. "Commitment and Social Organization: A Study of Commitment Mechanisms in Utopian Communities." *American Sociological Review* 33, 4 (August), pp. 499–517.

———. 1972a. *Commitment and Community: Communes and Utopias in Sociological Perspective*. Cambridge, Mass.: Harvard University Press.

———. 1972b. "Commitment and the Internal Organization of Millenial Movements." *American Behavioral Scientist* 16, pp. 219–243.

Kaplan, Marion. 1979. *The Jewish Feminist Movement in Germany: The Campaigns of the Judischer Frauenbund, 1904–1938*. Westport, Conn.: Greenwood Press.

Kaufman, Debra. 1985. "Women Who Return to Orthodox Judaism: A Feminist Analysis." *Journal of Marriage and the Family* (August), pp. 543–551.

———. 1987. "Coming Home to Jewish Orthodoxy: Reactionary or Radical Women?" *Tikkun* 2, 3, pp. 60–63.

Kelley, Dean. 1972. *Why Conservative Churches Are Growing*. New York: Harper & Row.

———. 1978. "Why Conservative Churches Are Still Growing." *Journal for the Scientific Study of Religion* 17 (June), pp. 165–172.

Kerr, Peter. 1985. "Singles Seek Social Life at Houses of Worship." *New York Times*, April 1, p. 82.

Klausner, Samuel. 1983. "The Ritual Role of Jewish Women: An Empirical Study." Paper presented at the meeting of the Society for the Scientific Study of Religion, Knoxville, Tennessee, November.

Koltun, Elizabeth. 1976. *The Jewish Woman: New Perspectives*. New York: Schocken Books.

Kovacs, Malcolm. 1977. " 'The Dynamics of Commitment': The Process of Resocialization of *Ba'alei Teshuvah*, Jewish Students in Pursuit of Their Identity at the Rabbinical College of America (Lubavitch)." Ph.D. diss., Union Graduate School.

Lasch, Christopher. 1977. *Haven in a Heartless World: The Family Besieged*. New York: Basic Books.

Lazerwitz, Bernard, and Michael Harrison. 1979. "American Jewish Denominations: A Social and Religious Profile." *American Sociological Review* 44 (August), pp. 656–666.

Lechner, Frank. 1985. "Fundamentalism and Sociocultural Revitalization in America: A Sociological Analysis." *Sociological Analysis* 46, 3, pp. 243–260.

Leventman, Seymour. 1969. "From Shtetl to Suburb." In Peter I. Rose, ed., *The Ghetto and Beyond*, pp. 33–56. New York: Random House.

Levy, Marion J., Jr. 1972. *Modernization: Latecomers and Survivors*. New York: Basic Books.

Leibman, Charles S. 1979. "Orthodox Judaism Today." *Midstream* 25 (August–September), pp. 19–26.

———. 1983. "Extremism as a Religious Norm." *Journal for the Scientific Study of Religion* 22 (March), pp. 75–86.

Liebman, Robert C., and Robert Wuthnow, eds. 1983. *The New Christian Right: Mobilization and Legitimation*. New York: Aldine.

Lofland, John A. 1977. *Doomsday Cult: A Study of Conversion, Proselytization, and Maintenance of Faith*, enlarged ed. New York: Irvington/Wiley.

———. 1978. "Becoming a World Saver Revisited." In James T. Richardson, ed., *Conversion Careers: In and Out of the New Religions*, pp. 10–23. Beverly Hills, Calif.: Sage.

Lofland, John A., and Lyn H. Lofland. 1984. *Analyzing Social Settings: A Guide to Qualitative Observation and Analysis*. Belmont, Calif.: Wadsworth.

Lofland, John A., and Norman Skovond. 1981. "Conversion Motifs." *Journal for the Scientific Study of Religion* 20 (September), pp. 373–385.

Lofland, John A., and Rodney Stark. 1965. "Becoming a World Saver: A

Theory of Conversion to a Deviant Perspective." *American Sociological Review* 30, pp. 863–874.

Long, Theodore, and Jeffrey K. Hadden. 1983. "Religious Conversion and the Concept of Socialization: Integrating the Brainwashing and Drift Models." *Journal for the Scientific Study of Religion* 22 (March), pp. 1–14.

Lubavitch Women's Organization. 1981. *The Modern Jewish Woman: A Unique Perspective*. New York: Lubavitch Educational Foundation for Jewish Marriage Enrichment.

Luckmann, Thomas. 1967. *The Invisible Religion*. New York: Macmillan.

Luker, Kristin. 1984. *Abortion and the Politics of Motherhood*. Berkeley and Los Angeles: University of California Press.

Lynch, Frederick. 1977. "Field Research and Future History: Problems Posed for Ethnographic Sociologists by the 'Doomsday Cult' Making Good." *American Sociologist* 12 (April–May), pp. 80–88.

———. 1978. "Toward a Theory of Conversion and Commitment to the Occult." In James T. Richardson, ed., *Conversion Careers: In and Out of the New Religions*, pp. 91–112. Beverly Hills, Calif.: Sage.

Magnus, Shulamit, and Saul Berman. 1981. "Orthodoxy Responds to Feminist Ferment." *Response* 40 (Spring), pp. 5–17.

Malnovich, Miriam. 1983. "A Haven Among the Hasidim." *Present Tense* 11 (Fall), pp. 41–44.

Marcus, George E., and Michael M.J. Fisher. 1986. *Anthropology as Cultural Critique: An Experimental Moment in the Human Sciences*. Chicago: University of Chicago Press.

Martin, David. 1978. *A General Theory of Secularization*. New York: Harper & Row.

Matthews, Jill Julius. 1984. *Good and Mad Women: The Historical Construction of Femininity in Twentieth-Century Australia*. Sydney: Allen & Unwin.

Mayer, Egon. 1979. *From Shtetl to Suburb: The Jews of Boro Park*. Philadelphia: Temple University Press.

Mayer, Egon, and Chaim Waxman. 1977. "Modern Jewish Orthodoxy in America: Toward the Year 2000." *Tradition* 16 (Spring), pp. 98–112.

McGuire, Meredith. 1981. *Religion: The Social Context*. Belmont, Calif.: Wadsworth.

———. 1982. *Pentecostal Catholics: Power, Charisma, and Order in a Religious Movement*. Philadelphia: Temple University Press.

McHugh, Peter. 1970. "Social Disintegration as a Requisite of Resocialization." In Gregory P. Stone and Harvey A. Farberman, eds., *Social Psychology Through Symbolic Interaction*, pp. 699–708. Waltham, Mass.: Ginn-Blaisdell.

Mester, Roberto, and Hillel Klein. 1981. "The Young Jewish Revivalist: A Therapist's Dilemma." *British Journal of Medical Psychology* 54, pp. 299–306.

Miller, Jean Baker. 1976. *Toward a New Psychology of Women*. Boston: Beacon Press.

244   *References*

————. 1984. *The Development of Women's Sense of Self*. Work in Progress Series. Wellesley, Mass.: Wellesley Center for Research on Women.

Mishler, Eliot. 1979. "Meaning in Context: Is There Any Other Kind?" *Harvard Educational Review* 49, pp. 1–19.

Mol, Hans. 1977. *Identity and the Sacred*. New York: Free Press.

Myerhoff, Barbara. 1978. *Number Our Days*. New York: Simon & Schuster.

Nash, Dennison. 1963. "The Ethnologist as Stranger." *Southwestern Journal of Anthropology* 19, 2, pp. 149–167.

Needleman, Jacob. 1970. *The New Religions*. Garden City, N.Y.: Doubleday.

Neitz, Mary Jo. 1987. *Charisma and Community: A Study of Religious Commitment Within the Charismatic Renewal*. New Brunswick, N.J.: Transaction Books.

Nelson, Hart M., Neil H. Cheek, Jr., and Paul Au. 1985. "Gender Differences in Images of God." *Journal for the Scientific Study of Religion* 24 (December), pp. 396–402.

Niebhur, Richard H. 1929. *The Social Sources of Denominationalism*. New York: Holt, Rinehart & Winston.

Nisbet, Robert. 1966. *The Sociological Tradition*. New York: Basic Books.

Parsons, Arthur S. 1986. "Messianic Personalism in the Unification Church." *Journal for the Scientific Study of Religion* 25 (June), pp. 141–161.

Petchesky, Rosalind Pollack. 1981. "Antiabortion, Antifeminism, and the Rise of the New Right." *Feminist Studies* 7, 2 (Summer), pp. 206–246.

Plaskow, Judith. 1977. "The Feminist Transformation of Theology." In Rita Gross, ed., *Beyond Androcentrism: New Essays on Women and Religion*, pp. 23–33. Missoula, Mont.: Scholars Press.

Poll, Solomon. 1962. *The Hassidic Community of Williamsburg*. New York: Basic Books.

Poupko, Chana K., and Dvora L. Wohlgelernter. 1976. "Women's Liberation—An Orthodox Response." *Tradition* 15 (Spring), pp. 45–52.

Quebedaux, Richard. 1978. *The Worldly Evangelicals*. San Francisco: Harper & Row.

Raphael, Marc Lee. 1984. *Profiles in American Judaism*. San Francisco: Harper & Row.

Reinharz, Shulamit. 1979. *On Becoming a Social Scientist*. San Francisco: Jossey-Bass.

————. 1983. "Experiential Analysis: A Contribution to Feminist Research." In Gloria Bowles and Renate Duelli Klein, eds., *Theories of Women's Studies*, pp. 162–191. London: Routledge & Kegan Paul.

Richardson, James T. 1985. "Studies of Conversion: Secularization or Reenchantment?" In Phillip E. Hammond, ed., *The Sacred in a Secular Age*, pp. 104–121. Berkeley and Los Angeles: University of California Press.

Richardson, James T., ed. 1978. *Conversion Careers: In and Out of the New Religions*. Beverly Hills, Calif.: Sage.

Richardson, James T., Mary White Stewart, and Robert B. Simmonds.

1979. *Organized Miracles: A Study of a Contemporary Youth, Communal Fundamentalist Organization.* New Brunswick, N.J.: Transaction Books.

Richardson, Laurel. 1985. *The New Other Woman: Contemporary Single Women in Affairs with Married Men.* New York: Free Press.

Rifkin, Jeremy, and Ted Howard. 1979. *The Emerging Order: God in the Age of Scarcity.* New York: Putnam's.

Rix, Sara E., ed. 1988. *The American Woman, 1988–1989: A Report in Depth.* New York: Norton.

Robbins, Thomas. 1988. *Cults, Converts, and Charisma.* London: Sage.

Robbins, Thomas, and Dick Anthony. 1972. "Getting Straight with Meher Baba: A Study of Mysticism, Drug Rehabilitation, and Postadolescent Role Conflict." *Journal for the Scientific Study of Religion* 11 (June), pp. 122–140.

———. 1979. "The Sociology of Contemporary Religious Movements." *Annual Review of Sociology,* vol. 5, pp. 75–89. Palo Alto, Calif.: Annual Reviews.

Robbins, Thomas, Dick Anthony, and James T. Richardson. 1978. "Theory and Research on Today's 'New Religions.'" *Sociological Analysis* 39, pp. 95–122.

Robertson, Roland. 1970. *The Sociological Interpretation of Religion.* Oxford: Blackwell.

———. 1978. *Meaning and Change: Explorations in the Cultural Sociology of Modern Societies.* New York: New York University Press.

Robertson, Roland, ed. 1969. *Sociology of Religion.* Hammondsworth, England: Penguin.

Rochford, E. Burke, Jr. 1985. *Hare Krishna in America.* New Brunswick, N.J.: Rutgers University Press.

Roiphe, Anne. 1981. *Generation Without Memory: A Jewish Journey in Christian America.* Boston: Beacon Press.

———. 1987. *Lovingkindness.* New York: Summit Books.

Rose, Susan. 1987. "Women Warriors: The Negotiation of Gender in a Charismatic Community." *Sociological Analysis* 48, *3,* pp. 245–258.

Rosen, Gladys. 1979. "The Impact of the Women's Movement on the Jewish Family." *Judaism* 28 (Spring), pp. 160–168.

Rudavsky, David. 1967. *Emancipation and Judgment: Contemporary Jewish Religious Movements, Their History and Thought.* New York: Diplomatic Press.

Ruddick, Sara. 1980. "Maternal Thinking." *Feminist Studies* 6, *2* (Summer), pp. 342–367.

Rudy, David R., and Arthur L. Greil. 1987. "Taking the Pledge: The Commitment Process in Alcoholics Anonymous." *Sociological Focus* 20, *1* (January), pp. 45–59.

Ruether, Rosemary Radford. 1978. *New Woman, New Earth: Sexist Ideologies and Human Liberation.* New York: Seabury Press.

Ryan, Mary P. 1975. *Womanhood in America: From Colonial Times to the Present.* New York: New Viewpoints.

Schatzman, Leonard, and Anselm L. Strauss. 1973. *Field Research: Strategies for a Natural Sociology*. Englewood Cliffs, N.J.: Prentice-Hall.

Schneerson, Yosef Yitzchak. 1990. *Likutei Dibburim*, vol. 3. Brooklyn, N.Y.: "Kehot" Publication Society.

Schneider, Susan Weidman. 1984. *Jewish and Female: Choices and Changes in Our Lives Today*. New York: Simon & Schuster.

Schreiber, Sara Chana. N.d. "The Minnesota Experience." Photocopied handout distributed by the Lubavitch.

Seidman, Steven. 1985. "Modernity and the Problem of Meaning: The Durkheimian Tradition." *Sociological Analysis* 46, 2, pp. 109–130.

Sennett, Richard. 1978. *The Fall of Public Man: On the Social Psychology of Capitalism*. New York: Vintage Books.

Sennett, Richard, ed. 1977. *The Psychology of Society*. New York: Vintage Books.

Shaffir, William. 1974. *Life in a Religious Community: The Lubavitcher Chassidim in Montreal*. Toronto: Holt, Rinehart & Winston.

———. 1978. "Witnessing as Identity Consolidation: The Case of the Lubavitcher Chassidim." In Hans Mol, ed., *Identity and Religion*, pp. 39–57. London: Sage.

———. 1983. "The Recruitment of Ba'alei Teshuvah in a Jerusalem Yeshiva." *Jewish Journal of Sociology* 25 (June), pp. 33–46.

Shupe, Anson D., Jr. 1981. *Six Perspectives on New Religions: A Case Study Approach*. New York: Edwin Mellen Press.

Shupe, Anson, and David G. Bromley. 1985. "Social Responses to Cults." In Phillip E. Hammond, ed., *The Sacred in a Secular Age*, pp. 58–72. Berkeley and Los Angeles: University of California Press.

Singer, Margaret. 1979. "Coming Out of the Cults." *Psychology Today* 12, 8, pp. 72–82.

Sklare, Marshall. 1971. *America's Jews*. New York: Random House.

———. [1955] 1972. *Conservative Judaism: An American Religious Movement*. New York: Schocken Books.

Sklare, Marshall, and Joseph Greenblum. 1979. *Jewish Identity on the Suburban Frontier: A Study of Group Survival in the Open Society*, 2nd ed. Chicago: University of Chicago Press.

Slater, Philip. 1970. *The Pursuit of Loneliness: American Culture at the Breaking Point*. Boston: Beacon Press.

Snow, David A., and Richard Machalek. 1982. "On the Presumed Fragility of Unconventional Beliefs." *Journal for the Scientific Study of Religion* 21 (March), pp. 15–26.

Stacey, Judith. 1983. "The New Conservative Feminism." *Feminist Studies* 9, 3 (Fall), pp. 559–583.

———. 1988. "Can There Be a Feminist Ethnography?" *Women's Studies International Forum* 11, 1, pp. 21–27.

Stark, Rodney, and William Sims Bainbridge. 1980. "Networks of Faith: Interpersonal Bonds and Recruitment to Cults and Sects." *American Journal of Sociology* 85, 6, pp. 1376–1395.

———. 1985. *The Future of Religion: Secularization, Revival, and Cult Formation*. Berkeley and Los Angeles: University of California Press.

Stone, Gregory P. 1970. "Appearance and the Self." In Gregory P. Stone and Harvey A. Farberman, eds., *Social Psychology Through Symbolic Interaction*, pp. 489–509. Waltham, Mass.: Ginn-Blaisdell.

Straus, Roger. 1976. "Changing Oneself: Seekers and the Creative Transformation of Life Experience." In John Lofland, ed., *Doing Social Life: The Qualitative Study of Human Interaction in Natural Settings*, pp. 252–272. New York: Wiley.

———. 1979. "Religious Conversion as a Personal and Collective Accomplishment." *Sociological Analysis* 40, 2, pp. 158–165.

Sugarman, Barry. 1975. "Reluctant Converts: Social Control, Socialization, and Adaptation in Therapeutic Communities." In Roy Wallis, ed., *Sectarianism: Analyses of Religious and Non-Religious Sects*, pp. 141–161. New York: Halsted Press.

Swidler, Ann. 1973. "The Concept of Rationality in the Work of Max Weber." *Sociological Inquiry* 43 (Spring), pp. 35–42.

Travisano, Richard V. 1970. "Alternation and Conversion as Qualitatively Different Transformations." In Gregory P. Stone and Harvey A. Farberman, eds., *Social Psychology Through Symbolic Interaction*, pp. 594–606. Waltham, Mass.: Ginn-Blaisdell.

Trebilcot, Joyce, ed. 1983. *Mothering: Essays in Feminist Theory*. Totowa, N.J.: Rowman & Allanheld.

Tremmel, William C. 1971. "The Converting Choice." *Journal for the Scientific Study of Religion* 10 (Spring), pp. 17–25.

Union of Orthodox Congregations of America/Orthodox Union. 1979–1980. *The Teshuva Issue*. Special Issue of *Jewish Life* 3, 4, Teves 5740 (Winter).

U.S. Bureau of the Census. 1981. *Statistical Abstract of the United States: 1981*. Washington, D.C.: Bureau of Labor Statistics.

U.S. Dept. of Labor, Bureau of Labor Statistics. 1989. *News Bulletin*, October 27.

Veroff, Joseph, Elizabeth Douvan, and Richard A. Kulka. 1981. *The Inner American: A Self-Portrait from 1957 to 1976*. New York: Basic Books.

Warner, R. Stephen. 1988. *New Wine in Old Wineskins: Evangelicals and Liberals in a Small-Town Church*. Berkeley and Los Angeles: University of California Press.

Wax, Rosalie H. 1971. *Doing Fieldwork: Warnings and Advice*. Chicago: University of Chicago Press.

Waxman, Chaim I. 1983. *America's Jews in Transition*. Philadephia: Temple University Press.

Weber, Max. 1946. "Religious Rejections of the World and Their Directions" and "The Social Psychology of World Religions." In *From Max Weber: Essays in Sociology*. Edited and translated by H. H. Gerth and C. Wright Mills, pp. 323–599, 267–301. New York: Oxford University Press.

―――. 1949. *The Methodology of the Social Sciences*. Translated and edited by Edward A. Shils and Henry A. Finch. New York: Free Press.

―――. 1958. *The Protestant Ethic and the Spirit of Capitalism*. New York: Scribner's.

―――. 1963. *The Sociology of Religion*. Boston: Beacon Press.

―――. 1968. *Economy and Society: An Outline of Interpretive Sociology*. Edited by Guenther Roth and Claus Wittick. New York: Bedminster Press.

Welter, Barbara. 1966. "The Cult of True Womanhood, 1820–1860." *American Quarterly* 18, pp. 151–174.

Wertheimer, Jack. 1989. "Recent Trends in American Judaism." In David Singer, ed., and Ruth R. Seldin, assoc. ed., *American Jewish Yearbook 1989*, vol. 89. New York: American Jewish Committee.

Wilson, Bryan. 1959. "An Analysis of Sect Development." *American Sociological Review* 24, 1, pp. 3–15.

―――. 1966. *Religion in Secular Society*. London: Watts.

―――. 1979. "The Return of the Sacred." *Journal for the Scientific Study of Religion* 18 (September), pp. 268–280.

―――. 1982. *Religion in Sociological Perspective*. New York: Oxford University Press.

―――. 1985. "Secularization: The Inherited Model." In Phillip E. Hammond, ed., *The Sacred in a Secular Age*, pp. 9–20. Berkeley and Los Angeles: University of California Press.

Wuthnow, Robert, James Davison Hunter, Albert Bergesen, and Edith Kurzweil. 1984. *Cultural Analysis: The Work of Peter L. Berger, Mary Douglas, Michel Foucault and Jurgen Habermas*. Boston: Routledge & Kegan Paul.

Zablocki, Benjamin. 1971. *The Joyful Community*. Baltimore, Md.: Penguin.

Index

Compositor: Braun-Brumfield, Inc.
Text: 10/13 Palatino
Display: Palatino
Printer: Braun-Brumfield, Inc.
Binder: Braun-Brumfield, Inc.